Kaplan Publishing are constantly finding new ways to support students looking for exam success and our online resources really do add an extra dimension to your studies.

This book comes with free MyKaplan online resources so that you can study anytime, anywhere. **This free online resource is not sold separately and is included in the price of the book.**

Having purchased this book, you have access to the following online study materials:

CONTENT	AAT	
	Text	Kit
Electronic version of the book	✓	✓
Knowledge Check tests with instant answers	✓	
Mock assessments online	✓	✓
Material updates	✓	✓

How to access your online resources

Received this book as part of your Kaplan course?
If you have a MyKaplan account, your full online resources will be added automatically, in line with the information in your course confirmation email. If you've not used MyKaplan before, you'll be sent an activation email once your resources are ready.

Bought your book from Kaplan?
We'll automatically add your online resources to your MyKaplan account. If you've not used MyKaplan before, you'll be sent an activation email.

Bought your book from elsewhere?
Go to **www.mykaplan.co.uk/add-online-resources**
Enter the ISBN number found on the title page and back cover of this book.
Add the unique pass key number contained in the scratch panel below.
You may be required to enter additional information during this process to set up or confirm your account details.

This code can only be used once for the registration of this book online. This registration and your online content will expire when the examinations covered by this book have taken place. Please allow one hour from the time you submit your book details for us to process your request.

Please scratch the film to access your unique code.

Please be aware that this code is case-sensitive and you will need to include the dashes within the passcode, but not when entering the ISBN.

CASH AND FINANCIAL MANAGEMENT

STUDY TEXT

Qualifications and Credit Framework

Q2022

This Study Text supports study for the following AAT qualifications:

AAT Level 4 Diploma in Professional Accounting

AAT Diploma in Professional Accounting at SCQF Level 8

CASH AND FINANCIAL MANAGEMENT

KAPLAN PUBLISHING'S STATEMENT OF PRINCIPLES

LINGUISTIC DIVERSITY, EQUALITY AND INCLUSION

We are committed to diversity, equality and inclusion and strive to deliver content that all users can relate to.

We are here to make a difference to the success of every learner.

Clarity, accessibility and ease of use for our learners are key to our approach.

We will use contemporary examples that are rich, engaging and representative of a diverse workplace.

We will include a representative mix of race and gender at the various levels of seniority within the businesses in our examples to support all our learners in aspiring to achieve their potential within their chosen careers.

Roles played by characters in our examples will demonstrate richness and diversity by the use of different names, backgrounds, ethnicity and gender, with a mix of sexuality, relationships and beliefs where these are relevant to the syllabus.

It must always be obvious who is being referred to in each stage of any example so that we do not detract from clarity and ease of use for each of our learners.

We will actively seek feedback from our learners on our approach and keep our policy under continuous review. If you would like to provide any feedback on our linguistic approach, please use this form (you will need to enter the link below into your browser).

https://forms.gle/U8oR3abiPpGRDY158

We will seek to devise simple measures that can be used by independent assessors to randomly check our success in the implementation of our Linguistic Equality, Diversity and Inclusion Policy.

CASH AND FINANCIAL MANAGEMENT

British Library Cataloguing-in-Publication Data

A catalogue record for this book is available from the British Library.

Published by
Kaplan Publishing UK
Unit 2, The Business Centre
Molly Millars Lane
Wokingham
Berkshire
RG41 2QZ

ISBN: 978-1-83996-883-9

The text in this material and any others made available by any Kaplan Group company does not amount to advice on a particular matter and should not be taken as such. No reliance should be placed on the content as the basis for any investment or other decision or in connection with any advice given to third parties. Please consult your appropriate professional adviser as necessary. Kaplan Publishing Limited and all other Kaplan group companies expressly disclaim all liability to any person in respect of any losses or other claims, whether direct, indirect, incidental, consequential or otherwise arising in relation to the use of such materials.

© Kaplan Financial Limited, 2024

Printed and bound in Great Britain.

All rights reserved. No part of this publication may be reproduced, stored in a retrieval system, or transmitted, in any form or by any means, electronic, mechanical, photocopying, recording or otherwise, without the prior written permission of Kaplan Publishing.

CASH AND FINANCIAL MANAGEMENT

CONTENTS

	Page number
Introduction	P.5
Unit guide	P.9
The assessment	P.20
Study skills	P.21

STUDY TEXT

Chapter

1	Cash and profit	1
2	Forecasting cash flows	39
3	Preparing cash budgets	85
4	Analysing and monitoring cash budgets	131
5	Liquidity management	183
6	Raising finance	205
7	Investing surplus funds	239
8	Impact of regulations and policies on financing and investment	271
9	Assumed knowledge	289
Mock Assessment Questions		315
Mock Assessment Answers		331
Glossary		343
Index		I.1

INTRODUCTION

HOW TO USE THESE MATERIALS

These Kaplan Publishing learning materials have been carefully designed to make your learning experience as easy as possible and to give you the best chance of success in your AAT assessments.

They contain a number of features to help you in the study process.

The sections on the Unit Guide, the Assessment and Study Skills should be read before you commence your studies.

They are designed to familiarise you with the nature and content of the assessment and to give you tips on how best to approach your studies.

STUDY TEXT

This Study Text has been specially prepared for the revised AAT qualification introduced in 2022.

It is written in a practical and interactive style:

- key terms and concepts are clearly defined
- all topics are illustrated with practical examples with clearly worked solutions based on sample tasks provided by the AAT in the new examining style
- frequent activities throughout the chapters ensure that what you have learnt is regularly reinforced
- 'pitfalls' and 'examination tips' help you avoid commonly made mistakes and help you focus on what is required to perform well in your examination
- 'Test your understanding' activities are included within each chapter to apply your learning and develop your understanding.

ICONS

The study chapters include the following icons throughout.

They are designed to assist you in your studies by identifying key definitions and the points at which you can test yourself on the knowledge gained.

 Definition

These sections explain important areas of Knowledge which must be understood and reproduced in an assessment.

 Example

The illustrative examples can be used to help develop an understanding of topics before attempting the activity exercises.

 Test your understanding

These are exercises which give the opportunity to assess your understanding of all the assessment areas.

 Foundation activities

These are questions to help ground your knowledge and consolidate your understanding on areas you're finding tricky.

 Extension activities

These questions are for if you're feeling confident or wish to develop your higher level skills.

Quality and accuracy are of the utmost importance to us so if you spot an error in any of our products, please send an email to mykaplanreporting@kaplan.com with full details.

Our Quality Co-ordinator will work with our technical team to verify the error and take action to ensure it is corrected in future editions.

Progression

There are two elements of progression that we can measure: first how quickly students move through individual topics within a subject; and second how quickly they move from one course to the next. We know that there is an optimum for both, but it can vary from subject to subject and from student to student. However, using data and our experience of student performance over many years, we can make some generalisations.

A fixed period of study set out at the start of a course with key milestones is important. This can be within a subject, for example 'I will finish this topic by 30 June', or for overall achievement, such as 'I want to be qualified by the end of next year'.

Your qualification is cumulative, as earlier papers provide a foundation for your subsequent studies, so do not allow there to be too big a gap between one subject and another.

We know that exams encourage techniques that lead to some degree of short term retention, the result being that you will simply forget much of what you have already learned unless it is refreshed (look up Ebbinghaus Forgetting Curve for more details on this). This makes it more difficult as you move from one subject to another: not only will you have to learn the new subject, you will also have to relearn all the underpinning knowledge as well. This is very inefficient and slows down your overall progression which makes it more likely you may not succeed at all.

In addition, delaying your studies slows your path to qualification which can have negative impacts on your career, postponing the opportunity to apply for higher level positions and therefore higher pay.

You can use the following diagram showing the whole structure of your qualification to help you keep track of your progress.

CASH AND FINANCIAL MANAGEMENT

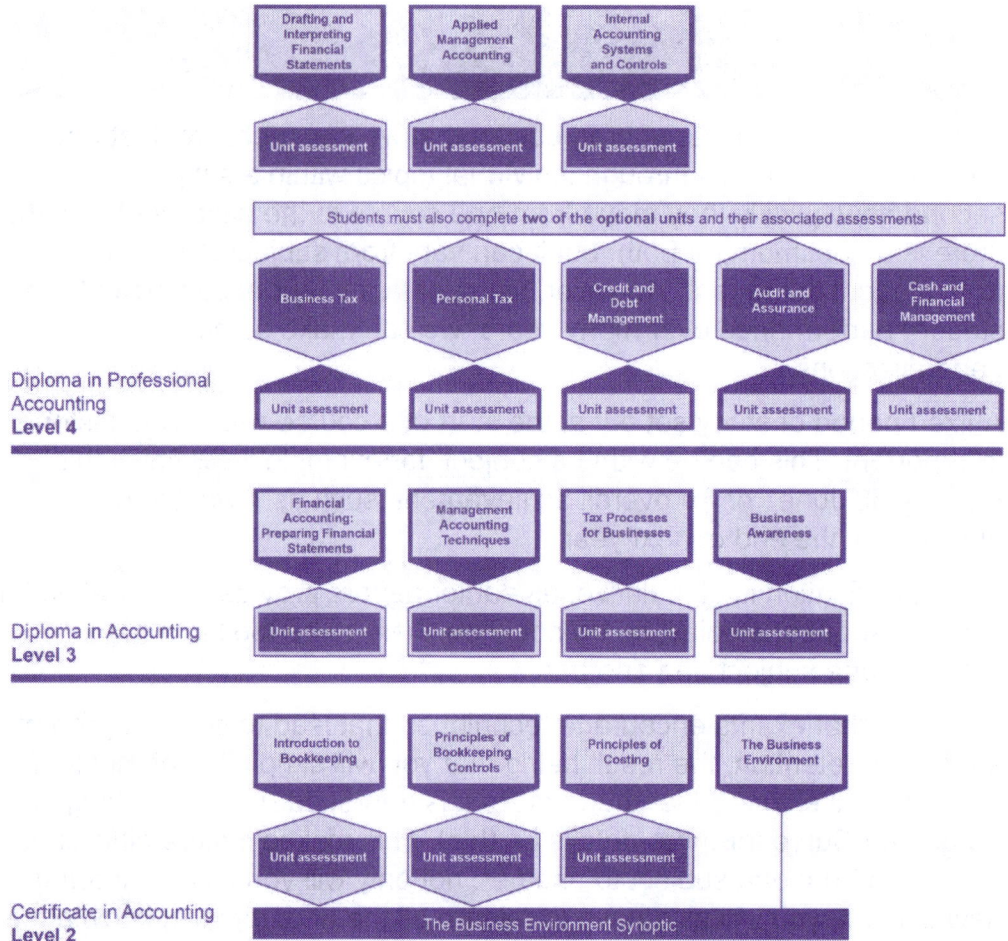

CASH AND FINANCIAL MANAGEMENT

UNIT GUIDE

Introduction

This unit focuses on the importance of managing cash within organisations and covers the knowledge and skills required to make informed decisions on financing and investment in accordance with organisational policies and external regulations.

Students will identify current and future cash transactions from a range of sources. They will learn how to eliminate non-cash items in the financial information provided. Using various techniques, students will prepare cash budgets considering the timing of transactions required to monitor the flow of cash into and out of organisations.

Understanding the importance of cash management is key to the sustainability of organisations, therefore students will identify shortfalls and surpluses in cash budgets and take appropriate action to deal with them. Students will understand how to reforecast cash budgets and reasons for deviations from budget.

Students will appreciate how an organisation needs to meet its financial obligation to avoid the risk of financial failure and the different methods of financing available to meet short and long term financing requirements, along with the types of investments available for surplus funds.

Students will gain an understanding of the external regulations and considerations that relate to cash and finance, including any financing and investment decisions, to comply with an organisation's policies and principles, which may not be purely focused on maximising wealth.

Cash and Financial Management is an **optional** unit.

CASH AND FINANCIAL MANAGEMENT

Learning outcomes

- Prepare forecasts for cash receipts and payments
- Prepare cash budgets and monitor cash flows
- Understand the importance of managing finance and liquidity
- Understand ways of raising finance and investing funds
- Understand regulations and organisational policies that influence decisions in managing cash and finance

Scope of content

To perform this unit effectively you will need to know and understand the following:

		Chapter
1	**Prepare forecasts for cash receipts and payments**	
1.1	**Types of cash receipts and payments:**	1
	Learners need to be able to:	
	• Understand types of cash receipts and cash payments, including regular, exceptional, capital, drawings, dividends, loan receipts and repayments and taxation payments and refunds	
1.2	**Reconcile profit with movement in cash**	1
	Learners need to be able to:	
	• Understand the differences between cash and profit	
	• Reconcile differences between accounting profits and cash by:	
	– adjusting for non-cash items,	
	– adjusting for non-operational items,	
	– adjusting for cash transactions included in the statement of financial position,	
	– adjusting for opening and closing balances in the financial statements and/or bank statements,	
	– calculating movements in cash	

CASH AND FINANCIAL MANAGEMENT

		Chapter
1.3	**Statistical techniques**	2

Learners need to be able to:

- Calculate the following
  - mark up,
  - margin,
  - percentages,
  - regression analysis (e.g. y = a + bx),
  - index numbers,
  - time series analysis,
  - trends,
  - seasonal variations

1.4	**Cash movement of non-current assets**	1

Learners need to be able to:

- Understand:
  - the carrying value of a non-current asset, including revaluation,
  - the effect of revaluation on cash on the disposal of a non-current asset

- Calculate:
  - the purchase price of the non-current asset
  - the sale proceeds of a non-current asset

2	**Prepare cash budgets and monitor cash flows**	
2.1	**Cash budgets and forecasts**	3, 4

Learners need to be able to:

- Understand relevant and non-relevant items when preparing cash budgets
- Understand the effect on cash flow of:
  - lagged or delayed receipts and payments in different periods of the cash budget
  - prompt payment discounts (PPD), irrecoverable debts and their timings
  - exchange rates, inflation and taxation when preparing cash budgets

CASH AND FINANCIAL MANAGEMENT

Chapter

- Prepare a cash budget to include:
  - all sources of cash receipts totalled to show receipts for the period
  - all sources of cash payments totalled to show payments for the period
  - net cash flow for the period
  - opening cash balance
  - closing cash balance

2.2 Sensitivity analysis on cash budgets   4

Learners need to be able to:

- Understand changes in assumptions, both controllable and non-controllable, that can affect the cash budget
- Calculate the impact of changes on the original cash budget due to volume, price, discounts and timings
- Make recommendations to management based on potential changes to the cash budget

2.3 Cash budgets and organisational policies   4

Learners need to be able to:

- Understand that policies of the organisation can avoid significant variances from the cash budget
- Understand the actions to take when addressing variances from the cash budget

CASH AND FINANCIAL MANAGEMENT

		Chapter
3	**Understand the importance of managing finance and liquidity**	
3.1	**Principles of finance and liquidity**	5
	Learners need to understand:	
	• The importance of cash budgeting in the management of liquidity	
	• Strengths and weaknesses of cash budgeting as a monitoring tool for organisations	
	• The importance of ensuring that an organisation can meet its financial commitments on time	
	• The repercussions of not meeting financial commitments on time	
	• How liquidity influences cash flow in respect of the timing of payments received and payments made when preparing the cash budget	
	• Signs of overtrading and overcapitalisation	
	• How to differentiate between liquid and non-liquid assets	
3.2	**Use calculations to support the management of finance and liquidity**	5
	Learners need to be able to:	
	• Understand the working capital cycle	
	• Understand the importance of liquidity and use of resources ratios in liquidity management	
	• Understand the usefulness of profitability ratios in the management of finance	
	• Understand the usefulness of gearing when considering financing options	

CASH AND FINANCIAL MANAGEMENT

Learners need to be able to calculate the following ratios:

- Liquidity ratios:
    - current ratio = current assets/current liabilities = X:1
    - quick ratio (acid test) = (current assets – inventories)/current liabilities = X:1

- Efficient use of resources ratios:
    - inventory holding period (days) = inventories/cost of sales × 365
    - trade receivable collection period (days) = trade receivable/revenue × 365
    - trade payables payment period (days) = trade payables/cost of sales × 365
    - working capital cycle = inventory holding period + trade receivable collection period – trade payables payment period

- Profitability ratios:
    - ROCE (return on capital employed) = operating profit/capital employed × 100
    - capital employed = total equity + non-current liabilities
    - return on shareholders' funds = profit after tax/total equity × 100
    - operating profit margin = operating profit/revenue × 100
    - interest cover = operating profit/ finance costs (i.e. interest) = X times

- Gearing ratio:
    - gearing = total debt/(total debt + total equity) × 100. Total debt in this unit is all non-current liabilities only

CASH AND FINANCIAL MANAGEMENT

4 **Understand ways of raising finance and investing funds**

4.1 **The basic terms and conditions associated with different types of financing**   6

Learners need to know:

- The different terms and conditions, as defined by the lender, surrounding the various types of financing:
    - fees
    - interest
    - penalties
    - lending restrictions
    - minimum/maximum amounts
    - minimum/maximum lending period
    - lending security

- The advantages and disadvantages of the different ways an organisation can raise finance:
    - bank and other loans
    - bank overdrafts
    - mortgages
    - leases
    - hire purchase agreements
    - loan stock
    - sale and leaseback
    - factoring
    - invoice discounting
    - shares
    - bonds
    - crowdfunding

CASH AND FINANCIAL MANAGEMENT

4.2 **Financing options to fund the organisation's cash requirements** — 6

Learners need to be able to:

- Understand the effect on gearing and liquidity for different financing options
- Understand the effect on credit rating for different financing options
- Understand the most appropriate financing option in a given situation
- Apply interest rates to financing options
- Calculate the total cost to an organisation for different financing options

4.3 **Surplus funds and the terms and conditions associated with each of these types of investments** — 7

Learners need to understand:

- The different terms and conditions, as defined by regulations, surrounding various types of investment:
    - fees
    - interest
    - penalties
    - investment restrictions
    - minimum/maximum amounts
    - minimum/maximum investment periods
- Advantages and disadvantages of different types of investment:
    - land
    - property
    - shares
    - bonds
    - gilts
    - various types of bank accounts
    - certificates of deposits and commodities

CASH AND FINANCIAL MANAGEMENT

4.4 Minimise the potential exposure to the organisation — 7

Learners need to understand:

- The impact of early withdrawal penalties and bonuses
- That various investments may have a minimum investment level
- That some investments may have conditions where withdrawal is restricted
- The relationship between risk, reward and liquidity
- The portfolio effect of diversifying investments
- How to measure the risk and return of different options

Learners need to be able to:

- Calculate the return on investment for different options
- Calculate the yield for different options

5 Understand regulations and organisational policies that influence decisions in managing cash and finance

5.1 Government monetary policies — 8

Learners need to understand:

- How the government, through monetary policy, can influence the rate of inflation and the supply of money through quantitative easing
- The main roles of the Bank of England

CASH AND FINANCIAL MANAGEMENT

5.2 Impact of financial regulations, guidelines and security procedures on an organisation's principles of cash management   8

Learners need to understand:

- Statutory regulations that relate to the management of cash balances
- That mandatory regulations must be adhered to and awareness of these regulations should be known, as included in the Companies Act 2006 and published by HM Treasury
- The regulations that cover anti-money laundering, counter financing of terrorism and bribery

5.3 Raising finance and investing funds according to organisational culture and policies   7, 8

Learners need to understand:

- How fundamental ethical principles, morals, sustainability or working practices could affect an organisation's reputation
- How to invest surplus funds to maximise the return on an investment, with due regard to the organisation's attitude to risk
- What the effect of the above restrictions could be in influencing decisions to raise finance and/or invest

5.4 Economic conditions that could affect various financial markets   8

Learners need to understand:

- The advantages and disadvantages of investing in local economies versus wider economies, or the global economy
- Whether to invest surplus funds or to reduce debt due to the change in economic conditions
- The effect of interest rates, exchange rates and commodity prices on financial markets
- The difference between fiscal and monetary policies and how a government can attempt to use these to manage an economy

Delivering this unit

This unit links with:

- Level 4 Applied Management Accounting
- Level 4 Drafting and Interpreting Financial Statements.

CASH AND FINANCIAL MANAGEMENT

THE ASSESSMENT

Test specifications for this unit assessment

Assessment type
Computer based unit assessment

Marking type
Partially computer/ partially human marked

Duration of exam
2 hours

Learning outcomes		Weighting
1	Prepare forecasts for cash receipts and payments	15%
2	Prepare cash budgets and monitor cash inflows	25%
3	Understand the importance of managing finance and liquidity	15%
4	Understand ways of raising finance and investing funds	20%
5	Understand regulations and organisational policies that influence decisions in managing cash and finance	25%
Total		100%

STUDY SKILLS

Preparing to study

Devise a study plan

Determine which times of the week you will study.

Split these times into sessions of at least one hour for study of new material. Any shorter periods could be used for revision or practice.

Put the times you plan to study onto a study plan for the weeks from now until the assessment and set yourself targets for each period of study – in your sessions make sure you cover the whole course, activities and the associated questions in the workbook at the back of the manual.

If you are studying more than one unit at a time, try to vary your subjects as this can help to keep you interested and see subjects as part of wider knowledge.

When working through your course, compare your progress with your plan and, if necessary, re-plan your work (perhaps including extra sessions) or, if you are ahead, do some extra revision/practice questions.

Effective studying

Active reading

You are not expected to learn the text by rote, rather, you must understand what you are reading and be able to use it to pass the assessment and develop good practice.

A good technique is to use SQ3Rs – Survey, Question, Read, Recall, Review:

1 **Survey the chapter**

   Look at the headings and read the introduction, knowledge, skills and content, so as to get an overview of what the chapter deals with.

2 **Question**

   Whilst undertaking the survey ask yourself the questions you hope the chapter will answer for you.

3 **Read**

   Read through the chapter thoroughly working through the activities and, at the end, making sure that you can meet the learning objectives highlighted on the first page.

CASH AND FINANCIAL MANAGEMENT

4 Recall

At the end of each section and at the end of the chapter, try to recall the main ideas of the section/chapter without referring to the text. This is best done after short break of a couple of minutes after the reading stage.

5 Review

Check that your recall notes are correct.

You may also find it helpful to re-read the chapter to try and see the topic(s) it deals with as a whole.

Note taking

Taking notes is a useful way of learning, but do not simply copy out the text.

The notes must:

- be in your own words
- be concise
- cover the key points
- well organised
- be modified as you study further chapters in this text or in related ones.

Trying to summarise a chapter without referring to the text can be a useful way of determining which areas you know and which you don't.

Three ways of taking notes

1 Summarise the key points of a chapter

2 Make linear notes

A list of headings, subdivided with sub-headings listing the key points.

If you use linear notes, you can use different colours to highlight key points and keep topic areas together.

Use plenty of space to make your notes easy to use.

CASH AND FINANCIAL MANAGEMENT

3   Try a diagrammatic form

The most common of which is a mind map.

To make a mind map, put the main heading in the centre of the paper and put a circle around it.

Draw lines radiating from this to the main sub-headings which again have circles around them.

Continue the process from the sub-headings to sub-sub-headings.

Annotating the text

You may find it useful to underline or highlight key points in your study text – but do be selective.

You may also wish to make notes in the margins.

Revision phase

Kaplan has produced material specifically designed for your final examination preparation for this unit.

These include pocket revision notes and a bank of revision questions specifically in the style of the new syllabus.

Further guidance on how to approach the final stage of your studies is given in these materials.

Further reading

In addition to this text, you should also read the 'Accounting Technician' magazine every month to keep abreast of any guidance from the examiners.

CASH AND FINANCIAL MANAGEMENT

Cash and profit

Introduction

This chapter demonstrates how important cash is to a business. It looks at how cash differs from profit.

ASSESSMENT CRITERIA	CONTENTS
Types of cash receipts and payments (1.1)	1 Types of cash flow
Reconcile profit with movement in cash (1.2)	2 Cash flow versus profit
	3 Calculating cash flows
Cash movements of non-current assets (1.4)	4 Reconciling profit to cash flow

1 Types of cash flow

1.1 The importance of cash flow

The term **cash** in this unit is used to describe bank account balances as well as coins and notes; and cash payments include cheque payments, BACS, direct debits and standing orders.

The majority of businesses will wish to make a profit. This means that, over a period of time, revenue needs to exceed costs. However, even if the business is making a profit, it must also have **cash funds** available to pay suppliers, employees and other expenses when due.

1.2 Types of cash flow

There are different types of cash flow that a business is likely to have:

- Regular receipts and payments such as sales, purchases and expenses.

- Receipts and payments of a long-term nature, known as capital receipts and payments, such as the raising of share capital or the purchase of non-current assets.

- Payments made to the owners of a business either in the form of drawings for a sole trader or partnership or dividends for a company.

- Other costs such as the payment of taxes to the government.

- Unusual or exceptional receipts or payments, for example, cash received from the sale of a non-current asset.

A business will have different types of receipts and payments. The typical types of cash flows that you will come across are described below.

1.3 Cash inflows

- **Regular revenue receipts** for a business will be cash sales and cash from customers that have purchased goods on credit.

- **Capital receipts** will include cash raised by issuing shares or raising a loan.

- Other types of capital cash inflow such as the proceeds from the sale of non-current assets, a tax refund or the receipt of government grants. These are likely to be **irregular cash inflows**.

1.4 Cash outflows

- **Regular revenue payments** will include payments for cash purchases, cash paid to payables, wage payments, payment of bills, and cash payments of expenses.

- **Capital payments** could include the repayment of loans or the purchase of non-current assets. When new non-current assets are purchased this may be for a large sum on just one date or it may take the form of regular payments if, for example, the asset is acquired under a lease or hire purchase agreement.

- Businesses will also be likely to make payments for corporation tax, VAT and PAYE. These may be regular such as the monthly PAYE payments or one-off payments each year such as the annual payment of corporation tax.

- Payments will also be made to providers of finance such as dividends to shareholders and interest payments to banks and other providers of finance. The timing of these payments will vary but, for example, companies usually pay any dividend twice a year; a small interim dividend during the year and a larger final dividend after the year end.

- Finally, in a sole trader's business or a partnership, there may be either regular or irregular payments made to the owner or partners in the form of drawings.

1.5 Exceptional cash flows

The cash flows described above are the normal, everyday types of cash flows that most businesses will have. However in some cases there will also be exceptional cash flows which are **not part of normal business** operations.

- Exceptional cash outflows might include payment of legal damages or redundancy costs.

- Exceptional cash inflows might include items such as receipts from an insurance company for damaged inventory.

Test your understanding 1

Cash receipts and payments take many different forms but they can be broadly categorised into regular, capital, exceptional and drawings.

Complete the table by selecting the correct description from the list of options below to match the type of cash receipt or cash payment (not all options need to be used).

Type of receipt or payment	Description
Irregular receipts	
Capital payment	
Regular revenue receipt	
Exceptional payment	
Exceptional receipt	
Regular revenue payment	
Annual disbursement	
Drawings	

Options:

A   Payment of electricity bill

B   Receipt from an insurance claim

C   Proceeds from the disposal of non-current assets

D   Payments made to the owners of the business

E   Lease new machinery

F   Pay corporation tax for the year

G   Payment of a redundancy package

H   Customer paying their debt

CASH AND FINANCIAL MANAGEMENT

 Test your understanding 2

Payments that relate to the purchase of non-current assets would be classified as:

A Capital payments
B Regular revenue receipts
C Drawings
D Exceptional receipts

 Test your understanding 3

Income received from an insurance claim for lost inventory would be classified as:

A Capital payments
B Regular revenue receipts
C Drawings
D Exceptional receipts

2 Cash flow versus profit

2.1 Cash flow and profit

Cash is not the same as profit. It is entirely possible for a profitable business to run short of cash.

- Profit is a figure on the Statement of Profit or Loss (SoPL).
- Cash is a current asset on the Statement of Financial Position (SoFP).

A typical Statement of Profit or Loss is shown below:

	£000
Revenue	X
Cost of sales	(X)
Gross profit	X
Distribution costs	(X)
Administrative expenses	(X)
Operating profit	X
Finance costs	(X)
Profit before tax	X
Tax	(X)
Profit for the period	X

A typical Statement of Financial Position is shown below:

	£000
Non-current assets	
Property, plant and equipment	X
Other tangible assets	X
Goodwill	X
	X
Current assets	
Inventories	X
Trade and other receivables	X
Cash and cash equivalents	X
	X
Total assets	X

Equity and liabilities
Equity
Share capital | X
Share premium account | X
Revaluation reserve | X
Retained earnings | X

Total equity | X

Non-current liabilities
Bank loans | X
Long-term provisions | X

| X

Current liabilities
Trade and other payables | X
Tax liabilities | X
Bank overdrafts and loans | X

| X

Total liabilities | X

Total equity and liabilities | X

2.2 The difference between cash and profit

There are several reasons why the profit of a business will not equate directly to cash. This is mostly due to financial statements being prepared on an accruals basis:

> **Definition**
>
> FRS 102 The Financial Reporting Standard applicable in the UK and Republic of Ireland defines the accruals basis as follows:
>
> 'The effects of transactions and other events are recognised when they occur (and not as cash or its equivalent is received or paid) and they are recorded in the accounting records and reported in the financial statements of the periods to which they relate.'

- **Revenue** is recognised in the Statement of Profit or Loss when it is earned but this is not necessarily when the cash is received. A business may make credit sales thus creating receivables.

- **Costs** are recognised in the Statement of Profit or Loss when incurred but this is not necessarily when the cash is paid. A business may have credit with suppliers creating payables.

- **Accruals** are an expense that has been incurred during the period but has not been paid by the period end, so will reduce profit but will not have impacted on cash flow.

- **Prepayments** are payments made during the period for an expense that relates to a period after the period end. This will impact the current period's cash flow as cash is being spent on an expense that will be accounted for in a future period's Statement of Profit or Loss.

- **Depreciation** is charged to the Statement of Profit or Loss, reducing profit, but it does not have any effect on cash. It is a non-cash expense.

- **Provisions for doubtful debts** are charged as expenses but they are not cash flows and will not reduce the cash balance of the business.

- **Purchases of non-current assets** are often large cash outflows of a business but the only amount that is charged to the Statement of Profit or Loss is the annual depreciation charge and not the entire cost of the non-current asset.

CASH AND FINANCIAL MANAGEMENT

- **Sale of non-current assets** will result in an inflow of cash to the business but the figure appearing in the Statement of Profit or Loss is not the sales proceeds but any profit or loss made on the sale.

- **Financing transactions,** such as issuing additional share capital and taking out or repaying a loan, will result in large cash flows in or out of the business with no effect on the profit figure.

- **Dividends or drawings** will result in cash outflows from the business but with no effect on the profit figure.

There are a number of different techniques that can be used to calculate the cash flows or changes in cash position.

3 Calculating cash flows

3.1 Introduction

To be able to produce cash budgets it is necessary to calculate the actual cash a business spends and receives during a time period. Figures from the Statement of Profit or Loss and Statement of Financial Position will be used for these calculations.

Note: Some of the concepts in this chapter are assumed knowledge. Please refer to Chapter 9 Assumed knowledge for more information.

3.2 Calculating cash flows

The adjustments include:

- calculating the **actual cash received from receivables** – using the opening and closing receivables balance and the sales revenue for the period

- calculating the **actual cash paid to payables** – using the opening and closing payables balance and the purchases for the period

- calculating the **actual cash paid for various expenses** – using accruals and/or prepayments to adjust the expense for the period.

3.3 Cash receipts from receivables

Example

Opening receivables are £10,000 and closing receivables are £14,000. Revenue for the period has been £12,000. Assuming that all the sales were on credit. How much cash has been received from receivables in the period?

Solution

To calculate the cash received in relation to sales it is possible to use the trade receivables control account:

Trade receivables

Opening balance	10,000	Cash received	8,000
Sales	12,000	Closing balance	14,000
	22,000		22,000

Instead of using a T account:

Cash received = sales + opening balance – closing balance

= 12,000 + 10,000 – 14,000

= 8,000

3.4 Cash payments to payables

 Example

Opening payables are £2,500 and closing payables are £3,250. Purchases for the period have been £2,250. Assuming that all the purchases were on credit. How much cash has been paid to payables in the period?

Solution

To calculate the cash paid in relation to purchases it is possible to use the trade payables control account:

Trade payables

Cash paid	1,500	Opening balance	2,500
Closing balance	3,250	Purchases	2,250
	4,750		4,750

Instead of using a T account:

Cash paid = purchases + opening balance – closing balance

= 2,250 + 2,500 – 3,250

= 1,500

3.5 Accruals

> **Example**
>
> Electricity has an opening accrual of £100 and a closing accrual of £50 relating to it. There is an amount of £200 recorded in the Statement of Profit or Loss for electricity.
>
> **Solution**
>
> To calculate the cash paid in relation to electricity complete the electricity account:
>
> **Electricity**
>
> | | | | |
> |---|---|---|---|
> | **Cash paid** | 250 | Opening accrual | 100 |
> | Closing accrual | 50 | Statement of Profit or Loss | 200 |
> | | 300 | | 300 |
>
> Instead of using a T account:
>
> Cash paid = expense + opening accrual – closing accrual
>
> = 200 + 100 – 50
>
> = 250

3.6 Prepayments

Example

Rent has an opening prepayment of £300 and a closing prepayment of £200 relating to it. There is an amount of £750 recorded in the Statement of Profit or Loss for rent.

Solution

To calculate the cash paid in relation to rent complete the rent account:

Rent

Opening prepayment	300	Statement of Profit or Loss	750
Cash paid	**650**	Closing prepayment	200
	950		950

Instead of using a T account:

Cash paid = expense − opening prepayment + closing prepayment

= 750 − 300 + 200

= 650

3.7 Non-current assets

A business may buy or sell a non-current asset and the cash paid or received for this will be classed as a cash outflow or inflow.

It may be necessary to calculate this cash flow with reference to the Statement of Profit or Loss and the Statement of Financial Position.

Example

New fixtures and fittings were purchased in a part exchange deal. The trade in allowance for the old fittings was £1,200 and the new fitting had a list price of £3,000. What was the cash outflow for this purchase?

Solution

£3,000 – £1,200 = £1,800 cash outflow.

Example

During the year a printing press was sold that had originally cost £35,000. When the press was sold the asset had a carrying value of £23,000. The loss on disposal was £5,000. What was the cash inflow from this sale?

Solution

Disposal

Printing press cost	35,000	Accumulated depreciation*	12,000
		Loss on disposal	5,000
		Cash received	**18,000**
	35,000		35,000

* calculated by subtracting the carrying value (£23,000) from the cost (£35,000).

Alternative working:

If the carrying value of the assets is £23,000 and a loss on disposal of £5,000 was made, then the cash received must have been £5,000 less than the carrying value. Therefore cash received = £18,000.

CASH AND FINANCIAL MANAGEMENT

 Example

The business decided to sell off one of its spare premises. The building had been depreciated at 5% on cost for the 5 years of ownership. The original purchase price was £50,000. There was a gain on disposal of £12,000. What was the cash received from this sale?

Solution

Disposal

Building cost	50,000	Accumulated depreciation*	12,500
Gain on disposal	12,000	**Cash received**	**49,500**
	62,000		62,000

* calculated by taking 5% of the original cost and multiplying it by the 5 years the building was owed for (50,000 × 5%) × 5 years = 12,500.

Instead of using a T account:

Cash received = Carrying value of the sold asset + gain on disposal

= (50,000 − (50,000 × 5% × 5 years)) + 12,000

= 37,500 + 12,000

= **49,500**

In some cases you may need to work out the cash paid for additions or received from a sale by looking at figures for total assets not individual ones as per the previous examples. In such cases make sure you include the depreciation charge for the period.

Example

The carrying value of non-current assets at the start of the period is £30,000 and the carrying value at the end of the period is forecast to be £37,000. Depreciation for the period will be £10,000. The company will pay for any additions immediately by cash. Calculate the cash to be paid for any additions.

Solution

Carrying value of NCA

Opening balance	30,000	Depreciation charge	10,000
Cash paid for additions	**17,000**	Closing balance	37,000
	47,000		47,000

Instead of using a T account:

Closing CV = Opening CV + additions – depreciation – CV of disposals

37,000 = 30,000 + additions – 10,000 – 0 (assume no disposals as none are mentioned in the question)

Additions = 17,000

CASH AND FINANCIAL MANAGEMENT

Non-current assets can be acquired by outright purchase (e.g. through raising a bank loan and paying cash) or via **leases**.

While the legal form is that the leased asset is still owned by the leasing company (the lessor) the commercial substance is that it is effectively the same as buying it. The accounting treatment reflects this (except for short term leases or for low value items – these will generally not be the case in CSFT):

- The leased non-current asset is recorded in the Statement of Financial Position and treated as a normal non-current asset.
- Lease and interest payments relating to the leased non-current asset are recorded in the Statement of Profit or Loss.

 Example

The carrying value of non-current assets at the start of the month is forecast to be £300,000 and the carrying value at the end of the month is forecast to be £370,000. Depreciation for the month was £30,000.

During the month the business will take out a new lease to acquire a new machine that would otherwise cost £40,000. The lease is payable at 5% per month.

The company will pay for any other additions immediately by cash. Calculate the cash to be paid for any additions in the month.

Solution

Carrying value of NCA

Opening balance	300,000	Depreciation charge	30,000
Additions	**100,000**	Closing balance	370,000
	400,000		400,000

The total additions are £100,000 of which £40,000 is the lease. The cash paid for additions is therefore £60,000.

Note: The cash paid for the lease will amount to £2,000 per month (£40,000 × 5%).

Companies may also revalue non-current assets. When accounting for revaluation of property, plant and equipment, the following procedure should be adopted.

- Restate the asset to the revalued amount (rather than at cost).
- Eliminate the accumulated depreciation to date on that asset.
- Establish or update the revaluation reserve.

The revaluation will change the carrying value of the non-current asset in the Statement of Financial Position, but has no cash effect. On disposal of the revalued asset, any gain or loss on disposal will be calculated by comparing the disposal proceeds with the carrying value as normal.

Example

A building was purchased at a cost of £100,000 on 1 January 20X5. It is depreciated over its useful life of 10 years on a straight line basis down to a nil residual value. At 31 December 20X5 the building was revalued at £126,000. The company does not make the annual transfer from revaluation reserve to retained earnings.

This revaluation will be account for as follows in the financial statements as at 31 December 20X5 and 20X6:

In the year ended 31 December 20X5, depreciation of £100,000 ÷ 10 = £10,000 would be charged so the carrying value at the date of revaluation is £90,000.

The revaluation gain is £36,000 (from a carrying value of £90,000 up to £126,000). This gain would be reported in other comprehensive income for the year and shown in the statement of financial position as a revaluation reserve within equity. There is no cash effect.

The revaluation is accounted for as follows:

	£	£
Dr Building (126 – 100)	26,000	
Dr Accumulated depreciation	10,000	
Cr Revaluation reserve		36,000

The revised depreciation charge for 20X6 would be £126,000/9 years = £14,000.

CASH AND FINANCIAL MANAGEMENT

At 31 December 20X6, the amounts to be included in the statement of financial position would be:

Carrying value of property (£126,000 – £14,000) = £112,000

Revaluation reserve would remain at £36,000

NOTE: If a non-current asset has been **revalued**, upon disposal any remaining balance on the revaluation reserve is transferred to retained earnings within the statement of changes in equity. This has no effect on the cash received from the sale of the asset.

Test your understanding 4

A car was purchased 3 years ago for £15,000 and depreciated on a straight line basis over 5 years with an expected scrap value of £3,000. It is now do be sold and is expected to make a gain on disposal of £500.

What is the expected cash receipt from the sale of the car?

A £8,300
B £7,300
C £6,500
D £6,000

Test your understanding 5

A building was originally purchased several years ago for £220,000. It was revalued 2 years ago (when the carrying value was £175,000) to £200,000 with an expected remaining life of 20 years and no residual value. The building is now to be sold and a loss on disposal of £5,000 is expected.

What is the expected cash receipts on the disposal of the building?

A £152,500
B £175,000
C £185,000
D £193,000

Test your understanding 6

Tariq had an opening carrying value of non-current assets of £150,000. During the year he charged £20,000 depreciation expense and ended the year with a non-current asset carrying value of £215,000. He disposed of one asset in the year which had a carrying value of £5,000

How much did Tariq spend on non-current asset additions in the year?

A £80,000
B £85,000
C £90,000
D £95,000

3.8 Other considerations

Non-cash items

Depreciation will be included in some of the expenses within the Statement of Profit or Loss. Depreciation is a non-cash item so it will need to be adjusted for.

Example

Expenses include a depreciation charge for £5,000. Total expenses are £14,000. All expenses are being settled on cash terms. Calculate the cash flow for expenses in the period.

Solution

The cash flow for expenses is: £14,000 – £5,000 = £9,000.

Tax payments

Tax will be shown in both the Statement of Financial Position and the Statement of Profit or Loss.

It is normally a current liability in the Statement of Financial Position as tax is usually owing to HMRC at the end of the financial year. In the Statement of Profit or Loss the tax figure is the expense for the period. The tax expense is not always the tax paid. It may be necessary to calculate the cash paid to the HMRC.

It could be that a receipt is expected from the tax authorities due to a recoverable VAT claim or a refund for overpaid tax. In this scenario, the amount would be shown as a current asset in the Statement of Financial Position.

CASH AND FINANCIAL MANAGEMENT

 Example

The tax payable at the start of the period shown on the Statement of Financial Position is expected to be £15,000 and at the end of the period it is expected to be £17,000. The tax expense show on the Statement of Profit or Loss is £16,000. Calculate the tax paid in the period.

Solution

Tax liability

Cash paid	14,000	Opening balance	15,000
Closing balance	17,000	Statement of Profit or Loss	16,000
	31,000		31,000

Instead of using a T account:

Cash paid = Expense + opening balance – closing balance

= 16,000 + 15,000 – 17,000

= **14,**000

Cash and profit: Chapter 1

Period expenses

There are some expenses that are paid as incurred. For example, wages tend to be paid in the month that they are earned by the employees so no adjustments are normally necessary to turn the Statement of Profit or Loss figure into a cash flow figure.

Test your understanding 7

The Statement of Profit or Loss for L Boy's business for the quarter ended 31 March is as follows:

	£	£
Revenue		210,325
Less: Purchases		(32,657)
Gross profit		177,668
Less: Expenses		
Wages	50,100	
Rent of office	15,000	
Insurance of machinery	7,851	
Electricity	12,352	
Depreciation	8,687	
		(93,990)
Profit for the year		83,678

Extracts from the Statement of Financial Position at 1 January and 31 March show the following:

	1 January	31 March
	£	£
Receivables	18,695	15,985
Payables	965	1,054
Accruals – Electricity	550	450
Prepayments – Rent of office	1,200	1,350

CASH AND FINANCIAL MANAGEMENT

Calculate the actual business cash receipts and cash payments for the quarter to 31 March.

	£
Sales receipts	
Purchases	
Wages	
Rent of office	
Insurance of machinery	
Electricity	
Depreciation	

Test your understanding 8

Catherine Olivia owns a dance school. Catherine prepares quarterly statements of profit or loss and statements of financial position. These are prepared on an accruals basis.

Catherine buys costumes for shows put on by the school and keeps these in inventory. She gets credit from her suppliers as she uses them on a regular basis. The dancers who attend her classes pay on a regular basis, but in arrears, so Catherine is owed money by them all of the time.

The Statement of Profit or Loss for Catherine's business for the quarter ended June is as follows:

	£	£
Revenue		3,000
Less: Purchases		(1,400)
Gross profit		1,600
Less: Expenses		
Wages	300	
Advertising expenses	100	
Travel expenses	400	
Fees for competitions	150	
		(950)
		650

KAPLAN PUBLISHING

Cash and profit: Chapter 1

Extracts from the Statement of Financial Positions at 1 April and 30 June show the following:

Statement of Financial Position at	1 April £	30 June £
Receivables	1,520	1,400
Payables	400	520
Accruals – travel costs	50	80
Prepayments – comp fees	80	110

Calculate the actual business cash receipts and cash payments for the quarter to 30 June.

	£
Sales receipts	
Purchase payments	
Wages paid	
Advertising expenses paid	
Travel expenses paid	
Competition expenses paid	

4 Reconciling profit to cash flow

4.1 Introduction

As discussed there is a difference between profit and cash flow. It is possible to calculate cash flow from profit, or vice versa, using information from financial statements and other information.

Items added to profit to get to cash:

- depreciation (a non-cash item)
- loss on disposal (a non-cash item)
- a decrease in the receivables balance
- a decrease in the inventory balance
- an increase in the payables balance
- any excess of the tax and or interest SoPL charge over the cash paid.

Items deducted from profit to get to cash:

- profit on disposal (a non-cash item)
- an increase in the receivables balance is deducted from profit
- an increase in the inventory balance
- a decrease in the payables balance
- any excess of the cash paid for tax and or interest over the SoPL charge.

Note: the opposite would be applied to calculate profit from cash.

4.2 Change in receivables

Operating profit contains items included within the balances in the Statement of Financial Position. For example, revenue in the Statement of Profit or Loss includes **all** sales made, whether the cash has been received or not, so the **change** in the receivables balance is calculated to identify the necessary adjustment to change profit into cash.

The receivables account allows us to calculate the cash received, as seen in section 3.3, by completing the following calculation:

Cash receipts = sales + opening receivables – closing receivables

This can be rewritten as:

Cash received = sales adjusted for the change in receivables

The Statement of Profit or Loss already includes the sales in the operating profit so the adjustment to change profit into cash is simply the 'change in receivables'.

Example

A company believes that 90% of sales will be on credit terms. The balance of trade receivables at 1 April is £8,000 and the company expects trade receivables at the end of June to be 30% of the credit sales for the quarter. The sales for the quarter are £10,000.

Calculate the adjustment required to change the profit figure into cash.

Solution

The opening balance = £8,000

The closing balance = £10,000 × 90% × 30% = £2,700

The difference = £5,300 decrease in balance

An addition of £5,300 will adjust the operating profit for the period for the cash received in excess of the credit sales made already included in the revenue.

	Receivables		
Opening balance	8,000	Cash received	14,300
Credit sales	9,000	Closing balance	2,700
	17,000		17,000

£9,000 sales are already recorded in the Statement of Profit or Loss within the Sales revenue amount. £14,300 has been received from the receivables. This means that to fully account for the cash receipts profit needs to be increased by £5,300.

4.3 Change in inventory

If the balance on the inventory account has increased it indicates that more inventory has been purchased therefore more cash has been spent reducing the cash flow and vice versa. The profit needs to be adjusted for the movement in inventory to calculate the cash flow for the period.

 Example

The opening inventory was £80,000 and the closing inventory is £90,000.

Calculate the adjustment required to change the profit figure into cash.

Solution

There has been an increase in the inventory balance. The difference is £10,000.

Profit will need to be reduced by £10,000.

4.4 Change in payables

Purchases in the Statement of Profit or Loss include all purchases made, whether the cash has been paid or not, so the change in the payables balance is calculated to identify the necessary adjustment to change profit into cash.

CASH AND FINANCIAL MANAGEMENT

Example

All purchases are to be made on credit terms. Purchases for the quarter are £2,400. The balance of trade payables at 1 April is £1,200. Total payments for purchases during the quarter will be £2,000.

Calculate the adjustment required to change the profit figure into cash.

Solution

The opening balance = £1,200

The closing balance = £1,200 + £2,400 − £2,000 = £1,600

The difference = £400 increase in balance

An addition of £400 will adjust the operating profit for the period for the extra payment recorded in the Statement of Profit or Loss under Purchases.

Payables

Cash paid	2,000	Opening balance	1,200
Closing balance	1,600	Purchases	2,400
	3,600		3,600

£2,400 purchases are already recorded in the Statement of Profit or Loss within the Cost of sales. Only £2,000 has actually been paid to the payables. This means that to fully account for the cash paid, profit needs to be increase by £400.

Test your understanding 9

Rico has total revenue for the year of £57,000, of which 20% were cash sales and the remainder on credit. Rico had opening trade receivables of £10,000 and closing trade receivables of £15,000.

What are the total cash receipts in respect of sales?

A £11,400
B £40,600
C £52,000
D £63,000

KAPLAN PUBLISHING

Test your understanding 10

The forecast Statement of Profit or Loss for A Business for the quarter ended June is as follows:

	£	£
Sales		7,500
Less: Cost of sales		
Opening inventory	600	
Purchases	1,200	
Closing inventory	(500)	
		(1,300)
Gross profit		6,200
Expenses		(940)
Operating profit		5,260
Tax		(1,350)
Profit after tax		3,910

Additional information

1. The company believes that 80% of sales will be on credit terms. 20% of total sales will be cash sales. The balance of trade receivables at 1 April is £5,000 and the company expects trade receivables at the end of June to be 30% of the credit sales for the quarter.

2. All purchases are to be made on credit terms. The balance of trade payables at 1 April is £600. Total payments for purchases during the quarter will be £1,000.

3. Expenses include a depreciation charge of £900. All other expenses are settled on cash terms.

4. The carrying value of the non-current assets at 1 April is forecast to be £10,000 and the carrying value at 30 June is forecast to be £12,000. The company will pay for any additions immediately by cash.

5. The tax payable shown in the Statement of Financial Position is expected to be £1,300 at 1 April and £1,400 at 30 June.

6. The forecast cash position at 1 April is £15,000.

CASH AND FINANCIAL MANAGEMENT

Calculate the closing cash position at 30 June. Use brackets or minus signs where appropriate.

	£
Operating profit	
Change in inventory	
Change in receivables	
Change in payables	
Adjustment for non-cash items	
Change in non-current assets	
Tax paid	
Net change in cash position	
Forecast cash position 1 April	
Forecast cash position 30 June	

Test your understanding 11

Labet is an office and industrial furniture manufacturer.

The statement of financial position below is stated as at 31 October 20X6, which is followed by a summary of Labet's cash book for the year ended 31 October 20X7.

Labet's Statement of financial position at 31 October 20X6

	£000	£000
Non-current assets		
Property, plant and equipment – cost	7,300	
– depreciation	1,110	
		6,190
Current assets		
Inventory	1,200	
Trade receivables	753	
Cash and cash equivalents	82	
		2,035
		8,225
Equity		
Share capital	3,000	
Retained earnings	1,425	
		4,425
Non-current liabilities		
Loan notes	2,260	
Deferred tax	180	
		2,440
Current liabilities		
Trade and other payables	573	
Tax payable	670	
Interest payable	117	
		1,360
		8,225

CASH AND FINANCIAL MANAGEMENT

Labet's summarised cash book for the year ended 31 October 20X7

	Note	Receipts/(Payment) £000
Cash book balance at 1 November 20X6		82
Interest paid during the year	(ii)	(160)
Administration expenses paid		(500)
Income tax	(iii)	(690)
Purchase cost of property, plant and equipment	(iv)	(3,460)
Receipt for disposal of land	(v)	1,200
Cash received from customers		7,500
Payments to suppliers of production materials, wages and other production costs		(3,000)
Distribution and selling costs		(730)
Cash received from increase in loan notes		2,500
Cash book balance at 31 October 20X7		2,742

Notes:

(i) All sales and purchases are on credit terms.

(ii) Interest outstanding at 31 October 20X7 was £130,000.

(iii) The tax liability as at 31 October 20X7 was £502,000.

(iv) The property, plant and equipment balance at 31 October 20X6 was made up as follows:

	Land £000	Premises £000	Plant & equipment £000	Total £000
Cost	2,000	1,500	3,800	7,300
Accumulated depreciation	0	350	760	1,110
Carrying value	2,000	1,150	3,040	6,190

During the year Labet purchased new premises at a cost of £1,600,000, and new plant and equipment for £1,860,000. Property, plant and equipment are depreciated on the straight line basis at 6% per year and are treated as a cost of sale. Labet charges a full year's depreciation in the year of acquisition.

(v) Land originally costing £1,000,000 was sold during the year for £1,200,000. Land is not depreciated.

(vi) Balances at 31 October 20X7:

Trade receivables	£620,000
Outstanding trade payables	£670,000
Inventory	£985,000
Deferred tax	£180,000

Prepare the Statement of Profit or Loss (all workings should be to the nearest £000).

Labet's Statement of Profit or Loss for the year to 31 October 20X7

£000

Revenue
Cost of sales

Gross profit   _____
Distribution costs
Administrative expenses
Disposal of land
                                                                       _____
Operating profit
Finance costs
                                                                       _____
Profit before tax
Income tax expense
                                                                       _____
Profit for the period

5 Summary

This chapter demonstrates the differences between cash and profit and how to reconcile between them. It shows how to use the Statement of Profit or Loss and the Statement of Financial Position figures to calculate cash flows.

Test your understanding answers

Test your understanding 1

Type of receipt or payment	Description
Irregular receipts	C
Capital payment	E
Regular revenue receipt	H
Exceptional payment	G
Exceptional receipt	B
Regular revenue payment	A
Annual disbursement	F
Drawings	D

Test your understanding 2

Answer A

Non-current assets would require a large capital payment to be made.

Test your understanding 3

Answer D

Income from an insurance claim would not be expected as part of day to day trading.

Test your understanding 4

Answer A

Depreciation each year = (15,000 − £3,000)/5 years = £2,400
Carrying value at disposal = £15,000 − (£2,400 × 3 years) = £7,800
Cash received = Carrying value + gain on disposal = £7,800 + £500 = £8,300

Test your understanding 5

Answer B

Depreciation after revaluation = 200,000/20 years = £10,000 per year
Carrying value at disposal = 200,000 − (10,000 × 2 years) = 180,000
Disposal proceeds = Carrying value − loss on disposal = 180,000 − 5,000 = 175,000

Test your understanding 6

Answer C

Closing CV = Opening CV + additions − disposal CV − depreciation
215,000 = 150,000 + additions − 5,000 − 20,000
Additions = 215,000 − 150,000 + 5,000 + 20,000 = 90,000

Test your understanding 7

	Working	£
Sales receipts	18,695 + 210,325 – 15,985	213,035
Purchases	965 + 32,657 – 1,054	32,568
Wages	As per income statement	50,100
Rent of office	15,000 – 1,200 + 1,350	15,150
Insurance of machinery	As per Statement of Profit or Loss	7,851
Electricity	12,352 + 550 – 450	12,452
Depreciation	Non-cash item	0

Test your understanding 8

	Working	£
Sales receipts	1,520 + 3,000 – 1,400	3,120
Purchases payments	400 + 1,400 – 520	1,280
Wages paid	As per SoPL	300
Advertising expenses paid	As per SoPL	100
Travel expenses	50 + 400 – 80	370
Competition fees paid	150 + 110 – 80	180

Test your understanding 9

Answer C

Cash received = Sales + opening receivables – closing receivables
Cash received = 57,000 + 10,000 – 15,000 = £52,000

Test your understanding 10

	Working	£
Operating profit		5,260
Change in inventory	600 – 500 reduction	100
Change in receivables	7,500 × 0.8 × 0.3 = 1,800 5,000 – 1,800 reduction	3,200
Change in payables	600 + 1,200 – 1,000 = 800 600 – 800 increase	200
Adjustment for non-cash items	Depreciation charge	900
Change in non-current assets	12,000 + 900 – 10,000 = 2,900 for additions	(2,900)
Tax paid	1,300 + 1,350 – 1,400 = 1,250 paid	(1,250)
Net change in cash position		5,510
Forecast cash position 1 April		15,000
Forecast cash position 30 June		20,510

Test your understanding 11

Labet's Statement of profit or loss for the year to 31 October 20X7

	£000
Revenue (W1)	7,367
Cost of sales (W2 – W4)	(3,838)
Gross profit	3,529
Distribution costs	(730)
Administrative expenses	(500)
Disposal of land (W5)	200
Profit from operations	2,499
Finance costs (W6)	(173)
Profit before tax	2,326
Income tax expense (W7)	(522)
Profit for the period	1,804

Workings

(W1) Revenue

	£000
Opening receivables	(753)
Cash received from receivables	7,500
Closing receivables	620
Revenue	7,367

(W2) Depreciation

	Premises £000	Plant £000	Total £000
Cost	1,500	3,800	5,300
Addition	1,600	1,860	3,460
	3,100	5,660	8,760
Depreciation charge for the year	186	340	526

(W3) Purchases

	£000
Opening payables	(573)
Cash paid	3,000
Closing payables	670
Purchases	3,097

(W4) Cost of sales

	£000
Opening inventory	1,200
Depreciation (W2)	526
Purchases (W3)	3,097
Closing inventory	(985)
	3,838

(W5) Disposal of land

	£		£
NBV	1,000,000	Accumulated depreciation	0
Gain	200,000	Proceeds	1,200,000
	1,200,000		1,200,000

(W6) Interest charge

	£000
Opening balance	117
Interest paid during the year	(160)
Closing balance	(130)
Statement of profit of loss charge	173

(W7) Tax charge

	£000
Opening balance	670
Tax paid during the year	(690)
Closing balance	(502)
Statement of profit of loss charge	522

CASH AND FINANCIAL MANAGEMENT

Forecasting cash flows

Introduction

This chapter considers statistical methods and techniques that can be used to forecast cash payments and cash receipts for inclusion within a cash budget.

One of the most common of these methods is time series analysis which can be used to forecast sales for future periods. Cash flow forecasts might also be affected by changes in quantities of sales or production and by inflation of costs and prices.

ASSESSMENT CRITERIA
Statistical techniques (1.3)

CONTENTS
1 Information for cash budgets
2 Time series analysis
3 Moving averages
4 Regression analysis
5 Inflation
6 Mark-ups and margins
7 Problems with forecasting

Information for cash budgets

1.1 Introduction

A lot of information is needed in order to produce a cash budget.

1.2 Sales information

The starting point for information for the cash budget will normally be sales, as this will be the basis for the production budget and expenses figures. This information will normally be provided by the **sales or marketing manager**. Both the quantity of sales and the price that will be charged are vital information for a cash budget.

1.3 Production information

Details such as the amount of production, the levels of closing inventories and the labour hours to be worked should all be available from the **production manager**. He, she or they may also have information about variable and fixed expenses of the factory and any planned capital expenditure but equally that information may come from the accountant.

1.4 Accounting information

Further information will come from the **accounts department** in the form of materials prices, labour hour rates, variable and fixed costs, details of sales of non-current assets. The accounts department or the credit control department will also have the information required to determine the payment pattern of receivables and payables.

1.5 Forecast information

The information provided by the different departments will be current or past information. This information will need to be amended to allow for any adjustments or alterations foreseen for future periods.

There are a number of different techniques that can be used to produce forecasted figures:

- **Time series analysis using moving averages** – removes peaks and troughs in time series data to produce a trend that can be extrapolated.

- **Regression analysis** – calculates the line of best fit, in a set of data, which can then be extrapolated.

- **Percentage change and index numbers** – to adjust prices and quantities by known percentages and to apply changes due to inflation.
- **Mark-ups and margins** – to calculate costs and revenues when a desired return is known.

2 Time series analysis

2.1 Introduction

 Definition

A time series is a set of values for some variable (e.g. monthly sales) which varies with time. A set of observations will be taken at specific times, usually at regular intervals.

Examples of figures which can be plotted as a time series are:

(a) train ticket sales each hour

(b) daily closing price of a share on the Stock Exchange

(c) weekly sales in a department store.

2.2 Time series graph

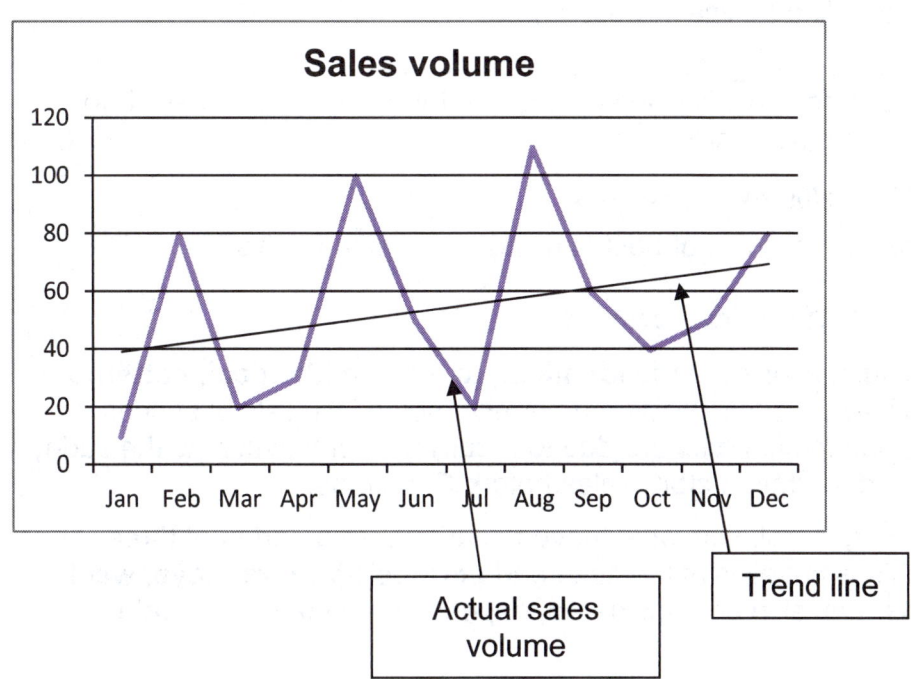

The graph shows the monthly sales volume for a year in a business. It can be seen that the sales have fluctuated month on month producing peaks and troughs in the data. For this graph to be useful for predicting cash flows the 'trend' or general movement of the data needs to be known – is it increasing, decrease or staying static?

The graph of a time series may be useful for investigating what happened in the past but the real value of producing a time series is to use it to forecast what will happen in the future.

In other words the past information is recorded, analysed and projected into the future to help with production planning, staff recruitment, etc.

2.3 Components of a time series

Analysis of time series has revealed certain characteristic movements or variations. These movements are the components of the time series. Analysis of these components is essential for forecasting purposes.

The four main components are:

- basic trend or long-term movement
- seasonal movement
- cyclical movement
- residual or random movements.

2.4 Basic trend

The basic trend shows the **general direction** in the graph over a long interval of time. This movement can be represented on the graph by a trend curve or line (a 'line of best fit').

One way of identifying the trend is simply to draw it in freehand on the graph. This is not usually good enough for forecasting purposes. Two more robust methods are:

- using moving averages
- calculating the line of best fit using regression analysis.

2.5 Seasonal variations

Seasonal fluctuations are the **identical, or almost identical, patterns** which a time series follows during corresponding intervals of successive periods. Such movements are due to recurring events, such as the sudden increase in department store sales before Christmas.

Although, in general, seasonal movements refer to a period of three months, this is not always the case and **periods of hours, days, weeks or months** may also be considered, depending on the type of data available.

2.6 Cyclical variations

Cyclical variations refer to **long-term oscillations** or swings about the trend line or curve. These cycles do **not necessarily follow exactly similar patterns** after equal intervals of time.

In business and economic situations, movements are said to be cyclical if they recur after time intervals of **more than one year**. A good example is the trade cycle, representing intervals of prosperity, recession, depression and recovery. For cyclical variations to be apparent, data must be available over very long periods of time since the periods of oscillation are so long. This is impractical for cash flows and, for that reason, the **calculation of cyclical variations is ignored in this chapter** although you must, of course, realise that they exist.

2.7 Random variations

Random variations are the **sporadic motions** of time series due to chance events such as **floods, strikes, elections**.

By their very nature they are **unpredictable** and therefore cannot play a large part in any forecasting, but it is possible to isolate the random variations by calculating all other types of variation and removing them from the time series data. It is important to extract any significant random variations from the data before using them for forecasting.

3 Moving averages

3.1 Introduction

The analysis of a time series consists of:

Step 1 Breaking the series down into trend and seasonal variations.

Step 2 Projecting the trend into the future.

Step 3 Applying the seasonal variation to the projected trend, to arrive at forecast figures.

3.2 Moving averages

By using moving averages, the **variations in a time series can be eliminated leaving a 'smoothed' set of figures** which is taken as the **trend**.

It is important that the correct cycle is chosen for the moving average; otherwise the result will not be as good as it should be.

For instance, if there are seasonal variations present in a time series and the pattern is repeated every third month (quarterly), the moving average should be calculated based on three months at a time to get the best results. It is possible to calculate a moving average based on any length of cycle.

3.3 Calculating moving averages

Example

The underlying trend is estimated using moving averages.

Month	Actual sales	3 point moving total	Trend
Jan	74		
Feb	100	267 (W1)	89 (W2)
Mar	93	279	93 (W3)
Apr	86	291	97
May	112	303	101
Jun	105	315	105
Jul	98	327	109
Aug	124	339	113
Sept	117	351	117
Oct	110	363	121
Nov	136	375	125
Dec	129		

Workings

(W1) Calculate the total of the sales for the first three months (month January to March).

74 + 100 + 93 = 267

(W2) Find the average sales for this three month period by dividing by 3.

267 ÷ 3 = 89

This represents the trend for February.

(W3) Repeat the process for the next three month period, moving on just one month (months February to April).

100 + 93 + 86 = 279

279/3 = 93

This represents the trend for March.

Repeat the calculation for each successive three-month period until the data has been fully analysed into three-month blocks.

Months March to May = 97 (trend for April).

Months April to June = 101 (trend for May).

Test your understanding 1

The following represents monthly output of a product.

What are the trend figures that would be obtained by a 3 point moving average?

Month	Sales volume	3 point moving total	Trend
Jan	4,000		
Feb	8,680		
Mar	5,260		
Apr	4,540		
May	9,220		
Jun	5,800		
Jul	5,080		
Aug	9,760		
Sept	6,340		
Oct	5,620		
Nov	10,300		
Dec	6,880		

3.4 Centred moving averages

In the previous example the period for the moving average was an odd number i.e. a three month moving average. This meant that it was possible to place each moving average against the central month for each calculation.

However if the moving average is taken with an even number of periods e.g. a four month moving average, then there is no central period. Instead the moving average total must be shown in the middle of the period which will be between the second and third periods of each calculation.

Therefore a further average must be taken known as the **centred moving average**. This is done by taking each successive pair of moving average figures and finding their own average which is then placed in the middle of their figures. This is the trend figure.

Example

Month	Actual sales	4 point moving average	Centred moving average (trend)
Jan	100		
Feb	118		
		120 (W1)	
Mar	125		121 (W2)
		122	
April	137		123
		124	
May	108		125
		126	
Jun	126		127
		128	
Jul	133		129
		130	
Aug	145		131
		132	
Sept	116		133
		134	
Oct	134		135
		136	
Nov	141		
Dec	153		

CASH AND FINANCIAL MANAGEMENT

Workings

(W1) Calculate the four point moving average for each successive period:

100 + 118 + 125 + 137 = 480   480/4 = 120

118 + 125 + 137 + 108 = 488   488/4 = 122

125 + 137 + 108 + 126 = 496   496/4 = 124

Place each of these figures in the central point of the four month period.

(W2) Calculate the centred moving average by taking each successive pair of four point moving averages and finding their average:

120 + 122 = 242   242/2 = 121

122 + 124 = 246   246/2 = 123

Show each of these centred moving averages in the centre of the two four-month figures used.

The final column, the centred moving average, is the trend of the data.

Be sure that you have understood the positioning of the moving averages in the above table. Each average has been written exactly opposite the middle of the figures from which it has been calculated. This results in the moving averages for even numbers of values (four in this case) being suspended halfway between two of the original figures.

Where you have a moving average for an even number of values, it is necessary to realign the moving averages so that they fall opposite an original value by calculating a centred moving average for every two moving average values.

Test your understanding 2

The table below provides details of Masham plc's quarterly sales in units.

Calculate the four point moving average of Masham's sales units.

Year	Quarter	Actual sales units	4 point moving average	Centred moving average (trend)
1	1	120		
	2	168		
	3	140		
	4	172		
2	1	136		
	2	184		
	3	156		
	4	188		
3	1	152		
	2	200		
	3	172		
	4	204		

3.5 Extrapolating the trend

Once the trend has been found it then needs to be projected into the future. If the trend is constant then extrapolation is easy to calculate as the difference between each value is the same.

This value can then be added to the final trend figure to extrapolate the trend into future periods.

Example

The trend for a set of data is as follows:

Month	Trend
Jan	85
Feb	89
Mar	93
Apr	97
May	101
Jun	105
Jul	109
Aug	113
Sept	117
Oct	121
Nov	125
Dec	129

What is the trend figure for March of the following year?

Trend is increasing by 4 each month 93 – 89 = 4, 105 – 101 = 4

129 + (4 × 3) = 141

If the trend is not constant then the average increase is calculated.

> ### Example
>
> The trend for a set of data is as follows:
>
> | Month | Trend |
> |-------|-------|
> | Jan | 100 |
> | Feb | 102 |
> | Mar | 106 |
> | Apr | 111 |
> | May | 114 |
> | Jun | 116 |
> | Jul | 118 |
> | Aug | 120 |
> | Sept | 123 |
> | Oct | 126 |
> | Nov | 129 |
> | Dec | 134 |
>
> What is the trend figure for March of the following year?
>
> Average trend
>
> = (Last known trend – first known trend) ÷ (number of sets of data – 1)
>
> = (134 – 100) ÷ (12 – 1) = 3.09
>
> Trend figure for March = 134 + (3 × 3.09) = 143.27

3.6 Seasonal variations

Once the trend has been calculated it is possible to calculate the **seasonal variation from the trend**. This is how much the actual data varies from the trend line. There are two ways of dealing with the seasonal variations:

(a) Using an **additive** model where variations are expressed in **absolute** terms with above and below average figures designated by plus and minus signs respectively. The sum of the seasonal variations should total zero (or are adjusted to equal zero).

(b) Using a proportional or **multiplicative** model where variations are represented in percentage terms with high and low figures being above or below 100%.

Both models can be used with a trend produced by any method.

The basic idea here will be to take a predicted trend figure and adjust it for an 'average' seasonal variation.

The additive model

In an additive model, the seasonal effect is the same (roughly constant) in the same period over different years.

 Example

The underlying trend has been estimated using a 3 point moving average.

Using the **additive** model:

Month	Actual sales	Trend	Seasonal variation
Jan	74		
Feb	100	89	11
Mar	93	93	0
Apr	86	97	−11
May	112	101	11
Jun	105	105	0
Jul	98	109	−11
Aug	124	113	11
Sept	117	117	0
Oct	110	121	−11
Nov	136	125	11
Dec	129		

When using the **additive** model **absolute** numbers are calculated. The seasonal variation is **from** the trend.

February's value is **greater than the trend** therefore the seasonal variation is **positive**. April's value is **less than the trend** therefore the seasonal variation is **negative**. If this data is plotted on a graph February's sales value would lie above the trend line and April's would lie below.

Test your understanding 3

Calculate the sales volume trend from this data using a 4 point moving average. Calculate the seasonal variation using the additive model.

Month	Sales volume	Moving average	Centred average	Seasonal variation
Jan	150			
Feb	310			
Mar	380			
Apr	420			
May	310			
Jun	470			
Jul	540			
Aug	580			
Sept	470			
Oct	630			
Nov	700			
Dec	740			
Jan	630			
Feb	790			
Mar	860			

The multiplicative model

Sometimes the seasonal variation is a **proportion** of the underlying trend value. It is then appropriate to use a **multiplicative model**.

Using the **proportional** or **multiplicative** model the variations are represented in percentage terms with high and low figures being above or below 100%.

CASH AND FINANCIAL MANAGEMENT

 Example

The underlying trend has been estimated using a 4 point moving average.

Using the **multiplicative** model:

Year	Quarter	Value	Trend	Proportion of the trend % (rounded to nearest whole number)
1	1	74		
	2	100		
	3	94	100	94 ÷ 100 × 100 = 94
	4	127	102	127 ÷ 102 × 100 = 125
2	1	84	106	84 ÷ 106 × 100 = 79
	2	106	111	106 ÷ 111 × 100 = 96
	3	120	114	105
	4	141	116	122
3	1	94	118	80
	2	112	120	93
	3	130	123	106
	4	147	126	117
4	1	112	129	87
	2	118	134	88
	3	148		
	4	169		

The seasonal variations in the proportional model are not true variations but percentage increases or decreases.

In some questions you may see multiplicative seasonal variations being stated as a positive or negative percentage from the trend.
For example:

- Year 1 quarter 3 would be referred to as 6% less than the trend.
- Year 2 quarter 4 would be referred to as 22% more than the trend.

Forecasting cash flows: Chapter 2

 Test your understanding 4

A company is preparing its forecast sales for the first quarter of next year.

Identify the sales volume trend from the data below using a 3 point moving average and calculate the monthly sales trend.

Calculate the seasonal variation using the multiplicative model.

Month	Sales volume	3 point trend	Seasonal variation %
Jan	4,000		
Feb	8,680		
Mar	5,260		
Apr	4,540		
May	9,220		
Jun	5,800		
Jul	5,080		
Aug	9,760		
Sept	6,340		
Oct	5,620		
Nov	10,300		
Dec	6,880		

3.7 Applying the seasonal variation

Once the seasonal variations have been calculated they can be used to forecast future values.

The trend line is extrapolated and the variations are applied to the trend.

Additive model forecast = Trend + Seasonal variation

Multiplicative model forecast = Trend × Seasonal variation (%)

Example

Using the **additive** model when the variations follow a repeating pattern.

Month	Actual sales	Trend	Seasonal variation
Jan	74		
Feb	100	89	11
Mar	93	93	0
Apr	86	97	−11
May	112	101	11
Jun	105	105	0
Jul	98	109	−11
Aug	124	113	11
Sept	117	117	0
Oct	110	121	−11
Nov	136	125	11

Step 1

The trend is increasing by 4 each month. Extrapolate the trend for future periods by adding 4 each time.

Step 2

Apply the seasonal variations. In this example the seasonal variations cycle 0, −11, 11, 0, −11, 11. We assume this continues for the forecast trend. The seasonal variation is **from** the trend so if there is a negative variation the forecast will be lower than the trend and a positive variation the forecast will be higher than the trend.

Forecast values			Forecast
Dec	129	0	129
Jan	133	−11	122
Feb	137	11	148
Mar	141	0	141

Example

Using the **additive** model when the seasonal variations do not follow a repeating pattern.

Year	Quarter	Trend	Seasonal variation
1	3	100	−6
	4	102	25
2	1	106	−22
	2	111	−5
	3	114	6
	4	116	25
3	1	118	−24
	2	120	−8
	3	123	7
	4	126	21
4	1	129	−17
	2	134	−16

Step 1

Average trend

= (Last known trend − first known trend) ÷ (number of sets of data − 1)

= (134 − 100) ÷ (12 − 1) = 3.09

Step 2

Since the seasonal variations, in this example, change, an average adjustment is computed, by adding together each quarter's variations and dividing by the number of observations.

CASH AND FINANCIAL MANAGEMENT

	Quarter			
Year	1	2	3	4
1	–	–	(6)	25
2	(22)	(5)	6	25
3	(24)	(8)	7	21
4	(17)	(16)	–	–
Sum	(63)	(29)	7	71
Average	(21)	(9.67)	2.33	23.7

Seasonal variations need to add up to zero so a small adjustment is made.

	1	2	3	4	Total
Average	(21)	(9.67)	2.33	23.7	–4.64
Adjustment	1.16	1.16	1.16	1.16	+4.64
Average adjusted	(19.84)	(8.51)	3.49	24.86	0

These figures can then be applied to the extrapolated trend.

Suppose we want to predict **year 5 quarter 3** sales. This would be done as follows.

Step 1 Trend figure

Starting from the last trend figure available, add on the appropriate number of trend increments.

Year 4	Quarter 2	=	134
Year 5	Quarter 3	=	134 + 5 movements
		=	134 + (5 × 3.09)
		=	149.45

Step 2 Adjust for average seasonal variation for quarter 3

Prediction   =   149.45 + 3.49 = 152.94

Example

Using the **multiplicative** model (assuming seasonal variations apply consistently from one year to the next):

Consider a business with the following results in a year:

Year	Quarter	Actual units sold	Trend	Multiplicative variation
20X1	1	65	60	+8.33%
20X1	2	80	70	+14.29%
20X1	3	70	80	−12.50%
20X1	4	85	90	−5.56%

Using the multiplicative model forecast unit sales in each quarter of year 2.

Year	Quarter	Trend	Variation	Forecast
20X2	1	100	+8.33%	108
20X2	2	110	+14.29%	126
20X2	3	120	−12.50%	105
20X2	4	130	−5.56%	123

Example

Using the **multiplicative** model when seasonal variations are not assumed to be consistent. **This is advanced knowledge**.

Seasonal variation = (Sales – Trend)/Trend × 100

Year	Time period	Sales	Centred moving average	Seasonal variation
		£000		
1	1	42		
	2	41		
	3	52	43.8750	+18.52% or 1.1852
	4	39	45.1250	–13.57% or 0.8643
2	5	45	47.1250	–4.51% or 0.9549
	6	48	49.1250	–2.29 or 0.9771
	7	61	50.8750	+19.90% or 1.1990
	8	46	52.1250	–11.75% or 0.8825
3	9	52	52.3750	–0.72% or 0.9928
	10	51	52.2500	–2.39% or 0.9761
	11	60		
	12	46		

Step 1

Identify the trend. The increase in the trend is not constant so the average increase per period is calculated.

Total increase over range: (52.2500 – 43.8750) ÷ (10 – 3) = 1.1964

Step 2

Since the seasonal variations, in this example, change, an average adjustment is computed, by adding together each period's variation and dividing by the number of observations.

Forecasting cash flows: Chapter 2

		Quarter		
Year	1	2	3	4
1	–	–	1.1852	0.8643
2	0.9549	0.9771	1.1990	0.8825
3	0.9928	0.9761	–	–
Sum	1.9477	1.9532	2.3842	1.7468
Average	0.9739	0.9766	1.1921	0.8734

Seasonal variations need to add up to four so a small adjustment is made.

	1	2	3	4	Total
Average	0.9739	0.9766	1.1921	0.8734	4.016
Adjustment	–0.004	–0.004	–0.004	–0.004	–0.016
Average adjusted	0.9699	0.9726	1.1881	0.8694	4.000

These figures can then be applied to the extrapolated trend.

Suppose we want to predict **year 4 quarter 3** sales. This would be done as follows.

Step 1   Trend figure

Starting from the last trend figure available, add on the appropriate number of trend increments.

Year 3	Quarter 2	=	52.2500
Year 5	Quarter 3	=	52.2500 + 5 movements
		=	52.2500 + (5 × 1.1964)
		=	58.2320

Step 2   Adjust for average seasonal variation for quarter 3

Prediction   =   58.2320 × 1.1881 = 69.1854

CASH AND FINANCIAL MANAGEMENT

 Test your understanding 5

A company is preparing its forecast sales for the first quarter of next year.

Identify the sales volume trend from this year's data using a 3 month moving average. Calculate the seasonal variation using the additive model. Use this information to predict March, April and May's sales volume for next year.

Month	Sales volume	3 point trend	Seasonal variation
Jan	4,600		
Feb	5,300		
Mar	5,100		
Apr	5,050		
May	5,750		
Jun	5,550		
Jul	5,500		
Aug	6,200		
Sept	6,000		
Oct	5,950		
Nov	6,650		
Dec	6,450		

Month	Forecast sales trend	Variation	Forecast sale volume
Mar			
Apr			
May			

Forecasting cash flows: Chapter 2

 Test your understanding 6

The managers of a company are preparing plans for the first quarter of next year. The figures below refer to the sales volumes for the year just past.

Complete the table to calculate the monthly sales volume trend, the monthly variations from the trend using the multiplicative model and then the prediction for the January to March for next year. Round all your figures to the nearest whole number.

Month	Sales volume	3 point trend	Seasonal variation
Jan	49		
Feb	37		
Mar	58		
Apr	50		
May	38		
Jun	60		
Jul	51		
Aug	40		
Sept	61		
Oct	53		
Nov	41		
Dec	61		

Month	Forecast sales trend	Variation	Forecast sale volume
Jan			
Feb			
Mar			

Test your understanding 7

Below is the sales data for January to December 20X1 and January to March 20X2. Calculate the 5 month trend and monthly variation using the additive model.

Month	Sales volume	5 point trend	Seasonal variation
Jan	150		
Feb	310		
Mar	400		
Apr	490		
May	750		
Jun	180		
Jul	340		
Aug	430		
Sept	520		
Oct	780		
Nov	210		
Dec	370		
Jan	460		
Feb	550		
Mar	810		

What will be the predicted sales volume for December 20X2?

A   610
B   476
C   526
D   482

Test your understanding 8

A company is preparing its forecast sales and purchase information for October of the current financial year.

The sales volume trend is to be identified using a 3–point moving average based on the actual monthly sales volumes for the current year.

(a) Complete the table below to calculate the current monthly sales volume trend and identify any monthly variations, using the additive model.

	Sales volume (units)	Trend	Monthly variation
May	11,000		
June	11,850		
July	12,550		
August	11,900		
September	12,750		

Additional information

The trend is assumed to be a straight line and the seasonal variations are cyclical.

The selling price per unit has been set at £21.

Monthly purchases are estimated to be 60% of the value of the forecast sales.

(b) Using the trend and the monthly variations identified in part (a) complete the table below to forecast the sales volume, sales value and purchase value for October.

	Forecast trend	Variation	Forecast sales volume	Forecast sales £	Forecast purchases £
October					

3.8 Disadvantages of moving averages

- Values at the beginning and end of the series are lost; therefore, the moving averages do not cover the complete period.
- The moving averages may generate cycles or other movements that were not present in the original data.
- The averages are strongly affected by extreme values. To overcome this, a weighted moving average is sometimes used, giving the largest weights to central items and small weights to extreme values.

4 Regression analysis

4.1 Introduction

Regression analysis is concerned with establishing the **relationship between two variables**.

Regression analysis finds the line of best fit or trend using formulae. It seeks to minimise the distance between each data point and the trend line.

Regression analysis is also useful for finding the **trend in a time series analysis** (as an alternative to moving averages).

4.2 The regression equation

The general equation for the regression line is given as:

$y = a + bx$

Where:

x is the independent variable

y is the dependent variable

a is the intercept on the y axis

b is the gradient of the line

You will be required to use the regression equation to forecast future values. When the regression equation is used for time series data the time periods are changed to numbers rather than specified days, months or years.

You must understand that the independent variable (x) in some way causes the dependent variable (y) to have the value given by the equation. For example, if we were calculating the cost of producing cars the number of cars produced would be the independent variable (x) and the cost would be the dependent variable (y) i.e. volume of production causes production cost to change and not vice versa.

Test your understanding 9

A company uses regression to forecast sales.

y = 220,000 + 500x

Where y is the sales value and x is the period. June 20X3 was period 18 (so x = 18). The forecast value of sales for September 20X3 using the regression equation is:

A £229,000
B £230,500
C £230,000
D £229,500

Test your understanding 10

Jump Ltd has two products, the Pole and the Plank. The Pole sells for £15 and the Plank for £50.

The sales volume of the Pole in Period 3 is forecast to be 1,200 units, using the regression line y = 450 + 250x (where x is the period).

(a) What is the forecast sales volume of Poles in Period 10?

Jump Ltd wants the sales revenue for Planks in Period 10 to match that predicted for Poles.

(b) What sales volume of Planks would they need to sell in order to achieve this?

4.3 The assumptions of regression analysis

Regression analysis is based on sample data and if we selected a different sample it is probable that a different regression equation would be constructed. For this reason, regression analysis is most suited to conditions where there is a relatively simple (and linear) relationship between cost and activity level.

Assumptions we are making:

- the relationship is a linear one
- the data used is representative of future trends.

5 Inflation

5.1 Introduction

Once the trend and forecasted values have been calculated it may be necessary to adjust them for inflation.

Inflation is a rise in the general level of prices of goods and services in an economy over a period of time.

Adjustments for inflation can be done using:

- percentages
- index numbers.

5.2 Percentage increases

One of the simplest ways of applying inflation to costs and revenues is to add a percentage increase that reflects the predicted level of inflation for the period compared to current figures.

> **Example**
>
> From past experience and knowledge of the market, a sales director predicts sales prices to rise by 2% due to inflation each month. So, if January sales are £100,000, then:
>
> February sales will be £100,000 × 1.02 = £102,000
> March sales will be   £102,000 × 1.02 = £104,040
> April sales will be   £104,040 × 1.02 = £106,121
>
> This can also be calculated using compounding. January sales are £100,000 by April interest will have been applied three times.
>
> April sales will be £100,000 × 1.02^3 = £106,121

Forecasting cash flows: Chapter 2

Test your understanding 11

If sales are forecast to be £3,000 in February and inflation is to be applied at 2.4% per month. What would be the forecast sales for June?

A   £3,299
B   £7,093
C   £3,221
D   £5,720

5.3 Percentage change

Calculating the percentage change from one period to another can also be used as a basis for forecasting. The difference between the two periods may be an indicator of the inflation rate that has been applied.

Example

A shopkeeper received the following amounts from the sale of radios:

```
           £000
20X1      1,000
20X2      1,100
```

The shopkeeper hopes to maintain the increase in revenue for the following years. Calculate the forecast revenue for 20X3, 20X4 and 20X5.

Solution

Step one

Calculate the difference in absolute figures:

1,100 – 1,000 = 100

Step two

Calculate the difference in percentage (relative) terms:

There has been a 10% increase from 20X1 to 20X2

100 ÷ 1,000 × 100 = 10%

CASH AND FINANCIAL MANAGEMENT

Step three

Apply this percentage increase year on year:

20X2		1,100
20X3	1,100 + (1,100 × 10%)	1,210
20X4	1,210 + (1,210 × 10%)	1,331
20X5	1,331 + (1,331 × 10%)	1,464

Test your understanding 12

The unit sales for a clock shop were as follows:

	Units
Jan	50
Feb	75
Mar	70
Apr	60
May	80

Calculate the percentage change month to month. Show a decrease in unit sales with a minus sign. Calculate to two decimal places.

	Percentage change
Jan to Feb	
Feb to Mar	
Mar to Apr	
Apr to May	

5.4 Index numbers

Index numbers can also be used to apply the effects of inflation.

Definition

An index number is a technique for comparing over time changes in some feature of a group of items (e.g. price or quantity) by expressing the change each year as a percentage of some earlier year.

An index is a useful method of comparing figures over time by simplifying data to a single index figure that can be compared to a base period (normally a year) which is given an index of 100. The index then shows the change in the figures each year compared to that base period.

5.5 Choosing a base year for an index

The year or period chosen for a base must be 'normal', e.g. if constructing an index to measure the number of foreign tourists in the UK then the choice of 2020 would not be representative of normal tourist levels due to the global covid virus pandemic impacting travel that year. It would give a misleading impression of the tourist levels, since any year compared to 2020 is likely to show a higher numbers of tourists.

The base period may be a single date, a month or a year.

The index number for the base period is given the value 100 and this might be allocated to:

- a year – 20X2 = 100
- a month – August 20X2 = 100
- a single date – 16 August 20X2 = 100

5.6 Calculating an index number

An index number is calculated as:

Current year figure ÷ base period figure × base index (usually 100)

Price could be used instead of cost in the calculation if sales prices are being considered.

Example

Given below are the production cost figures for a business for five months:

Month	Cost £000
May	138
June	149
July	158
August	130
September	136

You are required to calculate an index for these costs using May as the base month.

CASH AND FINANCIAL MANAGEMENT

Solution

Month	Cost £000	Calculation	Index
May	138	138/138 × 100	100.0
June	149	149/138 × 100	108.0
July	158	158/138 × 100	114.5
August	130	130/138 × 100	94.2
September	136	136/138 × 100	98.6

The indices that are above 100 show that the costs are higher than in May. The indices that are below 100 show that the costs are lower than in May.

We can see from the index figures that costs rose for two months then fell below May levels for two months.

The figures in the example above are the percentage change from May (the base month) e.g. the cost for July is 14.5% higher than that in May.

 Test your understanding 13

The price per unit of product is set on the first day of every month. The prices for the last three months were:

Month	5	6	7
Price	£52	£56	£50

The price in month 1 was £40. Create an index for the price per unit using month 1 as the base period.

Month	5	6	7
Price	£52	£56	£50
Index			

5.7 Using an index number

Index numbers can also be used to forecast future data to be in cash flows.

The formula for using an index is

Current value = Base value × Current index ÷ base index

Example

It is January and Aerials plc is forecasting future production costs. Given below are the forecast index numbers for the next 8 months:

Month	Index
January	103
February	108
March	115
April	94
May	99
June	109
July	112
August	117

January's production cost is £129,000

Calculate the forecast production cost for April, May and June to the nearest £.

Solution

April's forecasted production cost will be:

$\dfrac{94}{103}$ × £129,000 = £117,728

May's forecasted production cost will be:

$\dfrac{99}{103}$ × £129,000 = £123,990

April's forecasted production cost will be:

$\dfrac{109}{103}$ × £129,000 = £136,515

CASH AND FINANCIAL MANAGEMENT

 Test your understanding 14

A company uses an industry wage rate index to forecast monthly wage costs. Employees receive a pay rise in September each year. The current monthly cost of £7,800 was calculated when the wage index was 134. The forecast wage rate index for the next three months is:

August   152
September   162
October   168

What will the wage cost be for September, to the nearest £?

A   £6,452
B   £6,876
C   £9,430
D   £8,848

 Test your understanding 15

The company uses an industry sector index to calculate the selling price of its product. The price to due to be revised in March, in line with the index. The current selling price of £45 was set when the index was 132. The forecast index is as follows:

January   145
February   152
March   154
April   157

What will be the selling price, to the nearest penny in March?

A   £37.83
B   £51.82
C   £38.57
D   £52.50

6 Mark-ups and margins

6.1 Introduction

It is also possible to predict sales and costs by using mark ups and margins.

6.2 Mark-ups

A mark-up is a percentage added to the cost of a sale to calculate the selling price. The following proforma can help you work back from the sales price to calculate the cost of sales or vice versa.

	£	%
Revenue	X	100 + mark up
(Cost of sales)	(X)	(100)
Gross profit	X	Mark up

Example

If **revenue** is £2,750 and the mark up is 10% what is the cost of sales?

	£	%
Revenue	2,750	100 + 10 = 110
(Cost of sales)	(??)	(100)
Gross profit	??	10

The revenue of £2,750 is the equivalent of 110%. Therefore to calculate the cost of sales we need to divide the 2,750 by 110 and multiply it by 100.

2,750 ÷ 110 × 100 = £2,500

If the **cost of sales** is £3,500 and the mark up is 10% what is the revenue?

	£	%
Revenue	??	100 + 10 = 110
(Cost of sales)	(3,500)	(100)
Gross profit	??	10

The cost of sales of £3,500 is the equivalent of 100%. Therefore, to calculate the revenue we need to divide the 3,500 by 100 and multiply it by 110.

3,500 ÷ 100 × 110 = £3,850

6.3 Margins

A margin shows in percentage terms the amount of profit generated from revenue i.e. what percentage of the revenue eventually ends up as gross profit. The following proforma can help you work back from the sales price to calculate the cost of sales or vice versa.

	£	%
Revenue	X	100
(Cost of sales)	(X)	(100 – margin)
Gross profit	X	Margin

Example

If **revenue** is £10,000 and the margin is 5% what is the cost of sales?

	£	%
Revenue	10,000	100
(Cost of sales)	(??)	(100 – 5)
Gross profit	??	5

The sales value of £10,000 is the equivalent of 100%. Therefore to calculate the cost of sales we need to divide the 10,000 by 100 and multiply it by 100 – 5 which is 95, or multiply 10,000 by 95%.

10,000 ÷ 100 × 95 = £9,500

If the **cost of sales** is £4,500 and the margin is 10% what is the revenue?

	£	%
Revenue	??	100
(Cost of sales)	(4,500)	(100 – 10)
Gross profit	??	10

The cost of sales of £4,500 is the equivalent of 90%. Therefore to calculate the revenue we need to divide the 4,500 by 90 and multiply it by 100.

4,500 ÷ 90 × 100 = £5,000

> **Test your understanding 16**
>
> A company produces a product at a cost of £37.
>
> What sales price should it charge if it wants to achieve:
>
> (a) a mark up of 25%
>
> (b) a margin of 25%

7 Problems with forecasting

7.1 Problems with forecasting

Forecasting future cash flows has many problems which may limit their usefulness when producing a cash budget. These include:

- The assumption that past behaviour can be used as a basis for future activity.

- The volume of data available to base the forecast on may be limited this reduces the reliability of a forecast.

- The reliability of data provided. A supplier could change the selling price once the cash budget is completed. A competitor could drop their selling price leading to a decrease in the businesses selling price or volume.

- Data does not necessarily take into account outside influences on a business such as political, environmental, technological and social changes.

8 Summary

When preparing cash budgets a lot of forecast information is required.

There are various methods that can be used to try and predict future costs and revenues.

CASH AND FINANCIAL MANAGEMENT

Test your understanding answers

Test your understanding 1

Month	Sales volume (units)	3 point moving total	Trend
Jan	4,000		
Feb	8,680	17,940	5,980
Mar	5,260	18,480	6,160
Apr	4,540	19,020	6,340
May	9,220	19,560	6,520
Jun	5,800	20,100	6,700
Jul	5,080	20,640	6,880
Aug	9,760	21,180	7,060
Sept	6,340	21,720	7,240
Oct	5,620	22,260	7,420
Nov	10,300	22,800	7,600
Dec	6,880		

Forecasting cash flows: **Chapter 2**

Test your understanding 2

Year	Quarter	Actual sales value	Moving average	Centred moving average (T)
1	1	120		
	2	168		
			150	
	3	140		152
			154	
	4	172		156
			158	
2	1	136		160
			162	
	2	184		164
			166	
	3	156		168
			170	
	4	188		172
			174	
3	1	152		176
			178	
	2	200		180
			182	
	3	172		
	4	204		

Test your understanding 3

Month	Sales volume	Moving average	Centred average	Seasonal variation
Jan	150			
Feb	310			
		315		
Mar	380		335	45
		355		
Apr	420		375	45
		395		
May	310		415	−105
		435		
Jun	470		455	15
		475		
Jul	540		495	45
		515		
Aug	580		535	45
		555		
Sept	470		575	−105
		595		
Oct	630		615	15
		635		
Nov	700		655	45
		675		
Dec	740		695	45
		715		
Jan	630		735	−105
		755		
Feb	790			
Mar	860			

Test your understanding 4

Month	Sales volume (units)	3 Month trend	Seasonal variation %
Jan	4,000		
Feb	8,680	5,980	45.2
Mar	5,260	6,160	−14.6
Apr	4,540	6,340	−28.4
May	9,220	6,520	41.4
Jun	5,800	6,700	−13.4
Jul	5,080	6,880	−26.2
Aug	9,760	7,060	38.2
Sept	6,340	7,240	−12.4
Oct	5,620	7,420	−24.3
Nov	10,300	7,600	35.5
Dec	6,880		

Test your understanding 5

Month	Sales volume	3 Month trend	Seasonal variation
Jan	4,600		
Feb	5,300	5,000	300
Mar	5,100	5,150	−50
Apr	5,050	5,300	−250
May	5,750	5,450	300
Jun	5,550	5,600	−50
Jul	5,500	5,750	−250
Aug	6,200	5,900	300
Sept	6,000	6,050	−50
Oct	5,950	6,200	−250
Nov	6,650	6,350	300
Dec	6,450		

The monthly sales volume trend is an increase of 150 each month.

Month	Forecast sales trend	Variation	Forecast sale volume
Mar	6,950	–50	6,900
Apr	7,100	–250	6,850
May	7,250	300	7,550

The variation cycle is 300, –50, –250 therefore the variation for March is –50. The variation is negative therefore the sales will be less than the trend.

Test your understanding 6

Month	Sales volume	3 Month trend	Seasonal variation
Jan	49		
Feb	37	48	77%
Mar	58	48	121%
Apr	50	49	102%
May	38	49	78%
Jun	60	50	120%
Jul	51	50	102%
Aug	40	51	78%
Sept	61	51	120%
Oct	53	52	102%
Nov	41	52	79%
Dec	61		

Month	Forecast sales trend	Variation	Forecast sales volume
Jan	53	102%	54
Feb	54	78%	42
Mar	54	120%	65

Forecasting cash flows: **Chapter 2**

Test your understanding 7

Month	Sales volume	5 Month trend	Seasonal variation
Jan	150		
Feb	310		
Mar	400	420	(20)
Apr	490	426	64
May	750	432	318
Jun	180	438	(258)
Jul	340	444	(104)
Aug	430	450	(20)
Sept	520	456	64
Oct	780	462	318
Nov	210	468	(258)
Dec	370	474	(104)
Jan	460	480	(20)
Feb	550		
Mar	810		

What will be the predicted sales volume for December 20X2?

A 610

480 + (6 × 11) + 64 = 610

Test your understanding 8

(a)

	Sales volume (units)	Trend	Monthly variation
May	11,000		
June	11,850	11,800	50
July	12,550	12,100	450
August	11,900	12,400	−500
September	12,750		

(b)

	Forecast trend	Variation	Forecast sales volume	Forecast sales £	Forecast purchases £
October	13,000	450	13,450	282,450	169,470

Test your understanding 9

Answer B

y = 220,000 + (500 × 21) = £230,500

Test your understanding 10

(a) What is the forecast sales volume of Poles in Period 10?

Y = 450 + 250 × 10 = 2,950 units

(b) What sales volume of Planks would they need to sell in order to achieve this?

Poles sales revenue = 2,950 units × 15 = £44,250

Plank sales units = £44,250 ÷ 50 = 885 Planks

Test your understanding 11

Answer A

£3,000 × 1.024^4 = £3,298.53 rounded = £3,299

Test your understanding 12

	Working	Percentage change
Feb	(75–50)/50	50.00%
Mar	(70–75)/75	–6.67%
Apr	(60–70)/70	–14.29%
May	(80–60)/60	+33.33%

Test your understanding 13

Month	5	6	7
Price	£52	£56	£50
Index	130	140	125

Month 5 = 52 ÷ 40 × 100 = 130

Test your understanding 14

Answer C

162 ÷ 134 × 7,800 = £9,430

Test your understanding 15

Answer D

45/132 × 154 = £52.50

Test your understanding 16

(a) Mark up of 25% means the sales price is 125% of the cost.
Sales price = cost × 1.25 = £37 × 1.25 = **£46.25**

(b) Margin of 25% means the cost is 75% of the sales price.
Sales price = cost × 100/75 = £37 × 100/75 = **£49.33**

CASH AND FINANCIAL MANAGEMENT

Preparing cash budgets

Introduction

The preparation of a cash budget relies on identifying the expected payment patterns for receipts and payments by accounting for differences in timings arising from selling or purchasing goods and services on credit terms and on cash terms and deposits made in advance.

ASSESSMENT CRITERIA

Prepare cash budgets and monitor cash flows (2.1)

CONTENTS

1. Preparation of cash budgets
2. Receipts
3. Payments
4. VAT
5. Exchange rates
6. Interest received or payable
7. Loans

1 Preparation of cash budgets

1.1 Cash budgets

Cash is a business's most important asset as without cash it is not possible to pay for the running of the business. **Managers must forecast and monitor cash flows to ensure the business does not become bankrupt.**

A cash budget or cash flow forecast is an **estimate of all of the cash inflows and outflows for the period**. When these are applied to the opening cash figure, the closing cash balance at the end of each period can be estimated and management can plan to take any necessary action.

For example:

- if there is a cash deficit then agreement with the bank can be sought for an overdraft facility

- if there is a cash surplus then the treasury department may look into short-term investment.

Cash budgets are prepared by accountants, but operational managers are responsible for earning income and for spending.

When a cash budget is drafted, appropriate individuals (operational managers) should be consulted, to check:

- that they agree with the assumptions in the cash budget about income and expenditure, and receipts and payments

- whether there are any other exceptional items of receipt or payment that have been overlooked and so are missing from the draft cash budget.

CASH AND FINANCIAL MANAGEMENT

1.2 Proforma receipts and payments cash budget

Cash budget for the three months to September 20X4

	July £	Aug £	Sept £
RECEIPTS			
Cash sales			
Cash from receivables			
Capital introduced			
Total receipts			
PAYMENTS			
Fixed costs			
Payments to payables			
Purchases of non-current assets			
Total payments			
Net cash flow			
Opening cash balance			
Closing cash balance			

Example

At 1 March 20X4 Apple Ltd expects to have a cash balance of £2,000. It is estimated that cash from sales in March, April and May will be £24,000 each month. Cash payments for expenses each month are estimated to be £21,000 but some new equipment must be purchased at a cost of £12,000 paid for in May.

Prepare the cash budget for the next three months and determine the net cash position at the end of each of the three months.

Solution

Cash budget	March £	April £	May £
Cash inflows	24,000	24,000	24,000
Cash outflows:			
Expenses	(21,000)	(21,000)	(21,000)
Capital expenditure			(12,000)
Net cash inflow/(outflow)	3,000	3,000	(9,000)
Opening cash balance	2,000	5,000	8,000
Closing cash balance	5,000	8,000	(1,000)

The closing cash balance at the end of each month is derived by adding or deducting the net cash flow for the month to or from the cash balance at the start of the month. The closing cash balance of one month therefore becomes the opening cash balance the following month.

This indicates to management that although there will be cash in the bank at the end of March and April, there is expected to be a shortage at the end of May. Management can then use this information to plan for this eventuality by, for example, arranging for a bank overdraft or bank loan or selling some surplus assets.

Each cash budget has to be **amended to reflect** the particular circumstances of the business.

For example, other sources of income may arise, such as proceeds from the sale of non-current assets. There are many sorts of cash payments; possibly cash purchases as well as credit purchases, wages and salaries to employees or the drawings of a proprietor, and each must be detailed line by line under the payments heading.

Remember that a cash budget monitors cash – **do not include any non-cash items i.e. depreciation**.

CASH AND FINANCIAL MANAGEMENT

2 Receipts

2.1 Introduction

Sales are often made on credit and customers do not pay until subsequent periods.

The cash budget needs to show when the actual cash is expected to be received from receivables in the period rather than the actual sales made to receivables in the period.

2.2 Lagging of receipts

It will be necessary to use actual and forecast sales revenue and adjust it for the effects of lagging. This is the time it takes for receivables to pay their debts. Lagging of receipts affects a business's cash inflow as it will not match the sales revenue shown in the financial accounts.

From past experience it will be possible to estimate how the receivables of a business tend to pay and this can be used to estimate cash inflows to a business.

Example

A business makes sales on credit. From past experience the credit controller expects cash to be received as follows:

- 20% in the month of sale
- 50% in the month after sale
- 30% two months after sale.

Calculate the cash receipts for December to March.

	Dec £	Jan £	Feb £	Mar £
Sales revenue	10,000	12,000	14,000	16,000
In the month of sale (20%)	2,000	2,400	2,800	3,200
One month after sale (50%)	–	5,000	6,000	7,000
Two months after sale (30%)	–	–	3,000	3,600
Total receipts	2,000	7,400	11,800	13,800

The above example shows how receipts from receivables for a particular month are not the same as sales to receivables for that month. Note how the receipts follow a diagonal line.

2.3 Closing receivables

It is also possible to estimate the closing receivables figure for the period to be input into the Statement of Financial Position.

> **Example**
>
> Continuing from the previous example forecast the closing receivables balance as at 31 March.
>
> | | Dec £ | Jan £ | Feb £ | Mar £ |
> |---|---|---|---|---|
> | Sales revenue | 10,000 | 12,000 | 14,000 | 16,000 |
> | Received in December | 2,000 | | | |
> | Received in January | 5,000 | 2,400 | | |
> | Received in February | 3,000 | 6,000 | 2,800 | |
> | Received in March | | 3,600 | 7,000 | 3,200 |
> | Amounts outstanding | 0 | 0 | 4,200 | 12,800 |
>
> The closing receivables balance as at 31 March is £17,000. This is made up of 30% of February's and 80% of March's credit sales.

2.4 Opening receivables

The closing receivables balance for one period becomes the opening receivables balance for the next period.

When calculating the cash receipts from an opening balance, care must be taken to account for the proportion of cash that has already been received in prior months.

> **Example**
>
> Continuing with the previous example.
>
> From past experience the credit controller expects cash to be received as follows:
>
> - 20% in the month of sale
> - 50% are received in the month after sale
> - 30% two months after sale.

CASH AND FINANCIAL MANAGEMENT

		April £	May £	June £
Sales revenue		18,000	20,000	22,000
Opening balance £	17,000			
In the month of sale		3,600	4,000	4,400
One month after sale		8,000**	9,000	10,000
Two months after sale		4,200*	4,800***	5,400
Cash receipts		15,800	17,800	19,800

The opening receivables balance as at 31 March is £17,000. This consists of 30% (£4,200) of February's and 80% (£12,800) of March's credit sales.

*February's outstanding balance will all be received in April as this is two months after sale.

March's outstanding balance will be split between April and May:

The outstanding balance from March is 80% of March's total credit sales so the calculations are:

**April receipts from March = £12,800 ÷ 80 × 50 = £8,000

***May receipts from March = £12,800 ÷ 80 × 30 = £4,800

Test your understanding 1

Jason is preparing a cash budget. His credit sales are as follows.

	£
Opening receivables	24,000
May	30,000
June	20,000
July	25,000

His recent debt collection experience has been as follows:

In the month of sale	40%
One month after sale	60%

Required:

Forecast Jason's receipts from receivables for May to July and his closing receivables balance at the 31 July.

KAPLAN PUBLISHING

Preparing cash budgets: Chapter 3

> ### Test your understanding 2
>
> The following data and estimates are available for ABC Ltd:
>
> | | April £ | May £ | June £ | July £ | August £ |
> |---|---|---|---|---|---|
> | Sales | 30,000 | 37,000 | 45,000 | 50,000 | 60,000 |
>
> **Notes:**
>
> (1) 10% of sales are for cash.
>
> (2) The remainder is received 30% in the month following the sale and 70% two months after the sale.
>
> **Task**
>
> Prepare the cash receipts budgets for June, July and August.
>
> | | June £ | July £ | August £ |
> |---|---|---|---|
> | Receipts of cash | | | |
> | Cash sales | | | |
> | Credit sales | | | |

2.5 Sales volume and prices

It is also possible to calculate the forecast cash receipts when provided with information about sales volume and price.

The total monetary amount of the sales revenue for the period is calculated and then the cash receipts can be forecast using the technique described above.

CASH AND FINANCIAL MANAGEMENT

 Example

Kelly Limited sold 3,000 units of a product in June 20X3 at a selling price of £45 each. Due to an increase in production costs, this price will increase to £48 with effect from 1 July 20X3 and this is expected to reduce demand for July to 2,900 units. Thereafter demand is expected to increase by 10% per month.

All sales are on credit and receivables pay as follows:

10% in the month of sale

60% in the month following sale

30% two months after sale

Opening receivables for June 20X3 were:

Balance from April £33,750

Balance from May £85,050

What are the budgeted cash receipts in June, July and August 20X3?

	June £	July £	August £
Sales units	3,000	2,900	3,190
Selling price per unit	45	48	48
Sales	135,000	139,200	153,120
10% in the month of sale	13,500	13,920	15,312
60% in month after sale	56,700**	81,000	83,520
30% 2 months after sale	33,750*	28,350***	40,500
Total cash receipts	103,950	123,270	139,332

Notes

*All of April's outstanding balance will be received in June

**60/90 × May's outstanding balance will be received in June

***30/90 × May's outstanding balance will be received in July

Test your understanding 3

Major Inc has requested assistance with calculating sales receipts for entry into a cash budget.

Actual sales values are available for January and February and forecast sales values have been produced from March to June.

	Actual		Forecast			
	January	February	March	April	May	June
Total sales	£30,000	£32,000	£33,000	£35,000	£37,000	£40,000

It is estimated that cash sales are 17% of the total sales, the remaining are on credit.

Major Inc estimates that 40% of credit sales are received in the month after sale with the balance being received two months after sales.

Complete the table using the information above to calculate the timing of sales receipts that would be included in a cash budget for Major Inc for the period of March to June.

	March £	April £	May £	June £
Cash				
Credit sales receipts:				
Month after sale				
2 months after sale				
Total cash received				

CASH AND FINANCIAL MANAGEMENT

 Test your understanding 4

Shirley Ltd has been trading for a number of years. Shirley's owner, Kelly, has asked for help calculating their cash and credit sales.

Actual sales values achieved are available for October and November and forecast sales values have been produced for December to March.

Kelly estimates that cash sales account for 20% of the total sales. The remaining 80% of sales are made on a credit basis.

(a) Complete the table below to show the split of total sales between cash sales and credit sales.

	Actual		Forecast			
	Oct	Nov	Dec	Jan	Feb	Mar
Total sales (£)	11,000	14,000	16,000	18,500	19,900	22,100
Cash sales (£)						
Credit sales (£)						

Kelly estimates that 25% of credit sales are received in the month after sale with the balance being received two months after sale.

(b) Using your figures from part (a) calculate the timing of credit sales receipts that would be included in a cash budget for Shirley Ltd's for the period December to March.

	Dec £	Jan £	Feb £	Mar £
Monthly credit sales receipts				

 Test your understanding 5

A company has supplied information regarding its forecast sales.

Sales volume has been forecast for periods 1 to 5. Each product sells for £20.

The company estimates that 10% of sales are made on a cash basis with the balance made on a credit basis. An analysis of historical data shows that credit customers settle their debts on the basis of 20% one month after the date of sale and 80% two months after the date of sale.

	Period 1	Period 2	Period 3	Period 4	Period 5
Sales volume (units)	8,000	8,300	8,500	7,500	7,000

Preparing cash budgets: Chapter 3

Required:

Complete the table below to identify the total sales receipts forecast for periods 4 and 5. Identify the forecast trade receivables balance at the end of period 5.

	Period 4 £	Period 5 £
Total sales receipts		

The trade receivables balance at the end of period 5 is forecast to be:

£ ⬜

2.6 Irrecoverable debts

It is possible that some debts will not be collected. These are known as irrecoverable debts.

Example

A business has found that 30% of customers pay in the month of sale, 40% of customers pay in the month after the sale and 20% of customers pay two months after the month of sale. From past experience it is known that 10% of the customers do not pay.

Credit sales for the business are as follows:

	Actual			Budgeted	
	February £	March £	April £	May £	June £
Credit sales	10,000	20,000	30,000	25,000	30,000

Required:

Calculate the total irrecoverable debt for the period from February to June to be written off to the Statement of Profit or Loss.

Solution

Total credit sales =

£10,000 + £20,000 + £30,000 + £25,000 + £30,000 = 115,000

Total irrecoverable debt = £115,000 × 10% = £11,500

2.7 Discounts allowed

Prompt payment discounts or discounts allowed can be useful to improve the liquidity of a business in the short term, as cash should be received earlier, but in the long term less cash will be received overall from receivables.

When considering offering a settlement discount it is worth considering whether the cost outweighs the benefit i.e. the improvement in earlier cash flows outweighs the reduction in cash overall. This could be measured by the impact a settlement discount has on the overall cash balance of a business.

Example

A business is considering whether to offer a 3% discount for payment received from credit customers in the month of sale.

Credit sales for the business are as follows:

	February £	March £	April £	May £	June £
Credit sales	20,000	22,000	24,000	18,000	21,000

The business estimates that 60% of customers would take advantage of the settlement discount by paying in the month of sale, 30% of customers will pay in the month after the sale and 10% of customers will pay two months after the month of sale.

Required:

Calculate the value of the discount offered for February to June.

Solution:

Total credit sales =

£20,000 + £22,000 + £24,000 + £18,000 + £21,000 = £105,000

Total discount = £105,000 × 60% × 3% = £1,890

Test your understanding 6

A company's budgeted accounts show a figure of £4,000 for discounts allowed and £50,000 for total credit sales.

Calculate the settlement discount percentage that has been offered.

3 Payments

3.1 Introduction

A business will incur lots of expenditure when running a business such as wages, raw material purchases and overheads such as rent.

Some of the payments for these will be made in the month the cost is incurred, whereas others will be lagged payments. Lagged payments are calculated in the same way as lagged receipts.

3.2 Lagging of payments

Businesses will buy goods on credit and take time to make the payment to the supplier (payable). To be able to complete the cash budget for payments the timing and value of the payments needs to be calculated.

The calculation for the payments to payables is similar to that for receipts from receivables – calculate the total cost to be paid and then lag the payments in line with forecast timings.

Example

A business estimates that its credit purchases for February and March will be £14,000 but will increase by 10% each month thereafter. Its payment pattern to payables is that 60% are paid in the month after the purchases and the remaining 40% two months after the purchase.

What are the payments to payables for the three months of March, April and May?

	February £	March £	April £	May £
Purchases	14,000	14,000	15,400	16,940
Payments to payables				
One month after purchase		8,400	8,400	9,240
Two months after purchase			5,600	5,600
Cash payments		8,400	14,000	14,840

CASH AND FINANCIAL MANAGEMENT

3.3 Closing payables

It is also possible to estimate the closing payables figure for the period to be input into the Statement of Financial Position.

Example

Continuing from the previous example forecast the closing payables balance as at 31 May.

	February £	March £	April £	May £
Purchases	14,000	14,000	15,400	16,940
Paid in March	8,400			
Paid in April	5,600	8,400		
Paid in May		5,600	9,240	
Amount outstanding	0	0	6,160	16,940

The closing payables balance as at 31 May is £23,100. This is made up of 40% of April's and 100% of May's credit sales.

3.4 Opening payables

Just as with receivables, the closing payables balance for one period becomes the opening payables balance for the next period. When calculating the cash paid from an opening balance, care must be taken to account for the proportion of cash that has already been paid in prior months.

Example

Continuing from the previous example.

From past experience the credit controller expects cash to be paid as follows:

- 60% in the month after purchase
- 40% two months after purchase.

Preparing cash budgets: Chapter 3

	June £	July £	August £
Purchases		18,634	20,497	22,547
Opening balance £	23,100			
One month after purchase		10,164**	11,180	12,298
Two months after purchase		6,160*	6,776***	7,454
Cash payments		16,324	17,956	19,752

The opening payables balance as at 31 May is £23,100. This is made up of 40% (£6,160) of April's and 100% (£16,940) of May's credit sales.

*April's outstanding balance will all be paid in June as this is two months after purchase.

May's outstanding balance will be split between June and July:

The outstanding balance from May is 100% of May's total credit purchases so the calculations are:

**June payments from May = £16,940 ÷ 100 × 60 = £10,164

***July payments from May = £16,940 ÷ 100 × 40 = £6,776

Test your understanding 7

Remus's purchases in May were £100,000 and these are expected to increase by £10,000 per month for the next three months. All purchases are on credit terms. Payables are paid as follows:

- 50% in the month of purchase
- 30% in the month after purchase
- 20% two months after purchase.

Complete the table below to identify the total purchase payments forecast for July and August. Identify the forecast trade payables balance at the end of August.

	July £	August £
Total payments		

The trade payables balance at the end of August is forecast to be:

£ ☐

CASH AND FINANCIAL MANAGEMENT

 Test your understanding 8

A company pays its suppliers are follows:

- 30% one month after purchase
- 25% two months after purchase
- 45% three months after purchase.

At the end of period 3 the balance of trade payables is forecast to be:

	£
Balance from period 1	18,000
Balance from period 2	35,000
Balance from period 3	70,000
Trade payables at the end of period 3	123,000

Complete the table below to identify the value of trade payables at the end of period 3 that will be paid in periods 4 and 5.

	Period 4 £	Period 5 £
Total payments		

3.5 Discounts received

It may be possible to receive a discount from a supplier for prompt payment. Payment must be made within a specified time period for a discount to be applied to the amount due. This will reduce the overall amount paid to the payable but also reduces the length of time the money is in the bank gaining interest.

 Example

A business has been offered a discount of 2% if payment is received in the month of sale. The business forecasts purchases to be:

April £43,000

May £45,000

June £50,000

How much money can the business save by paying early?

Solution

Total purchases = £43,000 + £45,000 + £50,000 = £138,000

Total saving = £138,000 × 2% = £2,760

Preparing cash budgets: **Chapter 3**

 Test your understanding 9

One supplier has offered a discount to Box Co of 2% on an invoice for £7,500, if payment is made within one month, rather than the three months normally taken to pay. If Box's overdraft rate is 10% p.a., calculate if it is financially worthwhile for them to accept the discount and pay early?

3.6 Purchases expressed in terms of sales value

In some cases the information supplied about purchases will be expressed in terms of the sales value which has been budgeted. Purchases will be calculated based on a percentage of sales value. Once the purchases are known then the cash payments to the suppliers can be calculated.

Purchase prices could also be given in terms of a required **mark up or margin** (see Chapter 2 for more details).

 Example

A business has the following budgeted sales:

	February £	March £	April £	May £	June £	July £
Budgeted sales	38,000	40,000	44,000	46,000	45,000	50,000

The business expects purchases to be 60% of sales and its policy is to make purchases on credit each month which are enough to cover the following month's sales.

Payables are paid two months after the month of purchase. What are the payments to payables for each of the four months of April, May, June and July?

Solution

The first step is to calculate the cost of purchases incurred in each month.

	Feb £	March £	April £	May £	June £	July £
Budgeted sales	38,000	40,000	44,000	46,000	45,000	50,000
Purchases (60% of following month's sales)	24,000	26,400	27,600	27,000	30,000	

The next step is to apply the timing of the payment.

	Feb £	March £	April £	May £	June £	July £
Payments (two months after purchase)			24,000	26,400	27,600	27,000

3.7 Inventory levels

Another method of expressing information about purchase quantities is to include plans for any increases or decreases in inventory levels during the period.

> **Example**
>
> A business generally has purchases of £80,000 each month on credit. These are paid in the month following the purchase.
>
> However, it is budgeted to increase inventory levels at the end of May by £20,000 and that inventory levels will then remain at that value. There is no anticipated increase in sales.
>
> What are the cash payments to payables for each of the three months of April, May and June?
>
> **Solution**
>
> The first step is to calculate the amount of purchases each month. This will generally be £80,000 but May must be £100,000 in order to increase the inventory levels.
>
> As there is no anticipated increase in sales levels then purchases in June can revert to £80,000.
>
> | | March £ | April £ | May £ | June £ |
> |-----------|---------|---------|---------|--------|
> | Purchases | 80,000 | 80,000 | 100,000 | 80,000 |
>
> As payments are made in the month following the purchase then the cash payments will be as follows:
>
> | | April £ | May £ | June £ |
> |-----------|---------|--------|---------|
> | Purchases | 80,000 | 80,000 | 100,000 |

Inventory levels may also be used if we are calculating how much needs to be purchased or produced to meet sales demand.

This is calculated by subtracting the opening inventory and adding the closing inventory to the sales demand for the period.

Preparing cash budgets: **Chapter 3**

This is calculated as follows:

	Units
Sales	X
Less: Opening inventory of finished goods	(X)
Add: Closing inventory of finished goods	X
Production or purchases	X

If production is calculated then it will be necessary to convert this to purchases by calculating the total material needed for production and then how much these purchases are going to cost.

3.8 Labour costs

Labour costs are normally paid in the month in which they are incurred. Labour cost can be calculated based on units produced (piecework), standard hours worked and/or an annual salary.

Overtime payments/premiums may also be incurred in labour costs.

Example

Labour costs include hourly paid employees and four-weekly paid employees.

The labour costs for hourly paid employees are calculated based on the number of hours worked multiplied by a standard hourly rate of £10. Hourly paid employees are paid an overtime rate of £12 per hour.

The company also employs two supervisors who are paid every four weeks. They are each paid an annual salary of £20,800. The year is divided into 13 four-week periods.

Hourly paid employees are paid their standard hours in the period incurred and overtime hours in the following period. The supervisors are paid on the last day of each period.

CASH AND FINANCIAL MANAGEMENT

The forecast standard and overtime hours are given below.

	Period 1	Period 2	Period 3	Period 4	Period 5
Forecast standard hours	1,200	1,340	1,720	1,370	1,400
Forecast overtime hours	100	150	135	105	90

Complete the table below to identify the total payments for labour costs forecast for periods 4 and 5.

	Period 4	Period 5
Supervisors	£20,800/13 × 2 = £3,200	£20,800/13 × 2 = £3,200
Standard hours	1,370 × £10 = £13,700	1,400 × £10 = £14,000
Overtime hours	135 × £12 = £1,620	105 × £12 = £1,260
Total labour cost	£18,520	£18,460

Test your understanding 10

The production budget for a company shows the following monthly production:

	April Units	May Units	June Units
Production	6,200	6,800	7,000

Each unit of production requires two labour hours and the wage rate is £7.00 per hour for April and May increasing to £7.40 per hour in June. Normal working hours are 12,000 hours and, after that overtime is paid at time and a half. Overtime is paid in the following month.

Complete the table below to identify the total payments for labour costs for May and June.

	May £	June £
Total labour costs		

3.9 Other costs

Care should be taken with other costs, for example administration or distribution costs, as they may include a certain amount which relates to depreciation. **Depreciation is not a cash flow and therefore this amount should be excluded from the cash budget.**

Test your understanding 11

Housing plc is preparing cash payment figures to include in a cash budget.

The following information was provided by the production manager.

- Purchases are 35% of next month's forecast sales and are paid two months after the date of purchase.

	Actual			Forecast		
	February	March	April	May	June	July
Total sales (£)	70,000	72,000	77,000	80,000	83,000	85,000

- Wages are paid in the month that they are incurred and expenses are paid in the month after they are incurred. The figures are:

	Actual			Forecast		
	February	March	April	May	June	July
Wages (£)	15,000	17,000	17,000	18,000	18,000	18,500
Expenses (£)	6,000	6,500	6,750	7,000	7,000	7,750

- Expenses include £3,000 each month for depreciation.

- A new machine is to be purchased in May at a total cost of £40,000. Payment for the machine is to be made in 8 equal instalments starting in June. This machine is to be depreciated monthly on a straight line basis at 25% per annum.

Complete the table below for the payments section of the cash budget for Housing plc for the three months ended July.

	May £	June £	July £
Purchases			
Wages			
Expenses			
New machine			
Total payments			

CASH AND FINANCIAL MANAGEMENT

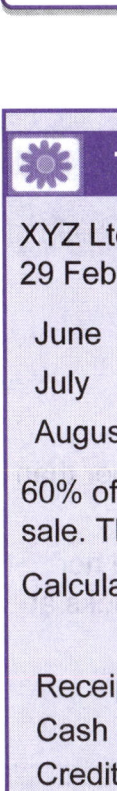 **Test your understanding 12**

XYZ Ltd has the following forecast sales for the nine months to 29 February 20X2:

June	£40,000	September	£48,000	December	£44,000
July	£44,000	October	£40,000	January	£42,000
August	£50,000	November	£45,000	February	£50,000

60% of the company's sales are on credit, payable in the month after sale. The remainder are cash sales.

Calculate the cash receipts for November to February.

	Nov £	Dec £	Jan £	Feb £
Receipts:				
Cash sales				
Credit sales				

Purchases amount to 40% of sales. XYZ buys and receives inventory to meet the following month's sales and these are paid for two months after delivery.

Wages comprise a fixed sum of £2,000 per month.

Fixed costs amount to £7,500 per month, payable one month in arrears, of which £1,500 is depreciation.

Calculate the cash payments for November to February.

	Nov £	Dec £	Jan £	Feb £
Payments:				
Purchases				
Wages				
Fixed costs				

KAPLAN PUBLISHING

4 VAT

4.1 Introduction

If a business is registered for VAT it must:

- charge VAT on its sales or services to its customers
- recover the VAT charged on its purchases and expenses rather than having to bear these costs as part of the business.

In such cases, as the VAT charged and incurred is neither revenue nor expense, the revenues and costs of the business are entered in books at their net of VAT value, and the VAT is entered in the VAT account.

4.2 Output VAT

Definition

The VAT charged on sales or taxable supplies is called **output VAT**.

4.3 Input VAT

When a business buys goods or pays expenses (inputs), then it will also be paying VAT on those purchases or expenses.

Definition

VAT paid by a business on purchases or expenses is called **input VAT**.

Businesses are allowed to reclaim their input tax. They do this by deducting the input tax they have paid from the output tax which they owe, and paying over the net amount only. If the input tax exceeds the output tax, then the balance is recoverable from HMRC.

4.4 Standard rated activities

Any taxable supply which is not charged at the zero or reduced rates is charged at the standard rate.

This is calculated by taking the VAT exclusive amount and multiplying by 20%.

If you are given the VAT inclusive rate then calculate the VAT amount by multiplying by 20/120.

CASH AND FINANCIAL MANAGEMENT

The following VAT structure can also be used to calculate VAT, VAT inclusive or VAT exclusive figures.

	£
VAT inclusive (gross)	120
VAT	20
VAT exclusive (net)	100

It may be necessary to calculate the VAT payment or refund from the HMRC for inclusion in the cash budget.

Test your understanding 13

A business that is registered for VAT makes credit sales of £220,000 in the period and credit purchases of £150,000. Each of these figures is net of VAT at the standard rate of 20%.

Calculate how much VAT is due to or from HM Revenue and Customs.

5 Exchange rates

5.1 Introduction

A change in exchange rates might affect a business in the following ways:

- Exchange rate changes can increase or reduce the price of a product sold abroad.
- The price of imported raw materials may change.
- The price of competitors' products may change in the home market.

5.2 Converting foreign currency to sterling

An exchange rate is the value of one currency expressed in terms of another. So, for example, £1 may be worth $1.35 in America and €1.15 in France.

Example

A business buys $4,000 of raw materials.

If the exchange rate is £1:$1.5000 then the sterling value of the raw materials is $4,000 ÷ 1.5000 = £2,667

If the exchange rate is $1:£0.6667 then the sterling value of the raw material is $4,000 × £0.6667 = £2,667

(rounded to the nearest whole £)

 Test your understanding 14

An English company is to purchase materials costing $100,000. You have the following information:

£1:$1.9000

What is the value of the purchase in £ (to the nearest whole £)?

 Interest received or payable

6.1 Introduction

One of the purposes of a cash budget is to identify the cash balance at the end of each period and to determine whether any interest is due to the business from the bank from a positive balance or whether an overdraft facility is required due to a negative balance.

If an overdraft is agreed with the bank and the facility is used then the bank will charge interest on the amount of the overdraft.

6.2 Interest received

In practice the amount of the interest will be calculated on a daily basis. However for cash budgeting purposes the amount of interest will normally be calculated on the basis of the amount of the credit balance at the end of the month.

The figure for interest will then be included in the following month's cash receipts.

CASH AND FINANCIAL MANAGEMENT

 Example

A business anticipates having a credit balance of £2,000 at the end of March. The budgeted cash receipts and payments (excluding interest) for the following three months are expected to be as follows:

	April	May	June
	£	£	£
Cash receipts	16,500	18,000	17,200
Cash payments	17,400	17,500	17,000

Interest is received at 0.5% per month on the balance at the start of each month.

Prepare the completed cash budget including the amount of interest.

Solution

		April £	May £	June £
Cash receipts		16,500	18,000	17,200
interest	(2,000 × 0.5%)	10		
	(1,110 × 0.5%)		6	
	(1,616 × 0.5%)			8
Cash payments		(17,400)	(17,500)	(17,000)
Net cash flow		(890)	506	208
Opening balance		2,000	1,110	1,616
Closing balance		1,110	1,616	1,824

6.3 Overdraft interest

In practice the amount of the overdraft interest will be calculated on a daily basis. However for cash budgeting purposes the amount of overdraft interest will normally be calculated on the basis of the amount of the overdraft outstanding at the end of the previous month.

This figure for interest will then be included in the following month's cash payments.

Example

A business anticipates having an overdraft of £2,000 at the end of March. The budgeted cash receipts and payments (excluding overdraft interest) for the following three months are expected to be as follows:

	April	May	June
	£	£	£
Cash receipts	16,500	18,000	17,200
Cash payments	17,400	17,500	17,000

Overdraft interest is charged at 0.5% per month on the overdraft balance at the start of each month.

Prepare the completed cash budget including the amount of overdraft interest.

Solution

		April £	May £	June £
Cash receipts		16,500	18,000	17,200
Cash payments		(17,400)	(17,500)	(17,000)
Overdraft interest	(2,000 × 0.5%)	(10)		
	(2,910 × 0.5%)		(15)	
	(2,425 × 0.5%)			(12)
Net cash flow		(910)	485	188
Opening balance		(2,000)	(2,910)	(2,425)
Closing balance		(2,910)	(2,425)	(2,237)

Note that you can only calculate the overdraft interest month by month once you have calculated the opening cash balance of the relevant month.

CASH AND FINANCIAL MANAGEMENT

 Test your understanding 15

Refer to the memos from Mark Bennett and Victoria Bartlett to prepare the cash flow forecast for the first 3 months of next year.

MEMO

To: Radhika Poriki
From: Mark Bennett
Date: 12 December
Subject: Next Year

Further to our conversation I have put together the forecast cash expenditure for next year:

- new equipment will cost a total of £200,000. We need to buy it in January and put down a deposit of £50,000 on 1 January. I have negotiated instalments for the remainder; three equal instalments payable on 1 February, 1 May and 1 September next year. We can get a grant for part of the cost (10% of total cost) and this will be received on 1 January

- rent for premises will amount to £5,000 per quarter payable in advance, with the first payment being 1 January

- wages will be £6,000 per month, payable on the last day of the month worked

- purchases are currently £10,000 each month, but will be increasing by 2% every two months for the rest of the year from March. Purchases will be paid for two months after they have been received

- the opening cash balance should be assumed to be £40,000

- the bank charges 1% interest on any overdraft at the end of a month. Payable in the following month.

I look forward to seeing the cash flow forecast and discussing it further.

With regards.

Mark

MEMO

To: Radhika Poriki

From: Victoria Bartlett

Date: 13 December

Subject: Future sales

I have put together some forecast sales for the first three months of next year for the new division. I have been quite conservative so these figures should be achieved with relative ease.

	December £	January £	February £	March £
Cash sales	16,000	18,000	18,500	20,000
Credit sales	7,000	6,000	7,000	6,000
Total	23,000	24,000	25,500	26,000

Credit sales will be payable by the end of the month after the sale was made. Selling and administration costs will amount to 10% of the sales made in the month and they are payable in cash as incurred.

With regards.

Victoria

CASH AND FINANCIAL MANAGEMENT

Cash flow forecast

	January £	February £	March £
CASH RECEIVED Sales: cash credit			
Grant			
Total			
CASH PAID Equipment: deposit			
Equipment: instalment			
Rent			
Wages			
Purchases			
Selling/administration			
Overdraft interest			
Total			
Net cash flow			
Opening cash balance			
Closing cash balance			

Preparing cash budgets: **Chapter 3**

7 Loans

7.1 Loans

A business may take out a bank loan to be able to pay for new purchases. The receipt of the loan would be included in the receipts section of the cash budget. A loan will need to be paid back to the bank.

There are 2 parts to a loan repayment – the **capital (principal) repayment** and the **interest charged** on the loan – these will both feature in the payments section of the cash budget.

Test your understanding 16

The cash budget for Sampras Construction for the three months ended May has been partially completed. The following information needs to be included to complete the cash budget.

- A bank loan of £60,000 has been arranged and it is to be received by Sampras Construction in March.

- The principal element is to be repaid in 60 equal monthly instalments beginning in April. This has been arranged as Sampras Construction is purchasing some new machinery for £58,000 in April.

- The loan has a 5% interest charge per annum calculated on the principal amount of the loan. The interest is to be payable monthly from March and should be rounded to the nearest £.

- There is a 2% monthly interest charge if Sampras uses its overdraft. The charge is calculated on the previous month end balance. Interest is rounded to the nearest £.

- On the 28 February the cash balance was £3,400 overdrawn.

CASH AND FINANCIAL MANAGEMENT

Complete the cash budget below. Use positive figures for cash inflows and negative figures are cash outflows. Enter zero where appropriate.

	March £	April £	May £
RECEIPTS			
Cash sales	6,200	6,700	7,500
Credit sales	35,000	38,000	39,000
Bank loan			
Total receipts			
PAYMENTS			
Purchases	−15,000	−10,000	−13,000
Wages	−10,000	−11,000	−10,500
Expenses	−5,600	−6,200	−6,800
Capital expenditure			
Bank loan principal repayments			
Bank loan interest			
Overdraft interest			
Total payments			
Net cash flow			
Opening cash balance			
Closing cash balance			

Test your understanding 17

Michael George Ltd is a new company with no trading history. They intend to sell plastic garden gnomes and have approached their bankers who have insisted on a cash flow forecast for the first 6 months to 30 June 20X6. The following data is predicted by the directors.

(a) They expect that 10% of sales will be settled in the month of sale, 50% in the month following, 35% two months after with 5% not collected.

(b) In January they only expect sales of £2,000 but these are expected to rise to £5,000 in February, £8,000 in March, £10,000 in April and peak at £15,000 in May and June.

(c) Purchases are 50% of the value of sales.

(d) The company has already bought, in December, sufficient gnomes to meet the January sales. It intends to continue to buy sufficient gnomes each month to cover the following month's sales. The December purchases are not due to be paid for until February, but all subsequent purchases are to be paid for in the month following purchase.

(e) The company will pay salaries of £1,500 per month, rent of £2,000 per quarter paid in advance commencing January, and general expenses of £750 per month.

(f) The company has been offered a government grant of £10,000 but it will not be received until June 20X6. The shareholders will pay £5,000 for their shares with the money being received in January. A truck costing £6,000 will be purchased in January and paid for on delivery.

(g) The bank has indicated that it would charge interest on any borrowing at the rate of 6% per annum. It should be calculated on the balance at the month end and paid in the following month.

Draw up the cash flow budget for the first 6 months of 20X6 and suggest what overdraft facility should be requested.

CASH AND FINANCIAL MANAGEMENT

	Jan £	Feb £	March £	April £	May £	June £
Cash receipts						
Sale of shares						
Receivables						
Government grant						
	___	___	___	___	___	___
Cash payments						
Purchase						
Salaries						
Rent						
General expenses						
Truck						
Interest						
	___	___	___	___	___	___
	___	___	___	___	___	___
Net cash flow						
Opening cash balance						
	___	___	___	___	___	___
Closing cash balance						
	___	___	___	___	___	___

8 Summary

Forecast sales revenue and purchases do not necessarily reflect the cash in and out flows required for a cash budget. This is because of a possible delay in receiving receipts from receivables and delays in paying payables. This lagging needs to be taken into account when producing the figures for inclusion into a cash budget.

Test your understanding answers

Test your understanding 1

The opening receivables balance will be 60% of April's credit sales as 40% of April's credit sales will have been collected in April. Any previous credit sales will have already been collected.

For example March's credit sales will be collected 40% in March and 60% in April therefore none should be outstanding.

	Opening £	May £	June £	July £
Sales	24,000	30,000	20,000	25,000
40% in month of sale		12,000	8,000	10,000
60% 1 month after sale		24,000	18,000	12,000
Total cash receipts		36,000	26,000	22,000

Closing receivables at 31 July = £25,000 × 60% = £15,000

Test your understanding 2

Cash budgets, June – August

	June £	July £	August £
Receipts of cash			
Cash sales	4,500	5,000	6,000
Credit sales 30%	9,990	12,150	13,500
Credit sales 70%	18,900	23,310	28,350
	33,390	40,460	47,850

CASH AND FINANCIAL MANAGEMENT

Test your understanding 3

	March £	April £	May £	June £
Cash	5,610	5,950	6,290	6,800
Credit sales receipts:				
Month after sale 40%	10,624**	10,956	11,620	12,284
2 months after sale 60%	14,940*	15,936***	16,434	17,430
Total cash received****	31,174	32,842	34,344	36,514

*January £5,100 is cash, £24,900 is credit. Of the credit sales 40% will be received in February leaving 60% in March £24,900 × 60% = £14,940

February £5,440 is cash, £26,560 is credit. 40% will be received in March £26,560 × 40% = £10,624** and 60% in April £26,560 × 60% = £15,936***

**** total cash received includes cash sales

Test your understanding 4

(a)

	Actual		Forecast			
	Oct	Nov	Dec	Jan	Feb	Mar
Total sales	11,000	14,000	16,000	18,500	19,900	22,100
Cash sales	2,200	2,800	3,200	3,700	3,980	4,420
Credit sales	8,800	11,200	12,800	14,800	15,920	17,680

(b)

	Credit sales £	Cash received				
		Nov £	Dec £	Jan £	Feb £	Mar £
October	8,800	2,200	6,600			
November	11,200		2,800	8,400		
December	12,800			3,200	9,600	
January	14,800				3,700	11,100
February	15,920					3,980
Monthly credit sales receipts			9,400	11,600	13,300	15,080

Test your understanding 5

	Period 1 £	Period 2 £	Period 3 £	Period 4 £	Period 5 £
Sales	160,000	166,000	170,000	150,000	140,000
Receipts					
Cash sales	16,000	16,600	17,000	15,000	14,000
Credit sales	144,000	149,400	153,000	135,000	126,000
One month after sale		28,800	29,880	30,600	27,000
Two months after sale			115,200	119,520	122,400
Total cash receipts				165,120	163,400

Closing receivables
80% of P4   = £108,000
All of P5   = £126,000
Total   = £234,000

Test your understanding 6

Settlement discount % = £4,000 ÷ £50,000 × 100 = 8%

Test your understanding 7

	May £	June £	July £	Aug £
Purchases	100,000	110,000	120,000	130,000
In the month of purchase	50,000	55,000	60,000	65,000
One month after purchase		30,000	33,000	36,000
Two months after purchase			20,000	22,000
Cash payments			113,000	123,000

Closing payables
July 20% × £120,000   = £24,000
August 50% × £130,000   = £65,000
Total   = £89,000

CASH AND FINANCIAL MANAGEMENT

 Test your understanding 8

	Period 4 £	Period 5 £
Total payments	51,500	40,000

Workings

Period 4

All of Period 1's outstanding amount = £18,000

Period 2 = 25 ÷ 70 × £35,000 = £12,500

Period 3 = 30 ÷ 100 × £70,000 = £21,000

Total = £51,500

Period 5

Period 2 = 45 ÷ 70 × £35,000 = £22,500

Period 3 = 25 ÷ 100 × £70,000 = £17,500

Total = £40,000

 Test your understanding 9

Discount saves 2% of £7,500 = £150

Financed by overdraft for extra two months in order to pay £7,350 early:

$$\text{Cost} = 10\% \times \frac{2}{12} \times £7,350 = £122.50$$

Net saving = £27.50

It is worth accepting the discount.

Test your understanding 10

	April	May	June
Time taken (hours)	12,400	13,600	14,000
Standard hours	12,000	12,000	12,000
Overtime hours	400	1,600	2,000
Forecast standard cost £	84,000	84,000	88,800
Forecast overtime cost £	4,200	16,800	22,200
Forecast labour cost		84,000 + 4,200 = **£88,200**	88,800 + 16,800 = **£105,600**

Test your understanding 11

	May £	June £	July £
Purchases (W1)	26,950	28,000	29,050
Wages	18,000	18,000	18,500
Expenses (W2)	3,750	4,000	4,000
New machine	0	5,000	5,000
Total payments	48,700	55,000	56,550

Workings

(W1) Purchases

May – payment is for purchases made in March based on the April forecast sales figures.

77,000 × 35% = £26,950

(W2) Expenses

Remove the depreciation as this is a non-cash item and then payment occurs in the following month.

May – April expenses less £3,000

£6,750 – £3,000 = £3,750

CASH AND FINANCIAL MANAGEMENT

Test your understanding 12

	Nov £	Dec £	Jan £	Feb £
Receipts:				
Cash sales (W1)	18,000	17,600	16,800	20,000
Credit sales (W2)	24,000	27,000	26,400	25,200
	42,000	44,600	43,200	45,200
Payments:				
Purchases (W3)	16,000	18,000	17,600	16,800
Wages	2,000	2,000	2,000	2,000
Fixed costs (W4)	6,000	6,000	6,000	6,000
	24,000	26,000	25,600	24,800

Workings

(W1) Since 60% of sales are credit sales, 40% are cash sales, e.g.

November cash sales = £45,000 × 40% = £18,000

(W2) October credit sales are paid in November, and so on.

Credit sales = 60% so the October receipt = 60% × £40,000 = £24,000.

(W3) 40% of the next month's sales paid 2 months later

i.e. the purchases in November will ordered and received in September and will be 40% of October sales

e.g. November: (40% × £40,000) = £16,000

(W4) Fixed costs: £6,000 (£7,500 − £1,500)

Test your understanding 13

Output VAT = £220,000 × 20% = £44,000

Input VAT = £150,000 × 20% = £30,000

The amount due to HM Revenue and Customs is the balance of these amounts = £44,000 – £30,000 = £14,000.

Test your understanding 14

$100,000 ÷ 1.9000 = £52,632

Test your understanding 15

Cash flow forecast for the first three months of next year

	January £	February £	March £
Cash received			
Sales: cash	18,000	18,500	20,000
Sales: credit	7,000	6,000	7,000
Grant	20,000	0	0
Total	45,000	24,500	27,000
Cash paid			
Equipment: deposit	–50,000	0	0
Equipment: instalment	0	–50,000	0
Rent	–5,000	0	0
Wages	–6,000	–6,000	–6,000
Purchases	–10,000	–10,000	–10,000
Selling/administration	–2,400	–2,550	–2,600
Overdraft interest	0	0	–324
Total	–73,400	–68,550	–18,924
Net cash flow	–28,400	–44,050	8,076
Opening cash balance	40,000	11,600	–32,450
Closing cash balance	11,600	–32,450	–24,374

CASH AND FINANCIAL MANAGEMENT

Test your understanding 16

	March £	April £	May £
RECEIPTS			
Cash sales	6,200	6,700	7,500
Credit sales	35,000	38,000	39,000
Bank loan	60,000	0	0
Total receipts	101,200	44,700	46,500
PAYMENTS			
Purchases	−15,000	−10,000	−13,000
Wages	−10,000	−11,000	−10,500
Expenses	−5,600	−6,200	−6,800
Capital expenditure	0	−58,000	0
Bank loan principal repayments	0	−1,000	−1,000
Bank loan interest	−250	−250	−250
Overdraft interest	−68	0	0
Total payments	30,918	86,450	31,550
Net cash flow	70,282	−41,750	14,950
Opening cash balance	−3,400	66,882	25,132
Closing cash balance	66,882	25,132	40,082

Test your understanding 17

	Jan £	Feb £	March £	April £	May £	June £
Cash receipts						
Sale of shares	5,000	0	0	0	0	0
Receivables (W1)	200	1,500	4,000	6,750	9,300	12,500
Government grant	0	0	0	0	0	10,000
	5,200	1,500	4,000	6,750	9,300	22,500
Cash payments						
Purchase (W2)	0	−3,500	−4,000	−5,000	−7,500	−7,500
Salaries	−1,500	−1,500	−1,500	−1,500	−1,500	−1,500
Rent	−2,000	0	0	−2,000	0	0
General expenses	−750	−750	−750	−750	−750	−750
Truck	−6,000	0	0	0	0	0
Interest	0	−25	−47	−58	−71	−74
	−10,250	−5,775	−6,297	−9,308	−9,821	−9,824
Net cash flow	−5,050	−4,275	−2,297	−2,558	−521	12,676
Opening cash balance	0	−5,050	−9,325	−11,622	−14,180	−14,701
Closing cash balance	−5,050	−9,325	−11,622	−14,180	−14,701	−2,025

Overdraft facility would need to be £15,000 to cover the cash shortfall in May.

Workings

(W1) Receipts from receivables

	Jan £	Feb £	March £	April £	May £	June £
Sales	2,000	5,000	8,000	10,000	15,000	15,000
Receipts						
Jan	200	1,000	700			
Feb		500	2,500	1,750		
March			800	4,000	2,800	
April				1,000	5,000	3,500
May					1,500	7,500
June						1,500
	200	1,500	4,000	6,750	9,300	12,500

(W2) Payments for purchases

	Jan £	Feb £	March £	April £	May £	June £
Sales	2,000	5,000	8,000	10,000	15,000	15,000

	Dec £	Jan £	Feb £	Mar £	Apr £	May £	June £
Purchases	1,000	2,500	4,000	5,000	7,500	7,500	
Paid							
Dec		1,000					
Jan		2,500					
Feb			4,000				
March				5,000			
April					7,500		
May							7,500
		3,500	4,000	5,000	7,500		7,500

CASH AND FINANCIAL MANAGEMENT

Analysing and monitoring cash budgets

Introduction

This chapter considers how cash budgets are prepared, and the impact on cash balances of changing individual assumptions. The chapter then looks at how cash flows should be monitored and compared to the actual cash flows, and the importance of this area for management.

ASSESSMENT CRITERIA

Cash budget and forecasts (2.1)

Sensitivity analysis on cash budgets (2.2)

Cash budget and organisational policies (2.3)

CONTENTS

1. Monitoring cash flow
2. Sensitivity of the cash budget
3. Changes in receipts from receivables
4. Changes in payments to payables
5. Comparison of actual to budget
6. Causes of variances and courses of action

Analysing and monitoring cash budgets: Chapter 4

1 Monitoring cash flow

1.1 Introduction

One of the objectives of a cash budget is to provide a basis or reference point against which actual cash flows can be monitored. Comparing actual cash flows with the budget can help with:

- identifying whether cash flows are much better or worse than expected (variance analysis)
- predicting what cash flows are now likely to be in the future, and in particular whether the business will have enough cash (or liquidity) to survive.

Monitoring against the cash flow forecast can take place over different timescales, depending upon:

- the nature of the business
- the scale of the cash flowing into and out of the business
- whether forecast assumptions require additional funding.

Just as cash flows can highlight shortfalls in funding within a business, so too can they highlight whether surplus funds are being generated.

The benefit from preparing timely cash flow forecasts is that you have early indications of both good and not so good events. This allows you to take early action to avoid possible problems and to maximise returns on cash generated within the business.

Possible decisions that could be taken to deal with forecast short-term cash deficits include:

- additional short-term borrowing
- negotiating a higher overdraft limit with the bank
- the sale of short-term investments, if the company has any
- using different forms of financing to reduce cash flows in the short term, such as leasing instead of buying outright
- changing the amount of discretionary cash flows, deferring expenditures or bringing forward revenues. For example:
    - reducing the dividend to shareholders
    - postponing nonessential capital expenditure
    - bringing forward the planned disposal of non-current assets

CASH AND FINANCIAL MANAGEMENT

- reducing inventory levels
- shortening the operating cycle by reducing the time taken to collect receivables, perhaps by offering a discount
- shortening the operating cycle by delaying payment to payables.

If the forecast shows cash surpluses, these will be dealt with according to their size and duration. Management should consider a policy for how surplus cash should be invested so as to achieve a return on the money, but without investing in items where the risk of a fall in value is considered too high.

Where long-term cash surpluses are forecast, management might consider other possible uses of the surpluses, such as paying a higher dividend or repaying loans and other debts.

1.2 Revising the cash budget or preparing a new cash forecast

It is important that comparisons of actual cash flows should be against meaningful targets. From time to time it may therefore be necessary to revise the cash budget or prepare a new cash flow forecast.

This should take account of the cash flows that have actually occurred and what future cash flows are now expected to be, in the light of revised estimates and management measures to deal with some of the problems.

2 Sensitivity of the cash budget

2.1 Sensitivity

Once a cash budget is produced it is important to know how much changes to the cash inflows and cash outflows affect the cash balance position. The cash flows could change due to:

- a change in price or volume in goods bought or sold or a change in another income or expense
- a change in payment or collection periods
- the introduction of a settlement discount
- irrecoverable debts.

Computer spreadsheets can be used, not only to speed up the preparation of cash budgets, but also to easily carry out a variety of forms of sensitivity analysis.

Analysing and monitoring cash budgets: Chapter 4

2.2 Percentage changes

In many cases managers may need to consider how the cash position will alter if there is a change in any of the receipt or expenditure items. What may seem a healthy positive cash position could change with a 1% increase in wages or a 2% fall in sales. It is therefore advisable to assess the sensitivity of the balance to such changes.

Example

Consider the following cash flow.

	January £	February £	March £
Receipts			
Sales	10,000	20,000	15,000
Payments			
Payables	10,000	10,000	20,000
Wages	2,000	3,000	2,000
Sundry	500	500	500
	12,500	13,500	22,500
Net cash flow	(2,500)	6,500	(7,500)
Opening cash balance	4,000	1,500	8,000
Closing cash balance	1,500	8,000	500

What would be the net cash position each month if:

(i) wages increased by 5% or

(ii) sales increased by 4%?

CASH AND FINANCIAL MANAGEMENT

Solution

(i) If wages increase by 5% the impact on the cash balance is as follows:

	£	£	£
Wages	2,100	3,150	2,100
(increase)/decrease	(100)	(150)	(100)
New net cash flow	(2,600)	6,350	(7,600)
Opening cash balance	4,000	1,400	7,750
Closing cash balance	1,400	7,750	150

Thus, although wages have increased, the cash balance is still positive and corrective measures are not yet required.

(ii) If sales increase by 4% the impact on the cash balance is as follows:

	£	£	£
Sales	10,400	20,800	15,600
Increase/(decrease)	400	800	600
New net cash flow	(2,100)	7,300	(6,900)
Opening cash balance	4,000	1,900	9,200
Closing cash balance	1,900	9,200	2,300

Test your understanding 1

	April £	May £	June £
Sales	2,600	3,100	1,600
Payables	1,300	1,550	700
Wages	1,000	1,000	1,000
Power	200	200	200
	2,500	2,750	1,900
Net cash flow	100	350	(300)
Opening cash balance	100	200	550
Closing cash balance	200	550	250

In the above cash flow, how sensitive is the cash balance at the end of June to a 1% increase and a 2% decrease in sales?

(a) **1% increase**

	April £	May £	June £
Sales			
Increase/(decrease)			
New net cash flow			
Opening cash balance	100		
Closing cash balance			

(b) **2% decrease**

	April £	May £	June £
Sales			
Increase/(decrease)			
New net cash flow			
Opening cash balance	100		
Closing cash balance			

CASH AND FINANCIAL MANAGEMENT

 Test your understanding 2

Marshtitch Ltd's latest statement of financial position is attached. After examining this and the memos from the Production Manager, Sales Manager and Chief Accountant, you are required to carry out the following tasks:

(a) Prepare a cash flow forecast for each of the three months ending 31 December 20X3.

(b) Calculate what effect a 10% reduction in the price charged to the other retailers would have. Suggest two courses of action the company could take to lessen the adverse impact this would have on the cash flow.

Marshtitch Ltd – Statement of Financial Position at 30 September 20X3

	£	£
Non-current assets		
Land and buildings		75,000
Plant and machinery	315,000	
Less: Depreciation	150,000	
		165,000
		240,000
Current assets		
Inventory		
Raw materials	72,000	
Finished goods	152,000	
Receivables	432,000	
	656,000	
Total assets		896,000

KAPLAN PUBLISHING

Equity		
Share capital		250,000
Retained earnings		362,400
		613,400
Current liabilities		
Bank overdraft	190,000	
Trade payables for raw materials	93,600	
	283,600	
Total equity and liabilities		896,000

MEMO

To: Accounting Technician

From: Production Manager

Subject: Budget data

Date: 2 October 20X3

You requested the following information recently:

1. The raw material cost of each 'Rose Bowl' is 90 pence. We have contracted for the next 6 months supplies at this price.

2. It takes 10 minutes for one member of staff to make each 'Rose Bowl' and we currently pay our staff £6.00 per hour.

3. Currently our fixed production overheads are running at £20,000 per month including depreciation of £4,000.

4. On 30 September we were carrying sufficient raw material inventory to make 80,000 'Rose Bowls'. We also held 40,000 'Rose Bowls' in inventory at that date.

5. We are anticipating an increasing demand for our product so I plan to increase our inventory of finished goods by 5,000 per month while maintaining raw material inventory at their present level.

CASH AND FINANCIAL MANAGEMENT

M E M O

To: Accounting Technician

From: Sales Manager

Subject: Budget data

Date: 2 October 20X3

You requested the following information recently:

1   We expect to sell 100,000 'Rose Bowls' to the retail trade in October, 110,000 in November and 120,000 in December. We also expect to sell 4,000 per month in our own shop.

2   We intend to sell the 'Rose Bowl' to the retail trade for £2.40 each and for £3.50 each from our own shop.

3   The cost of running the sales department is currently fixed at £10,000 per month including depreciation of £500 per month.

4   The fixed running costs of the shop are £8,000 per month including £1,000 in depreciation.

M E M O

To: Accounting Technician

From: Chief Accountant

Subject: Budget data

Date: 30 September 20X3

While preparing the budgeted cash flow to 31 December, please include the following assumptions:

1   Our credit policy for all trade customers is for payment in 30 days. For budgetary purposes please assume that 25% of retail trade customers pay one month after sale, 70% two months after sale and the remainder three months after sale.

2   You should assume that the debtors at 30 September will pay as follows:

	£
October	240,000
November	180,000
December	12,000
	432,000

Analysing and monitoring cash budgets: Chapter 4

> 3   Purchases of all raw materials will be paid for one month in arrears as at present. All other costs are paid in the month in which they occur.
>
> 4   All sales from our own shop will be made for cash.
>
> 5   Budget administration overheads at £20,000 per month.
>
> 6   The bank is charging us interest on the overdraft at a monthly rate of 0.75% of the balance at the end of the previous month.

	October £	November £	December £
Receipts			
Trade sales			
Shop sales			
	———	———	———
Total receipts			
	———	———	———
Payments			
Trade suppliers			
Production wages			
Production overheads			
Sales department costs			
Retail shop costs			
Administration costs			
Overdraft interest			
	———	———	———
Total payments			
	———	———	———
Net cash flow			
	———	———	———
Opening cash balance			
Closing cash balance			
	———	———	———

CASH AND FINANCIAL MANAGEMENT

3 Changes in receipts from receivables

3.1 Introduction

The cash flows that appear in the cash budget are heavily dependent upon the payment patterns of receivables. Managers may need information about the effect that a change in those payment patterns would have on the net cash position.

The cash received from receivables could change due to a number of reasons:

- change in volume
- change in price
- change in timing of receipts
- offering a settlement discount
- occurrences of irrecoverable debts.

3.2 Changes in volume, price and/or timing

Example

A business is producing its cash budget for the next three months. Credit sales in February and March were £50,000 and £58,000. Credit sales are forecast as £60,000, £70,000 and £50,000 respectively for each of the months of April, May and June. Credit customers are currently offered one month's credit and they all pay in the month after the sale.

Cash outflows in each month are estimated to be:

April	May	June
£48,000	£57,000	£60,000

At the end of March there is an overdraft of £10,000.

What would be the effect on the net cash position at the end of each month if credit customers were given two months' credit for sales from 1st April onwards?

Solution

Current policy cash budget (one month credit)

	April £	May £	June £
Receipts from receivables (previous month's sales)	58,000	60,000	70,000
Cash outflows	(48,000)	(57,000)	(60,000)
Net cash flow	10,000	3,000	10,000
Opening cash balance	(10,000)	–	3,000
Closing cash balance	–	3,000	13,000

New policy cash budget (two months credit)

	April £	May £	June £
Receipts from receivables (sales from two months ago)	50,000	58,000	60,000
Cash outflows	(48,000)	(57,000)	(60,000)
Net cash flow	2,000	1,000	–
Opening cash balance	(10,000)	(8,000)	(7,000)
Closing cash balance	(8,000)	(7,000)	(7,000)

The effect of receivables paying two months after the sale rather than one month has been to reduce a positive cash balance to an overdraft balance at the end of each month.

CASH AND FINANCIAL MANAGEMENT

 Test your understanding 3

MEMO

To: Henry Naem
From: Jenny Powell
Date: 14 January
Subject: Work for this week

Henry

I have left you a copy of the cash flow forecast for the next three months for a new venture.

Please can you calculate the effect on the balance if the receivables arising from January onwards were given an extra month's grace?

The original data was as follows:

	December £	January £	February £	March £
Cash sales	16,000	18,000	18,500	20,000
Credit sales	7,000	6,000	7,000	6,000
Total	23,000	24,000	25,000	26,000

Credit sales are currently payable by the end of the month after the sale was made.

November's credit sales were £10,000.

Analysing and monitoring cash budgets: Chapter 4

Cash flow forecast for the first three months of next year

	January £	February £	March £
CASH RECEIVED			
Sales: cash	18,000	18,500	20,000
Sales: credit	7,000	6,000	7,000
Grant	20,000	0	0
Total receipts	45,000	24,500	27,000
Total payments	–73,400	–68,500	–18,924
Net cash flow	–28,400	–44,000	8,076
Opening cash balance	40,000	11,600	–32,400
Closing cash balance	11,600	–32,400	–24,324

Impact on cash balance if receivables pay one month later

	January £	February £	March £
CASH RECEIVED			
Sales: cash			
Sales: credit			
Grant			
Total			
CASH PAID			
Net cash flow			
Opening cash balance			
Closing cash balance			

CASH AND FINANCIAL MANAGEMENT

 Test your understanding 4

A cash budget has been prepared for Maximillian Ltd for the next 4 periods for a new product. The budget was prepared based on the following sales volumes and a selling price of £12 per item.

	March	April	May	June
Sales volume units	1,300	1,500	1,700	1,900

The pattern of cash receipts used in the budget assumed 50% of sales were received in the month of sale and the remaining 50% in the month following sale.

	March	April	May	June
Original forecast sales receipts £	7,800	16,800	19,200	21,600

In the light of current economic trends Maximillian Ltd needs to adjust its cash budget to take account of the following:

- The selling price will be reduced by 5% per item
- The pattern of sales receipts changes to 25% of sales received in the month of sale, 30% in the month following sale and the remaining 45% two months after sale.

Complete the table below to show the effect of the changes in values and timing of receipts for March to June:

	Revised forecast sales £	Sales receipts				
		March £	April £	May £	June £	Total £
March sales						
April sales						
May sales						
June sales						
Revised forecast sales receipts						

Complete the sentence below:

Receipts from sales in March to June will increase/decrease by ___% if the sales price and timing of receipts change.

3.3 Settlement discounts

The payment pattern of receivables can also be altered by offering settlement discounts to credit customers. Settlement discounts should encourage earlier payment of debts as customers who pay earlier pay less.

> **Example**
>
> A business has the following budgeted credit sales and budgeted cash payments:
>
> | | Actual | | | Forecast | | |
> | --- | --- | --- | --- | --- | --- | --- |
> | | Jan | Feb | Mar | Apr | May | Jun |
> | | £ | £ | £ | £ | £ | £ |
> | Credit sales in £000s | 100 | 120 | 130 | 140 | 150 | 160 |
> | Payments in £000s | 80 | 94 | 108 | 110 | 120 | 135 |
>
> The current credit terms for customers are 60 days and the current payment pattern is that 20% of customers pay during the month following sale, 70% pay two months after the sale and 10% three months after the date of sale.
>
> The company is considering introducing a settlement discount of 2% for payment during the month after sale.
>
> This is anticipated to result in 60% of customers paying in the month after sale, 30% two months after the date of sale and 10% three months after the date of sale.
>
> The company anticipates a cash overdraft of £20,000 at the start of April.
>
> (i) Determine the net cash balance at the end of each of the months of April, May and June under the existing credit terms.
>
> (ii) Calculate the effect on the net cash balance at the end of each of the three months if the new policy of offering a settlement discount were introduced for credit sales made from 1 March onwards.
>
> (iii) Comment on how the new policy affects the net cash balance for each of the three months.

Solution

Under existing policy	April £	May £	June £
RECEIPTS			
Cash from receivables in one month 20%	26,000	28,000	30,000
Cash from receivables in two months 70%	84,000	91,000	98,000
Cash from receivables in three months 10%	10,000	12,000	13,000
Total receipts	120,000	131,000	141,000
PAYMENTS			
Payment to payables	110,000	120,000	135,000
Total payments	110,000	120,000	135,000
Net cash flow	10,000	11,000	6,000
Opening cash balance	(20,000)	(10,000)	1,000
Closing cash balance	(10,000)	1,000	7,000

Under new policy	April £	May £	June £
RECEIPTS			
Cash from receivables in one month **60%** × 98%	76,440	82,320	88,200
Cash from receivables in two months 30%	84,000*	39,000	42,000
Cash from receivables in three months 10%	10,000*	12,000*	13,000
Total receipts	170,440	133,320	143,200
PAYMENTS			
Payment to payables	110,000	120,000	135,000
Total payments	110,000	120,000	135,000
Net cash flow	60,440	13,320	8,200
Opening cash balance	(20,000)	40,440	53,760
Closing cash balance	40,440	53,760	61,960

* Note that the new policy is introduced for credit sales from 1 March onwards, so receipts relating to February and January sales will continue to follow the old policy.

Under the new policy of offering the settlement discount, the overdraft is removed much quicker. The overall cash balance has increased more rapidly under the new policy. The cash budget may need to be expanded to ensure that the 2% reduction in actual cash received does not have a negative effect later on.

Analysing and monitoring cash budgets: Chapter 4

Test your understanding 5

A business is considering whether to offer a 3% discount for payment received from credit customers in the month of sale.

This will only be offered to sales made after 1 April.

Credit sales for the business are as follows:

	Actual		Budgeted		
	February £	March £	April £	May £	June £
Credit sales	20,000	22,000	24,000	18,000	21,000

The current receivables collection forecast is:

- 15% in month of sale
- 75% in month after sale
- 10% two months after sale.

	April £	May £	June £
Original forecast sales receipts	22,100	22,900	19,050

The business estimates that 60% of customers would take advantage of the settlement discount by paying in the month of sale, 30% of customers will pay in the month after the sale and 10% of customers will pay two months after the month of sale.

Calculate the cash receipts for April, May and June if the settlement discount is offered.

Should this business offer a settlement discount?

	April £	May £	June £
New forecast sales receipts			

CASH AND FINANCIAL MANAGEMENT

3.4 Irrecoverable debts

It is possible that some debts will become irrecoverable debts i.e. the cash will not be received. The cash flows will need to be adjusted for this.

It may be that a business predicts that a certain percentage of outstanding amounts will not be received or that there is a specific receivable that will not be able to pay.

 Example

A business has found that 30% of customers pay in the month of sale, 40% of customers pay in the month after the sale and 20% of customers pay two months after the month of sale.

From past experience it is known that 10% of the customers do not pay.

Credit sales for the business are as follows:

	Actual			Budgeted	
	February £	March £	April £	May £	June £
Credit sales	10,000	20,000	30,000	25,000	30,000

	April £	May £	June £
The cash receipts will be:			
30% in month of sale	9,000	7,500	9,000
40% in subsequent month	8,000	12,000	10,000
20% two months after sale	2,000	4,000	6,000
10% irrecoverable debt	0	0	0
Giving:			
Total cash receipts	19,000	23,500	25,000

Irrecoverable debts are not recovered therefore no cash is received.

Analysing and monitoring cash budgets: Chapter 4

Example

It has come to the attention of the credit control manager that some of the credit customers are unlikely to pay. These customers are estimated to account for 5% of credit sales each month.

The credit manager has decided it is necessary to write off the amounts as an irrecoverable debt.

The current credit sales budget is as follows:

	Actual			Forecast		
	April	May	June	July	August	September
Total sales	82,000	84,000	85,000	90,000	92,000	95,000

The pattern of sales receipts are 30% in the month of sale, 45% in the month following sale and 25% two months after sale.

	June	July	August	September
Original value of sales	85,000	90,000	92,000	95,000
30% in month of sale	25,500	27,000	27,600	28,500
45% in subsequent month	37,800	38,250	40,500	41,400
25% two months after sale	20,500	21,000	21,250	22,500
Original timing of receipts	83,800	86,250	89,350	92,400
Revised value of sales	85,000	90,000	92,000	95,000
30% in month of sale	25,500	27,000	27,600	28,500
45% in subsequent month	37,800	38,250	40,500	41,400
20% two months after sale	16,400	16,800	17,000	18,000
5% irrecoverable debt (no cash flow)				
Revised timing of receipts	79,700	82,050	85,100	87,900
Change in receipts	–4,100	–4,200	–4,250	–4,500

CASH AND FINANCIAL MANAGEMENT

4 Changes in payments to payables

4.1 Introduction

The cash flows that appear in the cash budget are heavily dependent upon the payment patterns to payables. Managers may need information about the effect that a change in those payment patterns would have on the net cash position.

The cash paid to a payable could change due to a number of reasons:

- change in volume
- change in price
- change in timing of payments
- receiving a settlement discount.

4.2 Changes in volume, price and/or timing

Example

A business is producing its cash budget for the next three months. Credit purchases are forecast to be:

February	March	April	May	June
£50,000	£58,000	£48,000	£57,000	£60,000

Suppliers currently offer two month's credit.

Cash inflows in each month are estimated to be:

April	May	June
£58,000	£60,000	£70,000

At the end of March there is an overdraft of £10,000.

What would be the effect on the net cash position at the end of each month if the suppliers reduced the credit to one month from February?

Solution

Current policy cash budget (two months credit)

	April £	May £	June £
Cash inflows	58,000	60,000	70,000
Payments to payables	(50,000)	(58,000)	(48,000)
Net cash flow	8,000	2,000	22,000
Opening cash balance	(10,000)	(2,000)	–
Closing cash balance	(2,000)	–	22,000

New policy cash budget (one month credit)

	April £	May £	June £
Cash inflows	58,000	60,000	70,000
Payment to payables	(58,000)	(48,000)	(57,000)
Net cash flow	–	12,000	13,000
Opening cash balance	(60,000)	(60,000)	(48,000)
Closing cash balance	(60,000)	(48,000)	(35,000)

The effect of paying the payables one month earlier has meant that the cash balance has reduced dramatically.

CASH AND FINANCIAL MANAGEMENT

Test your understanding 6

Maximillian Ltd has managed to negotiate extended payment terms with its suppliers for purchases made from March onwards.

The original budget was to pay in the month after purchase.

	March	April	May	June
Forecast purchases (£)	8,000	8,200	8,400	8,600
Original forecast payment (£)		8,000	8,200	8,400

The settlement is now split over the 2 months after purchase, 50% is paid in the month after purchase and the remainder the month after that.

Complete the table below to show the new payments for April to June:

	April	May	June
Revised forecast payments			

Test your understanding 7

A cash budget has been prepared for Loadzmonie Ltd for the next 4 periods.

The budget was prepared based on the following sales volumes and a selling price of £15 per item.

	January	February	March	April
Sales volume	2,000	3,000	3,400	3,800

The pattern of cash receipts used in the budget assumed 40% of sales were received in the month of sale and the remaining 60% in the month following sale.

In the light of current economic trends Loadzmonie Ltd needs to adjust its cash budget to take account of the following:

- The selling price from period 1 will be reduced by 4% per item.

- The pattern of sales receipts changes to 20% of sales received in the month of sale, 30% in the month following sale and the remaining 50% two months after sale.

Analysing and monitoring cash budgets: **Chapter 4**

Complete the table below to show the effect of the changes in values and timing of receipts:

	January £	February £	March £	April £
Original value of sales				
Original timing of receipts				
Revised value of sales				
Revised timing of receipts				
Increase/(decrease) in receipts				

Loadzmonie Ltd has managed to negotiate extended payment terms with its suppliers.

The original budget was to pay in the month of purchase.

The settlement is now split over the 2 months after purchase – 40% is paid in the month after purchase and the remaining the month after that.

	January £	February £	March £	April £
Purchases	4,000	4,200	4,400	4,600

Complete the table below to show the effect of the changes in timing of the payments:

	January £	February £	March £	April £
Original timing of payments				
Revised timing of payments				
(Increase)/decrease in payment				

CASH AND FINANCIAL MANAGEMENT

Using the information above on receipts and payments complete the table below to show the revised budgeted cash balance for the months of February, March and April.

	February £	March £	April £
Original net cash flow	20,000	20,300	20,800
Changes in receipts			
Changes in payments			
Revised net cash flow			
Opening cash balance	7,500		
Closing cash balance			

4.3 Receiving a settlement discount

The payment pattern of payables can also be altered by receiving a settlement discount from the supplier.

Test your understanding 8

A company has managed to negotiate new payment terms with its suppliers.

The original budget was prepared based on paying suppliers in the month following purchase.

The revised payment terms allow for settlement of 40% in the month of purchase with a 5% settlement discount, 30% in the month following purchase with the remaining 30% two months after purchase. The budgeted purchases figures are:

	Period 1 (£)	Period 2 (£)	Period 3 (£)	Period 4 (£)	Period 5 (£)
Purchases	8,700	8,000	6,800	10,900	11,000

Complete the table to show the effect of the changes on the timing of purchase payments for periods 3, 4 and 5:

	3	4	5
Original forecast payments			
Revised forecast payments			
Increase/(decrease) in cash			

5 Comparison of actual to budget

5.1 Cash flow control reports

As well as using the cash budget to identify any anticipated surplus or deficit in future periods, it is also important to monitor the actual performance of the business compared to the budgeted performance.

This is part of the management process of control whereby the actual cash flows are compared to the budgeted cash flows and any significant variances between the two are highlighted and investigated.

> **Definition**
>
> An **adverse variance** occurs when the actual costs exceed the budgeted costs or when the actual revenue is less than the budgeted revenue.
>
> A **favourable variance** occurs when the actual cost is less than the budgeted cost or when the actual revenue exceeds the budgeted revenue.

Reporting of actual cash flows compared with budgeted cash flows should be carried out on a daily, weekly or monthly basis, depending on the size of the business and the frequency and value of its cash receipts and payments.

In common with all management reports, the purpose of a cash flow report is to provide a basis for management decision making. For this reason the report needs to be addressed to the manager who can control the cash flows.

5.2 Comparison of actual to budgeted cash flows

For each item in the cash budget the actual cash flow can be compared to the budgeted cash flow. Any significant differences should be investigated to determine why the variance happened and to consider how this can be dealt with in terms of future operations or future budgeting.

To identify significant variances it is possible to consider the size of the absolute value of the variance but also the percentage change when compared to the budget.

CASH AND FINANCIAL MANAGEMENT

Cash receipts

There are normally two main types of cash receipt to monitor: receipts from customers and investment income (e.g. interest).

Cash receipts from customers depend on:

- the volume and value of sales, and
- the time taken by customers to pay.

It is important to identify the cause of any difference in cash flow between budget and actual because the control action required will differ in each case.

If budgeted and actual cash receipts differ because budgeted and actual sales volumes are different, it should be remembered that the difference in volume should affect expenditures and cash payments too.

The implications for cash flow should therefore be considered in terms of net cash flows – in other words the difference in cash receipts less the difference in cash payments.

If budgeted and actual cash receipts differ because customers are taking more or less time to pay what they owe, action should be taken either to amend the budget or to take measures to speed up customer payments.

Cash payments

Payments can be divided into three categories:

- payments of a routine, recurring nature which are unrelated to activity level (e.g. rent, management salaries)
- payments of a routine nature which are related to activity level (e.g. payments to suppliers for purchases/expenses, wage payments, payments to sales staff of sales commissions)
- payments of a non-recurring nature (e.g. taxation, dividends, major capital expenditures).

Some payments will be committed and uncontrollable. Others might be reduced or deferred to improve cash flow.

Example

Given below are the actual and budgeted cash flows for the month of April:

	Budget £	Actual £
Cash sales	9,000	6,400
Receipts from receivables	34,000	27,800
Payments to payables	(16,700)	(20,500)
Production wages	(3,600)	(3,600)
Administration costs	(2,000)	(2,100)
Capital expenditure	(4,000)	(14,000)
Net cash flow	16,700	(6,000)

Calculate the percentage change from the budget and state what the most significant variance is?

Solution

- Cash sales show an adverse variance of £2,600, a drop of nearly 29% from budget (£2,600 ÷ £9,000 × 100 = 28.88%).

- Receipts from receivables are £6,200 adverse, a drop of just over 18% from budget (£6,200 ÷ £34,000 × 100 = 18.24%).

- Payments to payables are £3,800 adverse, an increase of nearly 23% on budget (£3,800 ÷ £16,700 × 100 = 22.75%).

- Production wages have matched budget.

- Administration costs are £100 adverse, an increase of 5% (£100 ÷ £2,000 × 100 = 5%).

- Capital expenditure is £10,000 adverse, an increase of 250% (£10,000 ÷ £4,000 × 100 = 250%).

The most significant variance is capital expenditure. This needs to be investigated.

Other significant variances include the reduction in cash sales with a 29% decline from budget and the payments to payable with an increase of 23% on budget.

CASH AND FINANCIAL MANAGEMENT

 Test your understanding 9

Given below are the actual and budgeted cash flows for the month of October for a business:

	Budget £	Actual £
Receipts from receivables	132,400	106,000
Payments to suppliers	(70,000)	(79,000)
Production wages	(17,000)	(17,500)
Production expenses	(1,000)	(1,500)
Selling expenses	(4,000)	(3,400)
Administration expenses	(4,100)	(4,100)
Net cash flow	36,300	500
Opening cash balance	10,000	10,000
Closing cash balance	46,300	10,500

Identify the variance value and whether it is adverse or favourable and calculate the percentage change (to the nearest whole %)

	£	Adverse/ favourable	% change
Receipts from receivables			
Payments to suppliers			
Production wages			
Production expenses			
Selling expenses			
Administration expenses			

Analysing and monitoring cash budgets: Chapter 4

5.3 Reconciliation of budgeted cash balance to actual cash balance

After determining the variances between the actual and budgeted cash flows for the period then it should be possible to use these differences to reconcile the budgeted cash balance at the end of the period to the actual cash balance.

This provides a useful summary, to the management of the business, of the causes of the unexpected actual position.

Example

Given below are the actual and budgeted cash flows for April:

	Budget £	Actual £
Cash sales	9,000	6,400
Receipts from receivables	34,000	27,800
Payments to payables	(16,700)	(20,500)
Production wages	(3,600)	(3,600)
Administration costs	(2,000)	(2,100)
Capital expenditure	(4,000)	(14,000)
Net cash flow	16,700	(6,000)
Opening cash balance	3,200	3,200
Closing cash balance	19,900	(2,800)

Prepare a reconciliation of the budgeted cash balance of £19,900 to the actual overdraft figure of £2,800 at the end of the month.

Reconciliation of budgeted cash balance to actual cash balance.

	£
Budged cash balance at 30 April	19,900
Cash sales	2,600 A
Receipts from receivables	6,200 A
Payments to suppliers	3,800 A
Administration costs	100 A
Capital expenditure	10,000 A
Actual cash (overdraft) balance at 30 April	(2,800)

CASH AND FINANCIAL MANAGEMENT

 Test your understanding 10

Following are the budget and actual figures for the last quarter.

	Budgeted £	Actual £
Receipts from receivables	94,875	98,214
Cash sales	10,250	9,750
Payments to payables	(52,741)	(56,254)
Cash purchases	(6,985)	(7,594)
Capital expenditure	–	(15,000)
Wages and salaries	(15,000)	(16,000)
General expenses	(19,584)	(18,745)
Net cash flow	10,815	(5,629)
Opening bank balance	8,800	8,800
Closing bank balance	19,615	3,171

Prepare the reconciliation below, selecting the appropriate description for each entry (adverse or favourable):

£

Budgeted closing bank balance

Receipts from receivables

Cash sales

Payments to payables

Cash payments

Capital expenditure

Wages and salaries

General expenses

————

Actual closing bank balance

————

Test your understanding 11

Fastinfo Ltd

MEMO

To: Henry Naem

From: Holly Powell

Date: 14 January

Subject: Work for this week

Henry

I have left a copy of the cash flow forecast and actual cash flow for the final three months of last year on my desk.

Please calculate the differences between actual and budget for the whole 3 months to reconcile the budgeted closing bank balance with the actual closing bank balance.

Please identify the most significant variance on a percentage basis.

CASH AND FINANCIAL MANAGEMENT

Cash flow forecast

	October £000	November £000	December £000
CASH RECEIVED			
Cash sales	1,200	1,100	1,100
Credit sales	1,100	1,150	1,200
TOTAL	2,300	2,250	2,300
CASH PAID			
Rent	250	250	250
Wages	38	35	37
Purchases	1,600	1,600	1,800
Selling/administration	28	29	29
TOTAL	1,916	1,914	2,116
Net cash flow	384	336	184
Opening cash balance	20	404	740
Closing cash balance	404	740	924

Actual cash flow

	October £000	November £000	December £000
CASH RECEIVED			
Cash sales	1,100	1,300	1,250
Credit sales	1,000	1,000	1,050
TOTAL	2,100	2,300	2,300
CASH PAID			
Rent	275	275	275
Wages	40	38	40
Purchases	1,500	1,650	1,750
Selling/administration	25	25	25
TOTAL	1,840	1,988	2,090
Net cash flow	260	312	210
Opening cash balance	20	280	592
Closing cash balance	280	592	802

Analysing and monitoring cash budgets: **Chapter 4**

Reconciliation of actual to budget

	Actual £000	Budget £000	£000 A or F	% change
Budgeted closing cash balance				
Cash sales				
Credit sales				
Rent				
Wages				
Purchases				
Selling/administration				
Actual closing cash balance				

The most significant variance is:

6 Cause of variances and courses of action

6.1 Cause of variances between budget and actual cash flow

Variances between budget and actual cash flows can occur for a number of reasons.

There are also a variety of courses of action available to minimise adverse variances or benefit from favourable variances.

Listed below are possible causes for adverse variances with possible courses of action.

Reduced receipts from receivables

Lower volume of sales than budgeted

- Increase marketing/advertising
- Reduce price to be competitive
- Offer deals e.g. Buy one get one free
- Improve the product

CASH AND FINANCIAL MANAGEMENT

Lower selling price than budgeted	• Check the deals being offered by sales staff
	• Check competition for their prices
Receipts taking longer to be collected from receivables	• Improve credit control/outsource debt collection
	• Change payment terms in contract
	• Offer a settlement discount for early payment

Increased payments

Higher price paid for raw materials	• Negotiate an early payment discount
	• Negotiate a trade or bulk discount
	• Change supplier
More materials required for production	• Change manufacturing techniques
	• Offer bonuses to employees for meeting usage targets
	• Investigate product requirement
Increase in labour costs	• Reduce overtime working
	• Offer bonuses to employees for meeting efficiency targets
	• Inexperienced staff take longer so look to increase training
	• Investigate the possibility of mechanisation/ computerisation of some tasks or processes

Analysing and monitoring cash budgets: Chapter 4

Increase in other costs
i.e. electricity, rent etc

- May be little action that can be taken as these are not very controllable by the business. It may be that the original budget did not take into account price rises

Capital expenditure/receipts

Payment or receipt made

- Make sure that all large items of expenditure are communicated to the budget manager

On the whole, favourable variances indicate that a working practice has improved i.e. labour costs are lower than budget; staff are working more efficiently therefore not working as much overtime to meet production or sales demand.

Unfortunately, sometimes a favourable variance may mean that there has been an adverse variance somewhere else in the business.

For example, labour costs are lower than expected (favourable); this could be caused by sales demand being lower than expected (adverse) so staff are not required to work as many hours. The favourable labour variance was not due to staff being more efficient, but due to a reduced demand for the product.

Generally, variances that are larger or showing a repeated trend need to be investigated more urgently to identify the cause and to take actions to correct them.

CASH AND FINANCIAL MANAGEMENT

 Example

Given below are the actual and budgeted cash flows for the month of April, along with the variances:

	Budget £	Actual £	Variance £
Cash sales	9,000	6,400	2,600A
Receipts from receivables	34,000	27,800	6,200A
Payments to payables	(16,700)	(20,500)	3,800A
Production wages	(3,600)	(3,600)	0
Administration costs	(2,000)	(2,100)	100A
Capital expenditure	(10,000)	(14,000)	4,000A
Net cash flow	16,700	(6,000)	

What may have caused these variances? How might the company have improved the cash flow for the period?

Solution

The most significant variance is the reduction in cash sales; this may be because more customers have taken credit. Receipts from credit sales have also declined so if more customers have taken credit sales then the collection of debts needs looking into.

Both cash and credit sales may have declined due to a drop in sales revenue.

Payments to payables have also increased, either due to increased purchase volume or cost or because payment is being demanded by the suppliers.

The combination of a reduction in receipts and an increase in payments may cause this business to have serious cash flow problems.

Production wages and administration costs are less of a concern.

The amount of capital expenditure that occurred in the period was not fully budgeted for. This may have been an oversight during budget creation or perhaps a machine failure occurred meaning that funds had to be spent to buy a replacement.

The company could have improved cash flow in the following ways:

- Better credit control and collection procedures leading to higher receipts from receivables.
- More advertising to keep the product in the public eye.

Analysing and monitoring cash budgets: Chapter 4

- Improvements to the products to increase the desirability of the product.
- Delaying payments to payables.
- Negotiating a settlement discount for prompt payments or longer credit terms with the suppliers.
- Postponing the capital expenditure.
- Purchasing the capital items using a lease or hire purchase terms rather than outright.
- Finding specific finance for the capital expenditure such as a bank loan.

Test your understanding 12

Match each cause of a variance listed on the left with a possible course of action from the list on the right.

Cause		Course of action
Receipts are not coming in as planned		Check the competition
Payments are being made late to suppliers		Change supplier
Sales volume has decreased		Outsource credit control
Payments to suppliers have increased in value		Improve staff efficiency
Labour costs have increased		Negotiate an early settlement discount

CASH AND FINANCIAL MANAGEMENT

Test your understanding 13

Variances between budget and actual cash flows can occur for number of reasons. Match the variance below with the possible course of action.

Variance	Course of action
Labour costs have increased	Negotiate early settlement discount
Prices of raw materials have increased	Improve the product
Payments to suppliers are being made earlier	Buy in bulk to achieve discounts
Sales volumes have decreased	Reduce overtime working

Test your understanding 14

Variances between budget and actual cash flows can occur for number of reasons. Match the variance below with the possible course of action.

Variance	Course of action
Suppliers are insisting on earlier payments	Improve communication
Customers are insisting on longer credit periods	Improve credit control
A new machine was bought that was not in the budget	Negotiate early settlement discount
Receipts from receivables is less than budget	Reduce discounts available

Test your understanding 15

Variances between budget and actual cash flows can occur for number of reasons. Match the variance below with the possible course of action.

Variance	Course of action
Customers are buying lower value products	Improve credit control by agreeing invoices before they are posted
Customers are taking more days to settle their debts	Actively market more expensive product lines
Electricity cost increases	Offer a settlement discount
Customers are delaying payments due to invoice queries	Install energy saving lights

7 Summary

As well as using cash budgets in order to plan for anticipated deficits or surpluses, management will also need to compare the actual cash flows for a period to the budgeted cash flows as part of the process of control.

Useful information for management will be a reconciliation between the budgeted cash balance at the end of the period and the actual cash balance, in order to highlight areas that can be improved in terms of operations or budgeting.

CASH AND FINANCIAL MANAGEMENT

Test your understanding answers

Test your understanding 1

(a) **1% increase in sales**

	April £	May £	June £
Sales (× 1.01)	2,626	3,131	1,616
Increase/(decrease)	26	31	16
New net cash flow	126	381	(284)
Opening cash balance	100	226	607
Closing cash balance	226	607	323

A 1% increase in sales results in the cash balance increasing from £250 to £323. This is an increase of £73 (i.e. 29%).

(b) **2% decrease in sales**

	April £	May £	June £
Sales (× 0.98)	2,548	3,038	1,568
Increase/(decrease)	(52)	(62)	(32)
New net cash flow	48	288	(332)
Opening cash balance	100	148	436
Closing cash balance	148	436	104

A 2% decrease in sales has not caused the cash balance to become overdrawn but cash has fallen to £104. This is a £146 (i.e. 58%) fall.

Test your understanding 2

(a) **Cash flow forecast for the three months ended 31 December 20X3**

	October £	November £	December £
Receipts			
Trade sales (W)	240,000	240,000	246,000
Shop sales (4,000 × £3.50)	14,000	14,000	14,000
Total receipts	254,000	254,000	260,000
Payments			
Trade suppliers (W)	93,600	98,100	107,100
Production wages (£1 per unit)	109,000	119,000	129,000
Production overheads	16,000	16,000	16,000
Sales department costs	9,500	9,500	9,500
Retail shop costs	7,000	7,000	7,000
Administration costs	20,000	20,000	20,000
Overdraft interest (at 0.75%)	1,425	1,444	1,572
Total payments	256,525	271,044	290,172
Net cash flow	(2,525)	(17,044)	(30,172)
Opening cash balance	(190,000)	(192,525)	(209,569)
Closing cash balance	(192,525)	(209,569)	(239,741)

Working

	October (units)	November (units)	December (units)
Sales			
Credit	100,000	110,000	120,000
Shop	4,000	4,000	4,000
	104,000	114,000	124,000
Closing inventory	45,000	50,000	55,000
Opening inventory	(40,000)	(45,000)	(50,000)
Production required	109,000	119,000	129,000

	£	£	£
Purchases (at 90p per unit)	98,100	107,100	116,100

	October £	November £	December £
Receipts			
B/fwd	240,000	180,000	12,000
October sales	0	60,000	168,000
November sales	0	0	66,000
December sales	0	0	0
	240,000	240,000	246,000

(b) **Effect of 10% reduction in price**

If price reduced from £2.40 to £2.16 on 1 October 20X3, the effect on sales will be:

	Volume	Reduction	Received October	November	December
		£	£	£	£
October	100,000	24,000	0	6,000	16,800
November	110,000	26,400	0	0	6,600
December	120,000	28,800	0	0	0
			0	6,000	23,400
Original overdraft			(192,525)	(209,569)	(239,741)
New overdraft			(192,525)	(215,569)	(269,141)
Interest charge			0	0	(45)
Final overdraft				(215,569)	(269,186)

Therefore, the final overdraft will increase by £29,445.

Action that could be taken:

(i) Receivables could be collected more quickly.

(ii) Additional credit could be taken from suppliers.

Test your understanding 3

Impact on bank balance if receivables arising from January onwards pay one month later

	January £	February £	March £
Cash received			
Sales: cash	18,000	18,500	20,000
Sales: credit	7,000		6,000
Grant	20,000	0	0
Total	45,000	18,500	26,000
Cash paid	–73,400	–68,500	–18,924
Net cash flow	–28,400	–50,000	7,076
Opening cash balance	40,000	11,600	–38,400
Closing cash balance	11,600	–38,400	–31,324

CASH AND FINANCIAL MANAGEMENT

Test your understanding 4

	Revised forecast sales £	Sales receipts				
		March £	April £	May £	June £	Total £
March sales	14,820	3,705	4,446	6,669	0	
April sales	17,100	0	4,275	5,130	7,695	
May sales	19,380	0	0	4,845	5,814	
June sales	21,660	0	0	0	5,415	
Revised forecast sales receipts		3,705	8,721	16,644	18,924	47,994

Receipts from sales in March to June will decrease by 26.6% if the sales price and timing of receipts change.

Test your understanding 5

	April £	May £	June £
Cash from receivables in month of sale	13,968	10,476	12,222
Cash from receivables in month after sale	16,500*	7,200	5,400
Cash from receivables in two months after month of sale	2,000*	2,200*	2,400
Total receipts	32,468	19,876	20,022

* Note that these amounts relate to the sales made before the new policy was introduced on 1 April (i.e. February sales and March sales). Therefore, they continue to follow the old policy.

At first glance it appears that this business should offer a settlement discount of 3% as cash receipts have increased by 13% over the 3 months in question.

Original total receipts £64,050

New total receipts £72,366

However, bear in mind that in the long term, overall cash receipts will be lower because of the discount.

Test your understanding 6

	April	May	June
Revised forecast payments £	4,000	8,100	8,300

Test your understanding 7

	January £	February £	March £	April £
Original value of sales	30,000	45,000	51,000	57,000
Original timing of receipts (W1)	12,000	36,000	47,400	53,400
Revised value of sales	28,800	43,200	48,960	54,720
Revised timing of receipts (W2)	5,760	17,280	37,152	47,232
Increase/(decrease) in receipts	–6,240	–18,720	–10,248	–6,168

	January £	February £	March £	April £
Original timing of payments	4,000	4,200	4,400	4,600
Revised timing of payments (W3)	0	1,600	4,080	4,280
(Increase)/decrease in payment	4,000	2,600	320	320

CASH AND FINANCIAL MANAGEMENT

	February £	March £	April £
Original net cash flow	20,000	20,300	20,800
Changes in receipts	−18,720	−10,248	−6,168
Changes in payments	2,600	320	320
Revised net cash flow	3,880	10,372	14,952
Opening bank balance	7,500	11,380	21,752
Closing bank balance	11,380	21,752	36,704

Workings

(W1)	January	February	March	April
In month	12,000	18,000	20,400	22,800
In following month	0	18,000	27,000	30,600
Total	12,000	36,000	47,400	53,400

(W2)	January	February	March	April
In month	5,760	8,640	9,792	10,944
One month following	0	8,640	12,960	14,688
Two months following	0	0	14,400	21,600
Total	5,760	17,280	37,152	47,232

(W3)	January	February	March	April
One month following	0	1,600	1,680	1,760
Two months following	0	0	2,400	2,520
Total	0	1,600	4,080	4,280

Analysing and monitoring cash budgets: Chapter 4

Test your understanding 8

	3	4	5
Original forecast payments £	8,000	6,800	10,900
In month of purchase 40% with 5% discount	2,584	4,142	4,180
Month following purchase 30%	2,400	2,040	3,270
2 months following purchase 30%	2,610	2,400	2,040
Revised forecast payments £	7,594	8,582	9,490
Increase/(decrease) in cash	406	(1,782)	1,410

Test your understanding 9

	£	Adverse/ favourable	% change
Receipts from receivables	26,400	A	20
Payments to suppliers	9,000	A	13
Production wages	500	A	3
Production expenses	500	A	50
Selling expenses	600	F	15
Administration expenses	0	–	0

CASH AND FINANCIAL MANAGEMENT

Test your understanding 10

	£
Budgeted closing bank balance	19,615
Receipts from receivables	3,339 F
Cash sales	500 A
Payments to payables	3,513 A
Cash payments	609 A
Capital expenditure	15,000 A
Wages and salaries	1,000 A
General expenses	839 F
Actual closing bank balance	3,171

Test your understanding 11

Reconciliation of actual to budget

	Actual £000	Budget £000	£000	% change
Budgeted closing bank balance			924	
Cash sales	3,650	3,400	250 F	7
Credit sales	3,050	3,450	400 A	12
Rent	825	750	75 A	10
Wages	118	110	8 A	7
Purchases	4,900	5,000	100 F	2
Selling/administration	75	86	11 F	13
Actual closing bank balance			802	

The most significant variance is: selling and administration cost.

KAPLAN PUBLISHING

Test your understanding 12

Receipts are not coming in as planned	Outsource credit control
Payments are being made late to suppliers	Negotiate an early settlement discount
Sales volume has decreased	Check the competition
Payments to suppliers have increased in value	Change supplier
Labour costs have increased	Improve staff efficiency

Test your understanding 13

Labour costs have increased	Reduce overtime working
Prices of raw materials have increased	Buy in bulk to achieve discounts
Payments to suppliers are being made earlier	Negotiate early settlement discount
Sales volumes have decreased	Improve the product

Test your understanding 14

Suppliers are insisting on earlier payments	Negotiate early settlement discount
Customers are insisting on longer credit periods	Reduce discounts available
A new machine was bought that was not in the budget	Improve communication
Receipts from receivables is less than budget	Improve credit control

Test your understanding 15

Customers are buying lower value products	Actively market more expensive product lines
Customers are taking more days to settle their debts	Offer a settlement discount
Electricity cost increases	Install energy saving lights
Customers are delaying payments due to invoice queries	Improve credit control by agreeing invoices before they are posted

CASH AND FINANCIAL MANAGEMENT

Liquidity management

Introduction

The effective management of cash is not something that can be undertaken in isolation or without an awareness of the general financial environment in which organisations operate.

ASSESSMENT CRITERIA
Principles of finance and liquidity (3.1)
Use calculations to support the management of finance and liquidity (3.2)

CONTENTS
1 Liquidity
2 Working capital cycle
3 Measuring liquidity
4 Gearing
5 Overtrading and overcapitalisation

1 Liquidity

1.1 Liquidity

Liquidity is the measure of surplus cash and near cash, over that level required to meet obligations. The main sources of liquidity are usually:

- cash in the bank
- short term investments that can be cashed in easily and quickly
- cash inflows from normal trading operations (cash sales and payments by receivables for credit sales)
- an overdraft facility or other ready source of extra borrowing.

Liquid assets consist of both cash and items that could or will be converted into cash within a short time, with little or no loss. They include some investments, for example:

- deposits with banks or building societies where a minimum notice period for withdrawal is required
- investments in government securities, which in the UK are called gilt-edged inventories (or 'gilts')
- other liquid assets are trade receivables and, possibly, inventory.

Trade receivables should be expected to pay what they owe within a fairly short time, so receivables are often considered a liquid asset for a business.

In some businesses, such as retailing, inventory will be used or re-sold within a short time, to create sales for the business and cash income. Inventory is less liquid than receivables.

A business has liquidity if it has access to enough liquid assets to meet its essential payment obligations when they fall due. This means that a business is extremely liquid if it has a large amount of cash, plus investments in gilts and funds in notice accounts with a building society, plus a large amount of trade receivables and inventory.

Liquidity is also boosted if a business has an unused overdraft facility, so that it could go into overdraft with its bank if it needed to.

1.2 Liquidity and the cash budget

A business that has good liquidity is unlikely to have serious cash flow problems. For all businesses, it is important to make payments when they fall due.

If financial commitments (for example paying suppliers, paying staff, paying rent, making payments to HMRC, loan repayments) are not satisfied, they can have serious repercussions for the business such as additional fees, recalled loans, suppliers refusing to provide goods and eventually liquidation.

A business with good liquidity is likely to be able to take advantage of early settlement discounts or bulk buy discounts from suppliers. They may also be able to offer additional credit to customers to attract more business and boost revenue. A business with poor liquidity, where cash flow is more restricted is less likely to be able to take advantage of these opportunities.

When a liquid business has to make a cash payment, it should be able to obtain the money from somewhere to do it. Normally, the cash to pay suppliers and employees comes from the cash received from trade receivables.

A cash budget should be used to assess a business's cash flow and hence liquidity. As we have seen in previous chapters, a cash budget will help a business identify periods when additional finance or management decisions are required to improve cash flow. It may also identify periods where a cash surplus could be used to earn additional interest or take advantage of an opportunity.

However, cash budgets include many assumptions such as the amount of future sales, customer payment patterns or when new non-current assets will be required. Cash budgets also do not include unexpected expenses such as a break down on a machine needing repairs, an unexpected rent increase or a sudden unexpected economic event impacting business (such as the global COVID pandemic in 2020).

The liquidity of a business, particularly its operational activities, is therefore related to its working capital and in particular its inventory, receivables and short-term payables.

2 Working capital cycle

2.1 Working capital

Definition

Working capital is the short-term net assets of the business made up of inventory, receivables, payables and cash.

Working capital is the capital available for conducting the day to day operations of an organisation. It is normally expressed as the excess of current assets over current liabilities.

Working capital management is the management of all aspects of both current assets and current liabilities, to minimise the risk of insolvency whilst maximising the return on assets.

2.2 Working capital cycle

The **working capital cycle** or the **cash cycle** is the length of time between the company's outlay on raw materials, wages and other expenditures and the inflow of cash from the sale of goods.

The faster a firm can 'push' items around the cycle the lower its investment in working capital will be.

Working capital is an investment which affects cash flows:

- when inventory is purchased, cash is paid to acquire it

- receivables represent the cost of selling goods or services to customers, including the costs of materials and the labour incurred

- the cash tied up in working capital is reduced to the extent that inventory is financed by trade payables. If suppliers give a company time to pay, the firm's cash flows are improved and working capital is reduced.

CASH AND FINANCIAL MANAGEMENT

The working capital cycle:

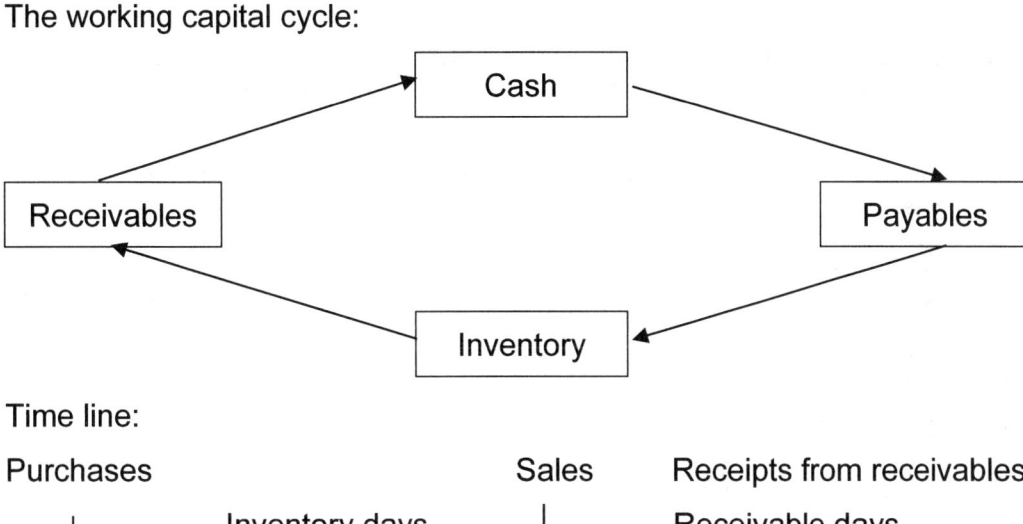

Time line:

Purchases · · · · · · · · · · · Sales · · · Receipts from receivables
· · · · · Inventory days · · · · · | · · · Receivable days
| Payable days · · · · · · · · Cash cycle
· · · · Pay payables

The length of the cycle depends on:

- how the balancing act between liquidity and profitability is resolved
- the efficiency of management
- the nature of the industry.

The optimum level is the amount that results in no idle cash or unused inventory, but that does not put a strain on liquid resources.

Trying to shorten the cash operating cycle may have detrimental effects elsewhere, with the organisation lacking the cash to meet its commitments and losing sales since customers will generally prefer to buy from suppliers who are prepared to extend trade credit, and who have items available when required.

Additionally, any assessment of the acceptability or otherwise of the length of the cycle must take into account the nature of the business involved. A supermarket chain will tend to have a very low or negative cycle – they have very few, if any, credit customers, they have a high inventory turnover and they can negotiate quite long credit periods with their suppliers.

Test your understanding 1

Which of the following is not part of the working capital cycle?

A   Receivables
B   Non-current assets
C   Payables
D   Inventory

Test your understanding 2

Fill in the blanks in the diagram of the working capital cycle below:

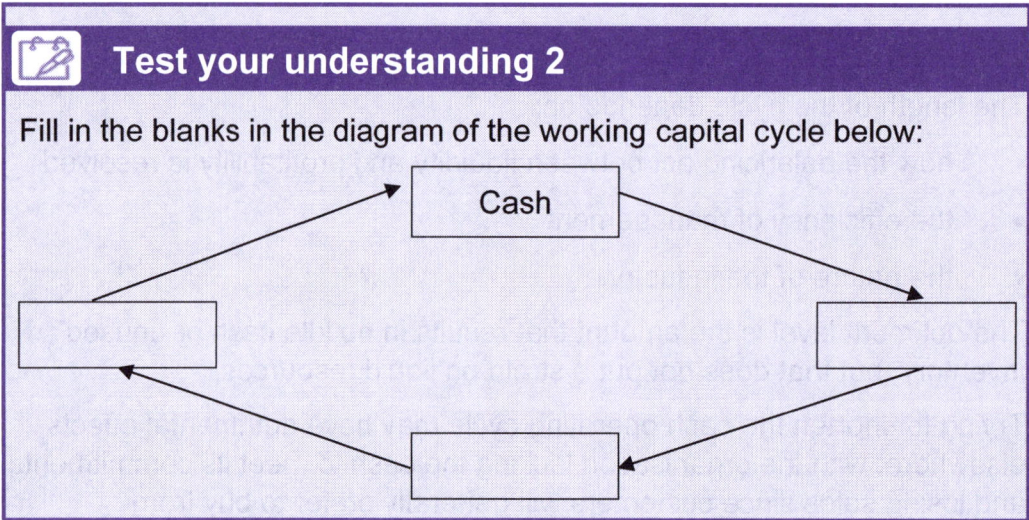

2.3 Calculating the working capital cycle

The working capital cycle (or cash cycle) can be calculated in days using the following formulae:

Receivables collection period (receivable days)

Average collection period (in days) = Trade receivables/revenue × 365

Payables collection period (payable days)

Average collection period (in days) = Trade payables/cost of sales × 365

Note: Sometimes credit purchases are used instead of cost of sales.

Inventory holding period (inventory days)

Average holding period (in days) = Inventory/cost of sales × 365

CASH AND FINANCIAL MANAGEMENT

Working capital cycle (cash cycle) is calculated as:

Inventory holding period + Receivables collection period – Payables payment period

Example

Below are the relevant details from the statement of financial position and statement of profit or loss from Josh plc. Calculate the working capital cycle.

Statement of Financial Position

	£000	£000
Current assets		
Inventories	500	
Trade receivables	1,000	
Cash and cash equivalents	200	
	1,700	
Trade payables	(900)	
		800

Statement of Profit or Loss

	£000
Revenue	5,000
Cost of sales	(3,000)
Gross profit	2,000
Operating expenses	(500)
Profit for the year	1,500

Inventory days = $\dfrac{\text{inventories}}{\text{cost of sales}} \times 365 = \dfrac{500}{3{,}000} \times 365 = 60.8$ days

Receivable days = $\dfrac{\text{receivables}}{\text{sales}} \times 365 = \dfrac{1{,}000}{5{,}000} \times 365 = 73.0$ days

Payable days = $\dfrac{\text{payables}}{\text{cost of sales}} \times 365 = \dfrac{900}{3{,}000} \times 365 = 109.5$ days

Working capital cycle (or cash cycle) = 60.8 + 73.0 – 109.5 = 24.3 days

Test your understanding 3

Which is the correct formula for the working capital cycle?

A Receivable days – inventory days – payable days
B Receivable days – inventory days + payable days
C Receivable days + inventory days – payable days
D Receivable days + inventory days + payable days

Test your understanding 4

A business has an average inventory holding period of 45 days, receives payment from its customers in 30 days and pays its payables in 38 days.

What is the working capital cycle (or cash cycle) in days for the business?

A 23 days
B 53 days
C 37 days
D 113 days

Test your understanding 5

A business has an average inventory holding period of 100 days, receives payment from its customers in 60 days and pays its payables in 80 days.

What is the working capital cycle in days for the business?

A 120 days
B 80 days
C 40 days
D 240 days

CASH AND FINANCIAL MANAGEMENT

Test your understanding 6

A business provides the following information:

Trade receivables	£4m
Trade payables	£2m
Inventory	£4.3m
Sales (80% on credit)	£30m
Cost of sales	£18m

Calculate the business's cash cycle?

Test your understanding 7

(a) If a business has an average inventory holding period of 30 days, a trade payable payment period of 45 days and a trade receivables collection period of 40 days, what is the working capital cycle?

(b) If the business above increased its inventory holding period by 3 days and increased the time it takes to pay its payables by 5 days, what is the impact on the working capital cycle?

3 Measuring liquidity

3.1 Return on capital employed (ROCE)

Return on capital employed indicates how successful a business is in utilising its assets.

$$\text{Return on capital employed \%} = \frac{\text{Operating profit}}{\text{Capital employed}} \times 100$$

Capital employed can be calculated as **working capital** (current assets less current liabilities) **plus non-current assets**.

It can also be calculated as **total equity plus non-current liabilities**; it represents the long-term investment in the business.

Working capital is part of capital employed so to boost ROCE we want to ensure we manage working capital and aim to get a good return if we have a surplus.

The aim of this calculation is to see how effectively the business is using the money invested in it.

Care should be taken with the interpretation of this ratio for the following reasons:

- It is based upon the statement of financial position values of the net assets rather than the true market value i.e. depreciation has been charged against the cost of the assets.

- A high ROCE may be solely due to accounting for depreciation reducing the capital employed figure rather than a high profit figure.

- As the statement of financial position values are based upon historical cost then the age structure of the assets of the business can also affect the return on capital employed.

- Often new investment does not bring immediate profits. This may be for a number of reasons. It may take time for the organisation's employees to learn how to use the new equipment.

    Alternatively it may take the organisation time to obtain enough orders to use the new facilities to the full. (This may result in a temporary reduction in the ROCE).

3.2 Current ratio

This is a common method of analysing working capital and is generally accepted as the measure of **short-term liquidity**. It indicates the extent to which the current liabilities of a business are covered by the current assets.

$$\text{Current ratio} = \frac{\text{Current assets}}{\text{Current liabilities}}$$

The aim is to ensure that current liabilities can be met as they fall due. Sometimes, textbooks suggest that if the current ratio is below a certain level (which is usually given as between 1.5 and 2), the business should become seriously concerned.

This should not be taken to be a strict rule, because:

(a) current liabilities include the bank overdraft which, in practice, is not repayable within one year (technically, of course, repayable on demand)

(b) different types of industry will have different typical current ratios. For example a supermarket will have high payable levels and high inventories but very few trade receivables; whereas a manufacturing business will not only have high payable and inventory levels but also significant levels of trade receivables.

Even considering the points above a current ratio of below 1:1 would be of concern to any business as it indicates that there are insufficient assets to cover the current liabilities as they fall due.

3.3 Quick ratio

The quick ratio is also known as the **acid test ratio**. It is calculated in the same way as for the current ratio but inventories are excluded from current assets.

$$\text{Quick ratio} = \frac{\text{Current assets} - \text{Inventory}}{\text{Current liabilities}}$$

This ratio is a much better test of the **immediate liquidity** of a business because inventory is assumed to be the least liquid of the current assets due to the length of time necessary to convert it into cash (via sales and trade receivables).

Although increasing liquid resources more usually indicate favourable trading, it could be that funds are not being used to their best advantage (e.g. a large unused cash balance). As with the current ratio, a quick ratio of less than 1:1 would be of concern to a business.

3.4 Operating profit margin

This ratio includes the costs incurred in running a business.

$$\text{Operating profit margin (\%)} = \frac{\text{Operating profit}}{\text{Revenue}} \times 100$$

A high margin is desirable. It indicates that either sales prices and/or volumes are high or that **ALL** costs are being kept well under control. Higher profits will usually (but not always) mean better liquidity.

Liquidity management: **Chapter 5**

3.5 Return on shareholders' funds

Return on shareholders' investment ratio is a measure of overall profitability of the business. It shows how much profit a company generates with the money shareholders have invested.

$$\text{Return on shareholders' funds \%} = \frac{\text{Profit after tax or net profit}}{\text{Total equity}} \times 100$$

A higher ratio means higher return on shareholders' investment and a lower ratio indicates otherwise. Investors always search for the highest return on their investment and a company that has higher ratio than others in the industry attracts more investors.

The ratio also indicates the **efficiency of the management in using the resources** of the business.

> **Example**
>
> The following illustration demonstrates some of the ratios
>
> **Summarised statement of financial position at 31 December 20X1**
>
> | | £000 | £000 |
> |---|---:|---:|
> | **Non-current assets**, at cost, less depreciation | | 5,200 |
> | **Current assets** | | |
> | Inventory | 1,200 | |
> | Trade receivables | 1,800 | |
> | Cash and other equivalents | 200 | |
> | | | 3,200 |
> | **Total assets** | | **8,400** |
> | **Equity** | | |
> | Ordinary share capital (£1 shares) | | 2,000 |
> | Preference share capital | | 400 |
> | Retained earnings | | 1,600 |
> | | | 4,000 |
> | **Non-current liabilities** | | |
> | Loan | | 2,800 |
> | **Current liabilities** | | |
> | Trade payables | 1,600 | |
> | | | 1,600 |
> | **Total equity and liabilities** | | **8,400** |

Summarised statement of profit or loss for the year ended 31 December 20X1

	20X1 £000
Revenue	12,000
Cost of sales	(8,000)
Gross profit	4,000
Operating expenses	(3,320)
Profit from operations	680
Finance cost	(148)
Profit before tax	532
Taxation	(212)
Net profit	320

Return on capital employed

$$\text{Return on capital employed} = \frac{\text{Operating profit}}{\text{Capital employed}} \times 100$$

$$= \frac{£680}{£4,000 + £2,800} \times 100 = 10\%$$

Current ratio

$$\text{Current ratio} = \frac{\text{Current assets}}{\text{Current liabilities}} = \frac{£3,200}{£1,600} = 2$$

Quick ratio

$$\text{Quick ratio} = \frac{\text{Current assets} - \text{Inventory}}{\text{Current liabilities}} = \frac{£3,200 - £1,200}{£1,600} = 1.25$$

Operating profit margin

$$\text{Margin} = \frac{\text{Profit from operations}}{\text{Sales revenue}} \times 100$$

$$= \frac{£680}{£12,000} \times 100 = 5.67\%$$

Return on shareholders' funds

$$\text{Return on shareholders' funds} = \frac{\text{Net profit}}{\text{Total equity}} \times 100$$

$$= \frac{£320}{£4,000} \times 100 = 8.00\%$$

To comment on how the business is maintaining its liquidity another years figures would need to be analysed for comparison or industry averages could be used.

4 Gearing

4.1 Gearing

Gearing is a measure of the company's capital structure – is the business being funded mainly by equity (repayable to shareholders) or by debt (repayable to banks)?

If there is a lot of debt compared to the equity it is thought that a business is **riskier** as debt must be paid back to the banks when requested whereas equity does not have to be paid back to the shareholders on demand.

$$\text{Gearing ratio} = \frac{\text{Total debt}}{\text{Total debt + equity}} \times 100$$

Total debt = All non-current liabilities ONLY

It is usual for all long term debt, such as loans and debentures, to be included in this calculation. In CSFT only long term debt is included in the gearing calculation, but you should be aware that some companies and banks will include short term debt (such as overdrafts) within total debt when calculating gearing.

CASH AND FINANCIAL MANAGEMENT

The impact on the gearing ratio will need to be considered when deciding on the type of finance as a highly geared business may find sourcing additional debt (and potentially additional equity) in the future harder than a company with less debt compared to equity. This is because a business with **higher gearing** is seen to be **more risky** by investors and lenders.

Example

The following illustration demonstrates some of the ratios

Summarised statement of financial position at 31 December 20X1

	£000	£000
Non-current assets, at cost, less depreciation		5,200
Current assets		
Inventory	1,200	
Trade receivables	1,800	
Cash and other equivalents	200	
		3,200
Total assets		**8,400**
Equity		
Ordinary share capital (£1 shares)		2,300
Retained earnings		1,600
		3,900
Non-current liabilities		
Loan		2,500
Current liabilities		
Trade payables	1,600	
Overdraft	400	
		2,000
Total equity and liabilities		**8,400**

> **Gearing**
>
> $$\text{Gearing ratio} = \frac{\text{Total debt}}{\text{Total debt} + \text{equity}} \times 100$$
>
> $$= \frac{£2{,}500}{£2{,}500 + £3{,}900} \times 100 = 39.1\%$$
>
> Gearing ratios vary between industries but generally a gearing ratio below 20% is low risk and a gearing ratio above 50% is quite high risk.
>
> However an all-round picture of the business needs to be examined including interest cover, liquidity and profitability.

4.2 Interest cover

Interest cover is a measure of how many times an entity could have afforded to pay its finance costs (i.e. interest).

If interest cover is low then there is a risk that the business may not be able to afford to pay the interest due, especially if the interest cover falls below 1.

$$\text{Interest cover} = \frac{\text{Operating profit (PBIT)}}{\text{Finance costs (Interest)}} = X \text{ times}$$

Very often loan covenants (conditions attached to a loan) will state a minimum level of interest cover (usually interest cover has to be above 2 or sometimes even 3).

Interest cover is something a lender will look at before deciding whether to lend additional finance to a business, but is also something the business itself should be monitoring to ensure interest can be paid as due. Certainly if interest cover falls to around (or below) one, it is likely to mean the business is in danger of not being able to meet its obligations to the bank/lender.

CASH AND FINANCIAL MANAGEMENT

 Test your understanding 8

Extracts from the financial statements of a business are as follows:

Operating profit	£5,000
Revenue	£25,000
Loans – 8% interest	£7,000
Share capital	£10,000
Retained earnings	£15,000
Trade payables	£3,000
Overdraft	£1,000

(a) What is the return on capital employed (ROCE)?

(b) What is the gearing ratio?

(c) What is the interest cover (assuming no interest on the overdraft)?

5 Overtrading and overcapitalisation

5.1 Overtrading

Overtrading usually occurs when a company tries to **expand too quickly** and **over-stretches its working capital** due to inadequate financing for its growth rate.

If **sales increase too rapidly**, then working capital requirements may increase as **more money is tied up in inventories** of raw materials to support the increased sales levels; **receivables will also rise**.

This can lead to a situation in which the company is operating at a profit but suffers a **liquidity crisis** as it has insufficient cash to pay its bills and expenses.

This problem happens over a period of time, with the working capital gradually being stretched and without the managers of the company realising what is happening as the company continues to be profitable. The statement of financial position eventually reveals the problem.

5.2 Identifying signs of overtrading

Signs of overtrading can be identified as follows:

- rapidly increasing sales volumes
- falling profit margins despite increased sales as higher discounts are given to attract more customers and production costs increase due to overtime costs, etc.
- greater reliance on short-term funding such as overdrafts
- longer receivable collection periods due to the inability to collect cash promptly
- increased payable payment period due to insufficient cash to pay debts.

5.3 Controlling overtrading

Planned overtrading is not dangerous; it is the unmanaged and undetected overtrading that causes company downfalls.

If, however, the symptoms of unmanaged overtrading are detected, then the problem may be averted by:

- issuing new share capital or loan stock
- taking out long-term loans rather than overdrafts
- reducing the operating cycle by controlling receivables and payables
- slowing down the company's expansion.

5.4 Over-capitalisation

Over-capitalisation is the opposite of overtrading. This is where a business has **too many resources** tied up in working capital than is required. If there are excessive inventories, trade receivable and cash, and very few trade payables, there will be an over-investment by the company in current assets. **Working capital will be excessive** and the company will be over-capitalised.

If working capital is too high (so the company is over-capitalised) then the company may have excess cash (which is earning a very low return) or has debt it does not require and therefore is paying unnecessary interest.

This usually results in lower profitability than could be achieved with an optimum level of working capital investment.

CASH AND FINANCIAL MANAGEMENT

Test your understanding 9

Overtrading can occur when working capital levels are too low.
True or false?

Over-capitalisation can occur when working capital levels are too high.
True or false?

Test your understanding 10

Which of the following are signs of overtrading?

A   Rapidly decreasing sales volumes
B   Rapidly increasing sales volumes
C   Increased profit margins
D   Falling profit margins
E   Short receivable collection periods
F   Longer receivable collection periods
G   Shorter payable payment periods
H   Longer payable payment periods
I   Greater reliance on short term funding
J   Less reliance on short term funding

6   Summary

In this chapter we have looked at how important the management of cash and liquid funds are the running and maintenance of a business.

Mismanagement of working capital can lead to a business overtrading and possibly going out of business due to a lack of cash to pay for debts. It is vital for a business to use cash budgets to manage their cash flows and identify periods of liquidity problems.

The chapter also covered the ratios that businesses and investors use to access liquidity, profitability and the gearing risk of a business.

Test your understanding answers

Test your understanding 1

Answer B

Non-current assets are not part of the working capital cycle – current assets are.

Test your understanding 2

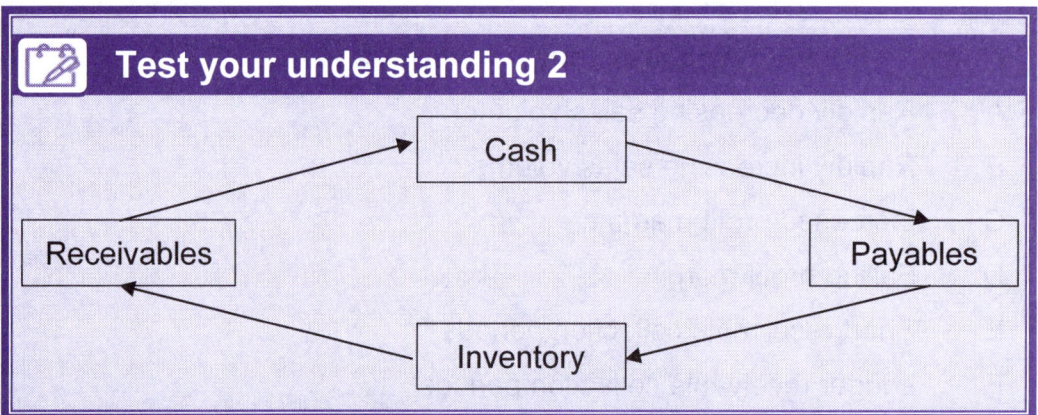

Test your understanding 3

Answer C

Receivable days + inventory days – payable days

Test your understanding 4

Answer C

45 + 30 – 38 = 37 days

Test your understanding 5

Answer B

100 + 60 – 80 = 80 days

CASH AND FINANCIAL MANAGEMENT

 Test your understanding 6

Receivable days = 4/(30 × 0.8) × 365 = 61 days

Inventory days = 4.3/18 × 365 = 87 days

Payable days = 2/18 × 365 = 41 days

Operating cycle = 61 + 87 – 41 = 107 days

 Test your understanding 7

(a) 30 days + 40 days – 45 days = 25 days

(b) 33 days + 40 days – 50 days = 23 days

The cash operating cycle will decrease by 2 days – the increase in inventory holding days increases the length of the cycle, the increase in the payment period decreases the length of the cycle – the net effect is a decrease of 2 days.

 Test your understanding 8

(a) ROCE = £5,000/(£7,000 + £10,000 + £15,000) = 15.6%

(b) Gearing = £7,000/(£7,000 + £10,000 + £15,000) = 21.9%

Remember total debt is all non-current liabilities only.

(c) Loan interest = £7,000 × 8% = £560.
Interest cover = £5,000/£560 = 8.9 times

The business could have paid its bank interest 8.9 times from its operating profits.

 Test your understanding 9

Overtrading can occur when working capital levels are too low.
True

Over-capitalisation can occur when working capital levels are too high.
True

> **Test your understanding 10**
>
> The following are signs of overtrading:
>
> B   Rapidly increasing sales volumes
> D   Falling profit margins
> F   Longer receivable collection periods
> H   Longer payable payment periods
> I   Greater reliance on short term funding

CASH AND FINANCIAL MANAGEMENT

Raising finance

Introduction

One of the purposes of preparing a cash flow forecast is to enable the management of a company to be able to forecast whether there is likely to be any cash surplus or cash deficit in the future periods.

If a cash deficit is forecast then management will need to arrange well in advance for how to deal with that deficit. In this chapter we consider different ways that finance can be raised.

ASSESSMENT CRITERIA

The basic terms and conditions associated with different types of financing (4.1)

Financial options to fund the organisation's cash requirements (4.2)

Minimise the potential exposure to the organisation (4.4)

CONTENTS

1. Raising finance
2. Interest rates and financing terminology
3. Bank overdrafts and loans
4. Factoring and invoice discounting
5. Hire purchase and leasing
6. Bonds and loan stock
7. Equity shares
8. Crowdfunding
9. Choosing the form of finance
10. Relationship between the bank and the customer

Raising finance

1.1 Introduction

Any business will have an initial amount of capital which is either contributed by the owner or, in the case of a company, is issued share capital. However at various stages in the business life cycle the management may find that there is a need to raise additional finance.

1.2 Reasons for additional finance

There are many reasons why a business may need to raise additional finance but the most common are:

- to fund working capital
- to increase working capital
- to reduce payables
- to purchase non-current assets
- to launch a new product or open more offices
- to acquire another business.

The need to raise the finance may be highlighted by a deficit in the cash budget, by management decisions regarding investment in non-current assets, or by the business strategy of growth by acquisition.

1.3 Controls on the raising of finance

Public organisations are organisations that are funded by the Government e.g. Schools, NHS trusts (hospitals etc.), Local Government. These organisations have **strict funding** (cash) controls.

They are required by Government to **balance their budgets** i.e. only spend the cash they have been granted and no more. Public organisations that fall into deficit are not allowed to source their own external finance.

Private organisations are allowed to source their own finance but they still have regulations to adhere to through the **Companies Act**.

1.4 The form of finance required

When deciding which type of finance to use, it is important to consider the specific circumstances of the business and the purpose for which the finance is required.

CASH AND FINANCIAL MANAGEMENT

In the rest of this chapter we will consider different types of finance but as a rule of thumb, the time scale of the finance should match the time scale of the reason for the finance. Therefore, if the finance is required for working capital reasons then the finance should be short term whereas if the finance is required for longer term investment in non-current assets or another business then the appropriate finance may be medium or long term.

The type of finance available may also depend on gearing levels (a business with find it easier to obtain debt if it has lower gearing), whether a business is listed or not, the amount of non-current assets they have to act of security on any loans and its level of profitability and trading success.

When raising finance it is also important to consider the impact on the liquidity of the business.

1.5 Gearing

In the previous chapter we saw that gearing is a measure of the company's capital structure – the ratio of debt to total funding

If there is a lot of debt compared to the equity it is thought that a business is a riskier investment.

$$\text{Gearing ratio} = \frac{\text{Total debt}}{\text{Total debt + equity}} \times 100$$

Total debt = All long term liabilities only (e.g. loans, debentures etc.)

The impact on the gearing ratio will need to be considered when deciding on the type of finance as a highly geared business may find sourcing funds in the future harder than a company with less debt compared to equity.

2 Interest rates and financing terminology

2.1 Introduction and terminology

- Interest – a regular return paid to the lender of debt finance.

- Fees – when arranging new finance a business may be charged an administration or 'arrangement' fee to set up the new finance. This could be on a loan or a share issue.

- Penalties – if a business breaches a loan condition (e.g. is late with a repayment or breaches a loan covenant) they may incur additional penalty fees.

- Minimum/maximum amounts – Some types of finance may have a minimum and/or maximum amount of finance that can be raised.

Raising finance: Chapter 6

- Minimum/maximum lending periods – Some types of finance may have a minimum and/or maximum length of time that finance can be borrowed.

- Base interest rate – the lowest interest rate a bank will charge. The rate is set by the **Bank of England**. Banks usually charge interest at 'an amount above base rate'.

- Fixed interest rate – provides an **unchanging** interest rate over the length of the borrowing/investing period.

- Variable interest rate – the rate **changes** in line with an agreed indicator (usually in line with base interest rate but it can be another agreed index).

- Flat rate interest – is calculated based on the **loan principal** or capital amount. It is applied to the whole of the loan every year and **does not** take into account any **repayments**. The flat rate of interest can seem to be a lower option but in reality can be quite expensive.

- Simple interest – Simple interest is calculated based on the original sum invested. Any interest earned in earlier periods is not included. Simple interest is often used for a single investment period that is less than a year. It can be calculated by taking the **total interest** as a **percentage** of the original **principal** or can be applied by using the following:

$V = X + (X \times r \times n)$

Where

V = Future value

X = Initial investment

r = Interest rate (expressed as a decimal)

n = Number of time periods

- Compound interest – to compound a sum, the figure is increased by the amount of interest it would earn over the period. Interest is earned on interest gained in earlier periods. Compounding can be calculated using the following:

$V = X(1 + r)^n$

Where

V = Future value

X = Initial investment

r = Interest rate (expressed as a decimal)

n = Number of time periods

CASH AND FINANCIAL MANAGEMENT

- Nominal interest rate – is the stated interest rate for a time period, for example a month or a year.

- Capped interest rate – an interest rate that has an upper limit.

- Effective interest rate – is the interest rate that includes the effects of compounding a nominal interest rate. It can be calculated using the following:

    $r = (1 + i/n)^n - 1$

    Where

    r = Effective interest rate

    i = Nominal interest rate

    n = Number of time periods

- Annual percentage rate (**APR**) – The APR is an annual rate that is charged for borrowing (or made by investing), expressed as a single percentage number. It is calculated on the loan principal outstanding so that the interest charge reduces each month in line with the reduction in the amount outstanding. It represents the actual yearly cost of funds over the term of a loan. This includes any fees or additional costs associated with the transaction. This is the **effective interest rate** that a borrower will pay on a loan.

 Example

Simple interest

£100 is invested in an account for six months. The interest rate is 10% per annum. Calculate the value of the account after six months.

Solution

$V = X + (X \times r \times n)$

$V = 100 + (100 \times 0.1 \times (6/12)) = \$105$

Compound interest

£100 is invested in an account for five years. The interest rate is 10% per annum. Calculate the value of the account after five years.

Solution

$V = X(1+r)^n$

$V = 100 \, (1.10)^5 = £161.05$

Nominal and effective interest

The nominal interest rate is 10% per year compounded on a monthly basis. A company is going to invest for 12 months what is the effective interest rate?

Solution

$r = (1 + i/n)^n - 1$

$r = (1 + 0.1/12)^{12} - 1$

$r = 0.1047 = 10.47\%$

The effective interest rate of receiving 10% interest per annum compounded on a monthly basis for 12 months is the same as receiving 10.47% interest per annum with no compounding.

These terms and calculations are also applicable when considering how to invest surplus funds (Chapter 7).

Test your understanding 1

A business invests £500,000 for 3 years.

What is the value of the investment after 3 years if the interest rate is:

(a) Simple interest of 7% per annum

(b) Compound interest of 6% per annum

2.2 Interest charged

It is worth considering the percentage cost and type of interest rate charges to work out the cheapest form of finance.

Fixed rate borrowing may be cheaper if the base rate is rising thus affecting the variable rate. Variable rate borrowing may be cheaper if the base rate is falling.

Example

The base rate is currently 1%.

It is possible to get a loan at a fixed rate of 5% or a variable rate of 2% above base rate.

The base rate would need to rise by more than 2% to make the fixed rate cheaper. The likelihood of this happening would have to be considered.

CASH AND FINANCIAL MANAGEMENT

It is also necessary to consider costs other than interest rates, such as fees and other charges that may be incurred.

Example

A one year loan of £30,000 is required.

Two options are available:

A loan with a fixed rate of 6.9%, with arrangement fees of 1% of the loan or a loan with an APR of 8%. Which is cheaper?

The total cost of the loan with the fixed rate is

£30,000 × 6.9% = £2,070

£30,000 × 1% = £300

Total cost £2,370

The total cost of the loan with an APR of 8% is

£30,000 × 8% = £2,400

The fixed rate loan is cheaper.

It is possible to use both an overdraft and a loan to meet a cash deficit. It may be that doing so actually reduces cost and meets the organisation's guidelines and regulations.

Test your understanding 2

Tianna takes out a £350,000 loan for 3 years. The (simple) interest rate is 1% above base rate and there is an arrangement fee of 1.5% of the loan amount. Base rate is 5% in years 1 and 2 but rises to 6% in year 3. What is the total cost of the finance?

2.3 Security

In some cases the bank may only be prepared to advance the money on the basis of some security given by the business. Security can be in the form of a personal guarantee, a fixed charge or a floating charge.

Definition

A **fixed charge** is where the security is a specific and identifiable asset or group of assets.

The bank would have the right to sell this specific asset if the business defaults on the loan repayments.

Definition

A **floating charge** is where the security is supplied by a group of assets of a relevant value, such as receivables or inventory. The value of the security is constant but the constituents of the security will be changing.

If the business defaults on the loan then the bank will seize assets to the value of the outstanding repayment.

Test your understanding 3

A fixed charge is security offered by a changing group of assets and a floating charge is security offered by a static asset.

True or false?

2.4 Credit rating

Before offering debt finance, a lender will usually consider a borrower's credit rating or credit score. This gives an indicator to lenders on how risky it is to lend that person or business money.

The credit rating looks at the borrower's previous history of paying debts on time and the borrower's financial status. For a business, this will include an assessment of their financial statements, looking at their profitability, gearing and liquidity ratios (see Chapter 5 for more details on these ratios).

Taking on additional debt finance will increase gearing and often decrease liquidity ratios such as the quick or current ratios. This may cause a credit rating to worsen, making it harder to obtain additional finance in the future.

CASH AND FINANCIAL MANAGEMENT

3 Bank overdrafts and loans

3.1 Bank overdraft

Bank overdrafts are most often negotiated for a **fixed period** in terms of a maximum available facility. In other words, the bank undertakes to advance anything up to, say £50,000, and the business can take advantage of the facility as and when it needs to.

The **interest** will generally be at a **variable** rate, calculated on a day-to-day basis with reference to the bank's base rate. Although the interest rate on an overdraft may be typically higher than on a loan, the important point about overdraft interest is that it is calculated daily on the amount of the actual overdraft rather than on a fixed amount as would be the interest on a loan.

The principal advantage of an overdraft is **flexibility**. The business only pays interest on the amount actually drawn, although there may be an additional flat charge of perhaps 0.25% on the maximum facility.

Overdrafts are (technically) **repayable on demand** and should never be regarded as substitutes for adequate medium term finance.

3.2 Effect on gearing and liquidity

In CSFT overdrafts are NOT included in total debt when calculating gearing, therefore a bank overdraft would have no impact on gearing.

However, an increased overdraft would usually be taken into consideration by a bank or an investor when deciding if to grant additional finance as it would increase the perceived risk of the business and lower its credit rating.

The use of a bank overdraft is an indication that the business does not have enough cash to cover its commitments therefore may be having liquidity problems.

However, having an overdraft facility does allow a business more flexibility with its cash flow and helps liquidity. An increased overdraft will also cause liquidity ratios such as the current or quick ratio to worsen.

> **Test your understanding 4**
>
> Which of the following best describes the main features of an overdraft?
>
> A   Interest rates are low; it is repayable on demand; it is useful for capital purchases
>
> B   Interest rates are high; it is repayable on demand; it is useful for capital purchases
>
> C   Interest rates are low; it is repayable on demand; it is a short term form of finance
>
> D   Interest rates are high; it is repayable on demand; it is a short term form of finance

3.3   Bank loans and mortgages

A term loan with a bank is a loan for a fixed amount, for an agreed period on pre-arranged terms. The loan can be tailored to meet the requirements of the borrower. It can be taken out for a period which matches the assets which it is financing and the repayment terms can be negotiated to match with the cash flows from the asset or the other business cash flows.

The loan will be governed by formal documentation which will include:

- The term (length) of the loan.
- The interest rate.
- The way in which the interest is charged.
- The repayment date/dates.
- Any security required for the loan.
- Any covenants (special conditions) attached to the loan.

Term loans can be for virtually any period and the repayment terms can be negotiated with the bank:

- Interest rates may be fixed or variable and they tend to be lower than that on an overdraft.
- There are a variety of methods of repaying interest and capital.
- The loan can be drawn upon in stages, e.g. 50% now and 50% in three months' time.

The **interest** on the loan will either be **fixed or variable**. If the interest is variable then the interest charged will depend upon market rates of interest and will normally be a certain percentage above the bank's base or central rate (previously known as LIBOR).

How the interest is charged will depend upon the method of repayment of the loan. With a bullet repayment loan the borrower does not pay off any of the loan capital during the repayment period. The entire loan capital amount is repaid at the end of the term of the loan. Therefore the interest that is charged each year is based upon the full loan amount.

With an amortising loan each periodic repayment is made up of interest and repayment of the capital of the loan in such a way that when the final repayment is made there is no capital amount outstanding. Interest on this type of loan is based upon the amount of the loan outstanding during the period since the last repayment.

In most cases a bank loan is most appropriate for the purchase of major assets which will hopefully provide income over the loan period out of which the loan interest and repayments can be made. However in some cases it may be necessary to raise a medium term loan to finance a working capital deficit.

A **mortgage** is a specific type of bank loan. A mortgage is always secured on a property, making it lower risk for the lender. Mortgages are usually long term in nature, in excessive of 10 years and often 20–30 years in length. Due to the good security available, the interest rates on a mortgage are usually quite low.

3.4 Effect on gearing and liquidity

A bank loan would be included in the calculation of gearing and it will **increase gearing** for a business as it is debt finance rather than equity finance.

The amount of loan recorded in the current liabilities will affect the liquidity ratios increasing the amount due versus the amount of current assets. This could have a bearing on the credit rating of a business.

Test your understanding 5

Which of the following best describes the main features of a bank loan?

A   Interest rates are low; it is useful for capital purchases
B   Interest rates are high; it is useful for capital purchases
C   Interest rates are low; it is a short term form of finance
D   Interest rates are high; it is a short term form of finance

Raising finance: Chapter 6

 Example

Enterprise Limited wants to take out a bank loan to cover the purchase of a new non-current asset.

They require £2 million for 4 years.

Interest will be charged on a flat rate on the initial balance at 8% and there is an arrangement fee of 2% of the initial loan.

Required

Calculate the cost of the loan to Enterprise Limited.

Solution

Arrangement fee = £2,000,000 × 2% = £40,000

Annual interest = £2,000,000 × 8% = £160,000

Total interest = £160,000 × 4 years = £640,000

Total cost of the loan = £40,000 + £640,000 = £680,000

4 Factoring and invoice discounting

4.1 Debt factoring

Debt factoring is an arrangement by which a factoring company purchases all the trade receivables due to a business as they arise. The business will be paid up to 80–85% of the value of invoices as they are raised, with the balance coming on the date the invoice is settled.

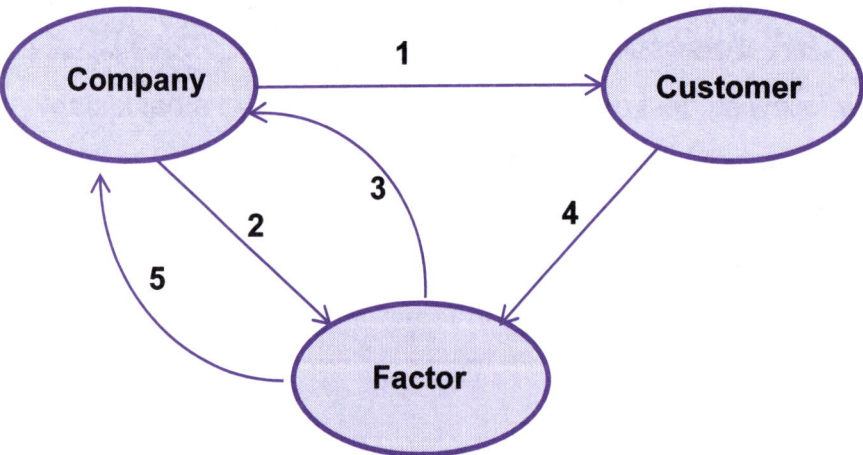

1   The company sells goods to the customer
2   The company sells the debt to the factor
3   Up to 80–85% of the debt is paid to the company in advance
4   The customer pays the factor
5   The factor pays the company the balance less an administration and finance fee

The factoring may be with recourse or without recourse.

Definition

With recourse factoring means that the business is liable to the factoring company if a debtor defaults.

Definition

Without recourse factoring means that the factor takes over all responsibility for bad debts as well as collected amounts.

In a factoring arrangement the factoring company will generally take over responsibility for debt collection and sales ledger accounting.

The factoring company will obviously make a charge which is proportional to the services it provides and the risk which it assumes.

One of the main disadvantages of debt factoring is the loss of relationships with customers who may not like dealing with the debt factoring company (who may be quite aggressive in their credit control).

4.2   Effect on gearing and liquidity

Gearing will not be affected by using a factor as there is no impact on the debt and equity of a business.

Factoring will improve short term liquidity as cash is advanced early by the factor. In the long term the company will receive less cash as the factor charges an administration fee and a finance fee.

4.3 Invoice discounting

Invoice discounting is another service provided by factoring companies.

It is similar to debt factoring, but the key difference is that with invoice discounting collection of the debt remains the responsibility of the selling business rather that the debt factoring company.

When a batch of debts is assigned for invoice discounting, the factoring company will advance up to 75% of the gross invoice value. The invoices act as security for the advanced money from the factoring company.

When the customer then pays the invoice (remember – debt collection remains the responsibility of the seller), the business then repays factoring company the advanced funds plus interest.

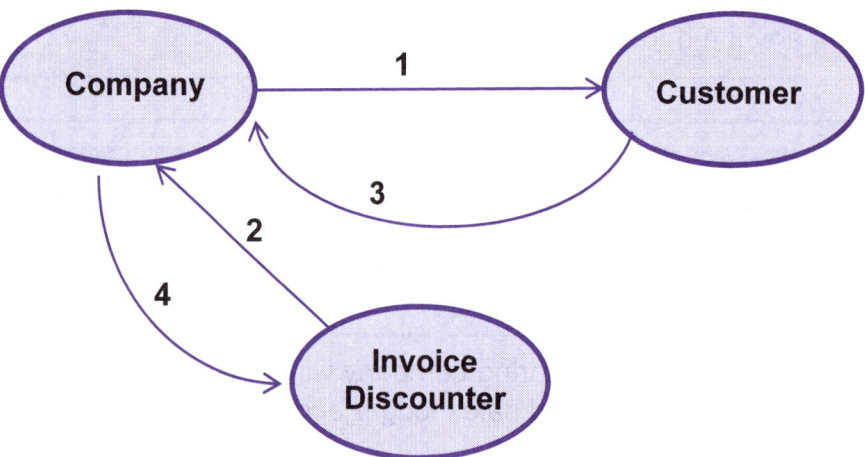

1. The company sells goods to the customer
2. Up to 75% of the debt is paid to the company in advance
3. The company receives payment
4. The company pays the invoice discounter the amount borrowed plus interest

Invoice discounting is simple and flexible, it can be used as and when short-term funds are needed and it enables the business to maintain a normal relationship with its customers (who need not know about the third party involvement).

Invoice discounting is very similar to having a short term loan secured on the receivables.

The key advantages are obtaining cash earlier and that the customer is unaware of the invoice discounting.

CASH AND FINANCIAL MANAGEMENT

4.4 Effect on gearing and liquidity

Gearing will not be affected by using an invoice discounter as there is no impact on the debt and equity of a business.

Invoice discounting will improve short term liquidity as cash is advanced early. In the long term the company has to repay the 'loan' plus interest so may have a bearing on long term liquidity.

Test your understanding 6

Mo Ltd plans to start using debt factoring to help manage its receivables and debt collection. Mo estimates their revenue for next year will be £3,000,000, cost of sales will be £2,000,000 and it currently has a trade receivable collection period of 45 days.

The debt factoring company will charge a fee of 0.5% of revenue for the debt collection and will advance 80% of the invoiced sales at an interest rate of 11%. They promise that all debts will be collected in 30 days.

What is the total cost to Mo of using the debt factoring company's services for next year (to the nearest £100)?

5 Hire purchase and leasing

5.1 Hire purchase

If a non-current asset is to be purchased by the business, but there is not enough cash available for an outright purchase, one simple method is to purchase the asset on a hire purchase scheme.

Hire purchase and instalment credit arrangements can be set up quickly and can generally offer fairly flexible repayment terms. The security for the 'advance' is clearly provided by the asset being purchased. If payment is not completed then the asset is re-possessed by the finance company.

The main disadvantage of a hire purchase agreement is that the total payment for asset can far outweigh the cash purchase price.

5.2 Effect on gearing and liquidity

The balance of the loan in non-current liabilities is classed as debt and will therefore be included in the gearing calculation and may have a bearing on whether the business is able to raise more finance if needed.

The amount of hire purchase recorded in the current liabilities will impact the liquidity ratio increasing the amount due versus the amount current assets. This could have a bearing on the credit rating of a business.

Example

Enterprise Limited is considering entering into a hire purchase agreement to purchase non-current assets of a value of £2 million.

The total amount of interest payable on the £2 million is £584,979. There are 47 regular monthly payments with an option to purchase the asset in the last month for an additional £53,888. Enterprise Limited wishes to own the asset at the end of the hire purchase agreement. The term is 48 months at an APR of 13.2%.

Required

Calculate the monthly and total cost of the hire purchase for Enterprise Limited.

Solution

Monthly cost

Enterprise Limited will be paying the £53,888 in the final month to own the asset so the cost that needs to be spread over 47 months = £2,000,000 + £584,979 − £53,888 = £2,531,091

Monthly repayments = £2,531,091 ÷ 47 = £53,853

Total cost

Total cost of hire purchase = (£53,853 × 47) + 53,888 = £2,584,979

Which can also be calculated as £2,000,000 + £584,979 = £2,584,979

5.3 Leasing

If a business is to buy a non-current asset such as plant and machinery or motor vehicles it may find that leasing the asset is a cheaper option than taking out a bank loan and purchasing the asset outright. Many financial intermediaries such as banks and insurance companies provide lease finance for a wide range of assets.

Definition

A contract is, or contains, a lease if it conveys the right to control the use of an identified asset for a period of time in exchange for consideration (IFRS 16)

Under a lease contract, the lessee has the use of the asset for some, if not all, of its useful life. The lessee may even be able to sell the asset at the end of its life with only a proportion of the sale proceeds being returned to the lessor.

The lessee will often, (but not necessarily) be responsible for the upkeep, maintenance and insurance of the asset.

The lessee will recognise a right-of-use asset and treat the asset in the Statement of Financial Position as if it is owned i.e. it will charge depreciation against the value of the asset. The lessee will also recognise a lease liability, and the lease payments will reflect the repayment of the liability and additional finance costs which will appear in the Statement of Profit or Loss.

The total cost of a lease is often more expensive than the outright purchase price, but may be cheaper than taking out a loan to purchase the asset outright.

Short term leases and low value items

Definition

A short term lease is one lasting 12 month or less.

Low value items are assets with a low monetary value such as tablet computers, telephones, personal computers or small items of office furniture.

When taking out a short term lease or a lease for a low value item a lessee can elect not to follow the usual lease treatment and instead expense the total lease payments (on a straight line basis) to the Statement of Profit or Loss. No asset or lease liability is recognised in the Statement of Financial Position in this case.

Raising finance: Chapter 6

5.4 Effect on gearing and liquidity

- **Normal lease** – The gearing of the company will increase because the asset base increases but so does the total debt. The increase in gearing could affect the company's ability to raise additional finance. The liquidity of the business will not be affected by the acquisition but will be reduced by the lease payments.

- **Short term/low value lease** – as the lease is 'off balance sheet' gearing will not be affected. A credit risk analyst will need to consider the size of the financial commitment. As there is no current liability there will be no effect on liquidity.

5.5 Sale and leaseback

Sale and leaseback arrangements most commonly relate to property and (less likely) large items of capital equipment. The company sells the asset to a financial institution (perhaps an insurance company or a pension fund) which is then leased back to the company for an agreed number of years.

This releases the value of the asset, but does commit the business to making ongoing lease payments and the business loses any future capital gain on the asset. It may also mean the loss of the asset at the end of the lease term.

5.6 Effect on gearing and liquidity

Although a sale and leaseback arrangement can provide an immediate source of cash (improving liquidity), often more than could be obtained from a mortgage, there are a number of disadvantages including:

- The company loses ownership of the asset and will therefore miss out on any appreciation in the asset's future value.

- The company will have to sign a rental agreement, thereby committing the company to occupying the property/using the asset for many years ahead. This can be restricting if a change of asset is required.

- Any rent charged will be subject to regular reviews and will probably increase over time.

The lease liability will affect the gearing of the company and the future borrowing capacity will reduce, as property (if that is what has been sold and leased back) is a common asset used to provide security for debt finance.

CASH AND FINANCIAL MANAGEMENT

6 Bonds and loan stock

6.1 Bonds

Any loan raised by the issue of a series of negotiable units could be described as **'loan stock'** (the term is not used with a precise meaning) or **'bonds'**.

Just as the total equity of a company is split into shares which are traded on a market, loans may be broken down into smaller units (e.g. one bond may have a face or par value of £100) and traded as well. Different varieties include **debentures** and **loan stock** and may be issued by companies, local authorities and governmental organisations.

Corporate bonds are used by many companies to raise funding for large scale projects – such as business expansion, takeovers, new premises or product development. They can be used to replace bank finance, or to provide long-term working capital.

The main features of a corporate bond are:

- the nominal value – the price at which the bonds are first sold on the market e.g. £100

- the interest (coupon) rate paid to the bond owner – this is usually fixed e.g. 5% the annual interest is the nominal value × coupon rate

- the redemption terms – when the nominal value of the bond must be repaid to the bond holder e.g. redeem at par in 2025.

Bonds can be sold on the open market to investment institutions or individual investors, or they can be sold privately.

If bonds are sold on the public market, they can be traded – similar to shares.

Some corporate bonds are structured to be convertible, which means they can be exchanged for shares at some point in the future.

Advantages of issuing bonds or loan stock

Bonds can be a very flexible way of raising debt capital. They can be secured or unsecured (a secured bond is often called a **debenture**), and you can decide what priority they take over other debts.

They can also offer a way of stabilising your company's finances by having substantial debts on a fixed-rate interest. This offers some protection against variable interest rates or economic changes.

Other advantages of using bonds to raise long-term finance include:

- it is generally cheaper to raise than a new issue of equity
- not diluting the value of existing shareholdings – unlike issuing additional shares
- it may be cheaper to finance than equity since debenture-holders suffer less risk and may be satisfied by a lower return. However, shareholders may perceive there to be a greater gearing risk if the company is already highly geared and may therefore require a higher return.
- the interest paid will be allowable for corporation tax.
- enabling more cash to be retained in the business – because the redemption date for bonds can be several years after the issue date.

Disadvantage of issuing bonds or loan stock

There are also some disadvantages to issuing bonds, including:

- regular interest payments to bondholders – though interest may be fixed, the interest will usually have to be paid even if you make a loss
- the potential for your business' share value to be reduced if your profits decline – this is because bond interest payments take precedence over dividends
- bondholder restrictions – because investors are locking up their money for a potentially long period of time, they can impose certain covenants or undertakings on your business operations and financial performance to limit their risk
- ongoing contact with investors can be somewhat limited so changes to terms and conditions or waivers can be more difficult to obtain compared to dealing with bank lenders, who tend to maintain a closer relationship.

6.2 Effect on gearing and liquidity

As the bond or loan stock is effectively a loan it will increase the debt finance and therefore increase the gearing of a company.

The interest on the bond will have an impact on liquidity as it is recorded as a current liability and the cash received will be recorded as a current asset.

7 Equity shares

7.1 Equity shares

The term equity relates to ordinary shares only. Equity finance is the investment in a company by the ordinary shareholders, represented by the issued ordinary share capital plus reserves. There are other types of share capital relating to various types of preferred share. These are not considered part of equity as their characteristics bear more resemblance to debt finance.

Companies issue shares to raise capital, usually in the form of cash although shares may be issued in exchange for assets.

Ordinary shareholders have voting rights in general meetings of the company but rank after all payables and preferred shares in rights to assets on liquidation.

Dividends are payable at the discretion of the directors (subject to sanction by shareholders) out of undistributed profits remaining after senior claims have been met. Amounts available for dividends but not paid out are retained in the company on behalf of the ordinary shareholders.

There are three main sources of equity finance:

- **internally generated funds** – comprise the cash retained from accumulated profits (i.e. undistributed profits attributable to ordinary shareholders) plus non-cash charges against profits (e.g. depreciation).

    For an established company, internally generated funds can represent the single most important source of finance, for both short- and long-term purposes.

    Such finance is cheap and quick to raise, requiring no transaction costs, professional assistance or time delay. However, it is essential that the company's dividend policy is taken into account when determining how much of each year's cash from earnings to retain.

- **new external share issues** – New shares can be issued by private negotiation, placing, or offer for sale, or by a rights issue.

- **rights issues** – A rights issue is an offer to the existing shareholders to subscribe for more shares, in proportion to their existing holding, usually at a relatively cheap price. A rights issue can be made by a quoted or an unquoted company seeking limited finance without offering shares to non-shareholders.

7.2 Effect on gearing and liquidity

There is less risk associated with ordinary share capital, since there are no penalties directly associated with not paying an ordinary dividend in one year. Issuing shares should have a positive effect on gearing as it increases the equity finance of a company hence reducing gearing.

Cash levels are increased when shares are issued so this will have a positive effect on liquidity of a company.

8 Crowdfunding

8.1 Crowdfunding

Crowdfunding is a modern and popular way for businesses to raise finance. Using an online platform such as Kickstarter, a business pitches their idea/product in an attempt to attract finance from a large number of investors. This is particularly popular for **small or start-up** businesses who often have difficulties raising more traditional methods of finance.

A successful crowdfunding pitch will need to be based on an attractive business plan to tempt investors.

Crowdfunding can be used to raise either debt or equity finance (or sometimes even in exchange for investors being given free/discounted products), and the use of an online platform enables millions of potential investors to be accessed. Raising debt in this manner is also called **'peer to peer lending'**.

Crowdfunding can be a quick process and as well as raising finance can help increase brand awareness and the profile of the business. Disadvantages are the fees payable to the online platform and any associated legal or administrative costs.

8.2 Effect on gearing and liquidity

The impact on gearing will depend on in crowdfunding is used to raise equity (which will decrease gearing) or debt (which will increase gearing).

The finance raised will boost cash and hence liquidity levels but if debt is raised then the additional liabilities may reduce the possibilities of raising further debt in the future.

CASH AND FINANCIAL MANAGEMENT

9 Choosing the form of finance

9.1 Introduction

As we have seen, there is a variety of forms of finance available to a business from the very short term to the long term. Each of these forms of finance has different characteristics and different costs and it is vital that the most appropriate and cheapest form of finance is chosen to meet the funding requirements of each situation.

In some situations a specific form of finance will be clearly the most appropriate, for example, the acquisition of a fleet of salesmen's cars under a leasing arrangement. However, in many cases, the choice is less obvious.

9.2 Which type of finance?

In general terms the financing method should be matched to the reason the cash is required or to life of the asset that is being purchased.

Therefore, in most cases, an overdraft is most suitable for increased working capital requirements but it may be possible to use debt factoring or invoice discounting to inject cash into the business when needed.

A loan or other longer term finance option is more suitable for the purchase of non-current assets or another business.

However, you do need to appreciate the advantages and disadvantages of each of the sources of finance to be able to make an informed decision. Consideration should be made of:

- Cost – interest, fees, early redemption penalties
- Timescale – how long will the cash be required for
- Security – fixed and floating charges
- Impact on the gearing of the company.

 Test your understanding 7

A business has produced its cash budget for the following six months. The cash budget shows that from month 4 onwards the current overdraft facility will be exceeded, largely due to the extension of additional credit to receivables in order to maintain market share in the face of stiff competition.

List the options the business has in dealing with this situation.

KAPLAN PUBLISHING

9.3 Considering the finance options

If a company is unable to raise money by the mainstream methods, then more desperate options may have to be considered.

Companies performing badly may not be able to borrow further money from their bank, nor raise money from capital disposals.

(a) The sale/leaseback of assets is often the first of the more desperate options to be considered. This may realise funds in the short term, although freehold rights will be lost.

(b) A company might consider running its inventory levels down to a very minimum quantity or alternatively not holding any inventory at all. The disadvantages of this step are considerable:

- The company runs the risk of a stock-out, i.e. customer demand exceeds the goods in inventory, so goodwill and customers are lost.

- The production cycle will have to be altered and staff possibly made redundant.

- Bulk purchase discounts will no longer be available.

- The company's scale of operation usually has to be reduced.

- Consequently, this is a step which is only taken when no other finance is available and the directors are trying to keep the business operating.

Test your understanding 8

Steinburgs are planning to expand their manufacturing facilities. The expansion plans require new machinery at a cost of £60,000 and a working capital injection of £10,000.

There are 3 different options for funding the expansion:

Option 1

- A bank loan of £60,000 secured on the new machinery. Capital repayments are to be made of equal amounts over 3 years. The interest rate is fixed at 4% per annum calculated on the capital balance outstanding at the beginning of each year.

- An arrangement fee equal to 0.5% of the bank loan is payable at the beginning of the loan term.

- The bank is also offering an overdraft facility of £15,000 which attracts an annual interest rate of 13%. Steinburgs believe that they will have an average overdraft of £8,000 for the first 7 months of the first year.

CASH AND FINANCIAL MANAGEMENT

Option 2

- A bank loan of £80,000 secured on the assets of the partnership. Capital repayments are to be made over 3 years, with a 3 month payment holiday at the beginning of the loan term.

- The interest rate is fixed at 8% of the principal amount per annum for the first 2 years and will then revert to a variable interest rate 3% above the base rate.

- An arrangement fee equal to 0.9% of the bank loan is payable at the beginning of the loan term.

- No overdraft facility will be required.

Option 3

- Steinburgs' two owners each take out a personal secured loan for £35,000 repayable over 4 years at an interest rate of 4%. These monies will then be loaned to the partnership as increased capital. Interest of 7% per annum is payable by the business to the two owners.

- No overdraft facility will be required.

Required:

Calculate the cost of each of the above options for the first year. Which of the 3 methods would you recommend?

	Loan interest £	Arrangement fee £	Overdraft interest £	Total cost £
Option 1				
Option 2				
Option 3				

Recommendation:

Raising finance: Chapter 6

 Test your understanding 9

A company has two options available to raise finance to buy a new machine.

Option 1

A bank loan of £100,000 with capital repayments made over 5 years. The interest rate is fixed at 7% per annum for the first year and will then revert to a variable interest rate of 3% above the base rate for rest of the loan term.

Option 2

A bank loan of £100,000 with capital repayments made over 8 years. The interest rate is fixed at 5% for the first year and will then revert to a variable interest rate of 4% above the base rate for the rest of the loan term.

Required:

Calculate the total cost of both these options for the first 2 years. The base rate is predicted to be 1% in year 2.

	Option 1			Option 2		
Year	Loan interest	Capital repayments	Total	Loan interest	Capital repayments	Total
1						
2						
Total						

Which option should be chosen?

The company wishes to consider the whole life of the loans. Interest rates are as above but from year 3 to the term end the base rate will be 1.5%.

Which option should be chosen?

Test your understanding 10

Finalite are planning to expand their production facilities. The expansion plans require new machinery at a cost of £55,000 and a working capital injection of £20,000.

There are 3 different options for funding the expansion:

Option 1

- A bank loan of £55,000 secured on the new machinery. Capital repayments are to be made of equal amounts over 5 years. The interest rate is fixed at 5% per annum calculated on the capital balance outstanding at the beginning of each year.
- An arrangement fee equal to 0.7% of the bank loan is payable at the beginning of the loan term.
- The bank is also offering an overdraft facility of £22,000 which attracts an annual interest rate of 11%. Finalite believes that they will have an average overdraft of £11,000 for the first 6 months of the first year.

Option 2

- A bank loan of £75,000 secured on the assets of the partnership. Capital repayments are to be made over 5 years, with a 5 month payment holiday at the beginning of the loan term.
- The interest rate is fixed at 7% of the principal amount per annum for the first 2 years and will then revert to a variable interest rate 2% above the base rate.
- An arrangement fee equal to 0.8% of the bank loan is payable at the beginning of the loan term.
- No overdraft facility will be required.

Option 3

- Finalite's two owners each take out a personal secured loan for £37,500 repayable over 3 years at an interest rate of 5%. These monies will then be loaned to the partnership as increased capital. Interest of 8% per annum is payable by the business to the two owners.
- No overdraft facility will be required.

Required:

Calculate the cost of each of the above options for the first year. Which of the 3 methods would you recommend?

	Loan interest £	Arrangement fee £	Overdraft interest £	Total cost £
Option 1				
Option 2				
Option 3				

Recommendation:

Test your understanding 11

A business has paid £3,000 in interest on a £30,000 loan in one year. Calculate the flat rate applied to the loan.

Test your understanding 12

A bank has offered to lend a company £90,000 to be repaid in 12 monthly instalments of £7,815. Calculate the flat rate of interest being applied to the loan.

10 Relationship between the bank and the customer

10.1 Introduction

Whether an overdraft or a loan or a combination of the two is chosen to finance a deficit, a relationship is formed between the bank providing the finance and the company using the finance.

10.2 Fiduciary relationship

The bank and the customer also have a fiduciary relationship which means that the **bank is expected to act with the utmost good faith** in its relationship with the customer.

10.3 The duties of the customer

The customer has two main duties:

- to exercise care in drawing cheques such that fraud is not facilitated
- to tell the bank of any forgeries known of.

10.4 The rights of the bank

The rights of the bank are:

- to charge reasonable charges and commissions over and above interest
- to use the customer's money in any way provided that it is legal and morally acceptable
- to be repaid overdrawn balances on demand
- to be indemnified against possible losses when acting on a customer's behalf.

11 Summary

There are many choices facing a business that needs to raise finance but it is important that the right choice of the form of finance is made. This will start with an initial consideration of the reason for the additional finance.

If it is due to the need for increased working capital then a form of short-term or possibly loan finance would be most appropriate. If the finance is required for the purchase of non-current assets then long-term finance to match with the life of the asset is probably the best option.

Test your understanding answers

Test your understanding 1

(a) Simple interest per year = £500,000 × 0.07 = £35,000

Total after 3 years = £500,000 + (£35,000 × 3 years) = **£605,000**

(b) Compound interest:

Total after 3 years = £500,000 × 1.06^3 = **£595,508**

Test your understanding 2

Interest year 1 = £350,000 × 0.06 (5% + 1%) = £21,000

Interest year 2 = £21,000 (same as year 1) = £21,000

Interest year 3 = £350,000 × 0.07 (6% + 1%) = £24,500

Arrangement fee = £350,000 × 0.015 = £5,250

Total cost = **£71,750**

Test your understanding 3

False

A fixed charge is security offered by a specific asset

A floating charge is security offered by a group of assets

Test your understanding 4

Answer D

Test your understanding 5

Answer A

Test your understanding 6

Mo Ltd will incur two costs – the debt factoring company's fee and the interest on the advanced funds.

If receivable days are reduced to 30 days then the trade receivables would now be:

£3,000,000 × 30/365 = £246,575

Of which 80% will be advanced: £246,575 × 80% = £197,260

Costs

Fee: £3,000,000 × 0.5%	£15,000
Interest: £197,260 × 11%	£21,699
Total cost	£36,699

Therefore to the nearest £100 the cost is **£36,700**. Administrative savings and an improvement in cash flow (due to earlier cash collection) which will reduce any overdraft charges will hopefully offset this cost.

Raising finance: Chapter 6

 Test your understanding 7

- negotiate an increased overdraft
- delay payment to payables
- take out a short term bank loan
- debt factoring
- invoice discounting
- Hire purchase or leasing

 Test your understanding 8

	Loan interest £	Arrangement fee £	Overdraft interest £	Total cost £
Option 1	2,400	300	607	3,307
Option 2	6,400	720	0	7,120
Option 3	4,900	0	0	4,900

Recommendation: Option 1 as it is the cheapest.

 Test your understanding 9

| | Option 1 ||| Option 2 |||
Year	Loan interest	Capital repayments	Total	Loan interest	Capital repayments	Total
1	7,000	20,000	27,000	5,000	12,500	17,500
2	3,200	20,000	23,200	4,375	12,500	16,875
Total	10,200	40,000	50,200	9,375	25,000	34,375

Recommendation: Option 2 as it is the cheapest over the first 2 years.

When the whole life of the loan is considered the capital repayments will be same – £100,000. The total interest paid will be the relevant cost.

CASH AND FINANCIAL MANAGEMENT

	Option 1			Option 2	
Year	Interest		Year	Interest	
1	100,000 × 7% = 7,000		1	100,000 × 5% = 5,000	
2	80,000 × 4% = 3,200		2	87,500 × 5% = 4,375	
3	60,000 × 4.5% = 2,700		3	75,000 × 5.5% = 4,125	
4	40,000 × 4.5% = 1,800		4	62,500 × 5.5% = 3,438	
5	20,000 × 4.5% = 900		5	50,000 × 5.5% = 2,750	
Total	15,600		6	37,500 × 5.5% 2,063	
			7	25,000 × 5.5% = 1,375	
			8	12,500 × 5.5% = 688	
			Total	23,814	

If total interest cost is considered then Option 1 is the cheapest but taking longer to pay back a loan may be more beneficial to the company.

Test your understanding 10

	Loan interest £	Arrangement fee £	Overdraft interest £	Total cost £
Option 1	2,750	385	605	3,740
Option 2	5,250	600	0	5,850
Option 3	6,000	0	0	6,000

Recommendation: Option 1

Workings

Option 1

Loan interest 55,000 × 5% = £2,750

Arrangement fee 55,000 × 0.7% = £385

Overdraft interest 11,000 × 11% × 6/12 = £605

Option 2

Loan interest 75,000 × 7% = £5,250

Arrangement fee 75,000 × 0.8% = £600

Option 3

Loan interest (37,500 × 8%) × 2 = £6,000

Test your understanding 11

3,000 ÷ 30,000 × 100 = 10%

 Test your understanding 12

£7,815 × 12 = £93,780
3,780 ÷ 90,000 × 100 = 4.2%

CASH AND FINANCIAL MANAGEMENT

Investing surplus funds

Introduction

In this chapter we will consider the ways in which any cash surplus can be invested and the factors that should be considered to determine the best type of investment.

KNOWLEDGE
Surplus funds and the terms and conditions associated with each of these types of investment (4.3)
Minimise the potential exposure to the organisation (4.4)
Raising finance and investing funds according to organisational culture and policies (5.3)

CONTENTS
1   Business requirements for investing
2   Investment terminology
3   Investment objectives
4   Types of investment
5   Making the right decision

Investing surplus funds: Chapter 7

1 Business requirements for investing

1.1 Introduction

Cash budgets can be used to forecast if there are going to be any surplus funds available to the company.

Surplus funds comprise liquid balances held by a business, which are neither needed to finance current business operations nor held permanently for short-term investment.

Surplus funds can fall into two categories:

- **Long-term surpluses.** Permanent cash surpluses and long-term cash surpluses are rare. These are cash surpluses that a business has no foreseeable use for. When they arise, the business is likely to repay liabilities, reinvested in growing the business or pay out the money to its owners in the form of dividends or drawings.

- **Short-term surpluses** that need to be invested temporarily (perhaps in short-term securities or deposit accounts) until they are required.

The availability of surplus cash is temporary, awaiting employment either in existing operations or in new investment opportunities (whether already identified or not).

The 'temporary' period can be of any duration from one day to the indefinite future date at which the new investment opportunity may be identified and seized. The business will need its cash at some point in the not-too-distant future, but for a short time, perhaps several months, the business has more cash than it needs.

Cash surpluses should be used, and should not be left in a current bank account earning no interest.

The cash might be transferred to a deposit account that does pay interest, or it might be invested in 'financial securities' such as government bonds (in the UK, gilt-edged securities or gilts). When cash surpluses are large, the interest income from investing the money can be quite large, adding to cash flow and profit.

Opportunities like this should always be taken; money **invested just overnight will be worth more than money left idle**. Surplus cash will therefore require an investment decision.

CASH AND FINANCIAL MANAGEMENT

1.2 Investment strategy

Many companies will have regulations and procedures to ensure that the liquidity of the business is safeguarded, for example:

- a certain amount of cash must be available immediately at any point in time
- investments in certain types of instrument may be limited to a financial amount or a percentage of total investment
- investment of surplus funds might only be allowed in certain specified types of investment
- all investments must be convertible into cash within a certain number of days.

These procedures, regulations and limits must be followed at all times.

1.3 Treasury activities and risk

Whoever is in charge of the treasury function must ensure that, although surplus cash is invested profitably, excessive risks are not taken.

There are many highly speculative and highly risky financial instruments on the market, which although they may yield very high returns, can also have huge losses.

The aim of the treasury activities in a trading company is to earn a reasonable return on any surplus cash but not to speculate.

1.4 External influences on cash balances

Cash balances will be affected by internal controls, business performance, planning etc. but they will also be affected by the uncontrollable, external environmental and financial environment.

Treasury managers therefore need to consider the external economic and financial environment as well at their internal business performance and policies when managing cash.

This is looked at in more detail in chapter 8.

Investing surplus funds: **Chapter 7**

2 Investment terminology

2.1 Investment terminology

- Interest – a regular return paid to the lender of debt finance. For more details on types of interest such as fixed rate, variable rate, simple interest and compound interest see chapter 6.

- Fees – when arranging new investment a business may be charged an administration or 'arrangement' fee to set up the new investment.

- Penalties – if a business wishes to withdraw funds from an investment before the agreed maturity date it will likely incur penalty fees. This is normally in the form of lost interest (e.g. if funds are withdrawn early then the penalty is the loss of 2 months' interest).

- Minimum/maximum amounts – Some types of investments may have a minimum and/or maximum amount of money that can be invested.

- Minimum/maximum lending periods – Some types of investments may have a minimum and/or maximum length of time that money can be invested.

3 Investment objectives

3.1 Investment considerations

The main factors that should be considered when determining how to deal with surplus funds are:

- **Risk** – the degree of risk attached to the investment in terms of variability of return and potential loss of the principal sum invested.

- **Liquidity** – the cash must be available for use when needed. How quickly the investment can be converted back to cash is of major importance. Factors such as how good a market exists for the chosen investment and the settlement period on any transaction should be considered.

- **Maturity** – means the length or duration of investments.

- **Return** – the income and capital gain from the chosen security. The aim is to earn the highest possible after tax returns.

- **Diversification** – the portfolio effect. By investing in different types of investments the portfolio of investments is more diverse which helps to reduce the overall risk.

3.2 Risk

Risk refers to the probability that the investment might rise or fall in value. As a general rule risk and return should be related. The **higher the risk** of an investment the **higher the potential return should be**.

Companies need to manage risk. It is present whenever there are two or more possible future outcomes. Risk can manifest itself as:

- an unexpected change in interest rates, relevant for companies that have to pay interest on loans or earn interest on investments
- an unexpected change in exchange rates, relevant for companies with overseas operations
- an unexpected change in the company's business environment e.g. the market for its products or services changes which can significantly impact the company's cash flows.

Sound financial planning, both in the short and long term, is the key to survival.

There are two main categories of risk:

- **Systematic**: it affects a large number of assets and is practically impossible to protect yourself against. Systematic risk is the variability of returns caused by factors affecting the whole market. Examples of systematic risk are political events or changes to tax rates.

- **Unsystematic**, or 'specific risk': it affects a small number of assets – a workers' strike or bad press, for example.

    Types of unsystematic risk include:

    - credit or default risk (the company cannot pay the contractual interest and principal on debt obligations)
    - country risk (a country cannot honour its financial obligations)
    - interest rate risk (an increase of interest rates hurts the price of bonds and stocks)
    - political risk (changes in government policies, which are more common in second- and third-world countries)
    - market risk (the volatility of the stock market or fluctuations in stock prices which are the effect of market forces).

The **amount of risk a business takes directly corresponds with the rate of return**. For instance, a higher risk yields a higher potential return and a lower risk yields a lower rate of return.

> **Example**
>
> A business has £10,000 of surplus cash to invest for a period of one month until it is needed to pay the quarterly VAT bill. The money could be paid into a bank deposit account earning 0.4% interest per month or it could be invested in shares purchased through a broker.
>
> Consider the risks of these two options.
>
> **Solution**
>
> If the money is paid into the bank deposit account there is virtually no risk at all. The withdrawal in one month's time will total:
>
> £10,000 + (0.4% × £10,000) = £10,040
>
> The investment has earned £40 of income for the business.
>
> If the £10,000 were to be invested in shares then in one month's time the share value may have increased to say £13,000, in which case the shares could be sold for that amount earning £3,000 of profit.
>
> However it is also possible that the share values have fallen and the shares can only be sold for £7,500 in one month's time meaning not only that a loss has been made but also that there is no longer enough cash available to pay the VAT bill.

3.3 Liquidity and maturity

Liquidity refers to the ease with which an investment can be cashed in or realised without significant loss of value or interest.

When any surplus cash is invested it is important to ensure that it can be **realised when needed**. The ease of realisation will be reflected in the return that the investment gives.

For example a bank deposit is easily and quickly turned into cash and so is seen as very liquid. However, a stock in a small company may not be easy to sell at short notice so is deemed to be far less liquid.

Term to maturity refers to the remaining time to maturity for a financial instrument. At maturity the instrument is repaid by the borrower. Term to maturity ranges from zero in the case of bank deposits that are easily withdrawn on demand to instruments such as shares which have no maturity date.

A cash surplus is usually temporary and may only available for some weeks or months. If an investment is cashed in or sold before it reached maturity there is a risk that there will be some **loss in value or interest received**. Some investments will not allow funds to be withdrawn before the maturity date, or will only allow an early withdraw with **penalty fees** (such as the loss of several months' interest).

If a company knows that it will need the funds in three days (or weeks or months), it simply invests them for just that period at the best rate available with safety. The solution is to match the maturity of the investment with the period for which the funds are surplus.

- The exact duration of the surplus period is not always known. It will be known if the cash is needed to meet a loan instalment, a large tax payment or a dividend but it will not be known if the need is an unidentified cash requirement.

- Expected future trends in interest rates affect the maturity of investments. For example, if interest rates are forecast to fall, the returns on longer term investments might well be lower than those on short term investments.

- Bridging finance may be available to bridge the gap between the time when the cash is needed and the subsequent date on which the investment matures.

- An investment may not need to be held to maturity if either an earlier withdrawal is permitted by the terms of the instrument without excessive penalty, or there is a secondary market and its disposal in that market causes no excessive loss. A good example of such an investment is a certificate of deposit, where the investor 'lends' the bank a stated amount for a stated period, usually between one and six months. As evidence of the debt and its promise to pay interest the bank gives the investor a certificate of deposit (CD). There is an active market for CDs issued by the commercial banks and turning a CD into cash is easy and cheap.

3.4 Return

Return on an investment is the interest received over the period of time the investment is held for. A business that has surplus funds to invest will wish those funds to earn a good profit or return but what is also paramount is the safety of the asset.

Although the whole purpose of investing cash is to receive a return, the rate of return is really the last factor to consider when investing cash surpluses.

This is because it is largely dictated by the risk, liquidity and maturity. Once management has decided on the appropriate level of risk, liquidity and maturity, it has substantially narrowed down the types of investment that are appropriate. The market then dictates the rates of return on these investments.

3.5 Diversification

There is a general rule that a business should not put all its surplus funds into one investment. It is much better to diversify by investing in a number of different investments. This would lead to the business spreading the risk. It is known as the portfolio effect.

3.6 Organisational policy

Many companies will have regulations and procedures to ensure that the liquidity of the business is safeguarded.

For example, a certain amount of cash must be available immediately at any point in time, that investments in certain types of instrument may be limited to a financial amount, that surplus funds might only be allowed to be invested in certain specified types of investment or that all investments must be convertible into cash within a certain number of days. These procedures, regulations and limits must be followed at all times.

Most organisations want to avoid the high risk investments. What they will choose to invest in depends on the following:

- **Value** of funds available for investment.
- Length of **time** for which the funds are available.
- **Certainty** of funds and **accuracy** of cash budget.
- **Return** on invested funds – is it adequate? Does it compensate for the risk involved?
- **Risk** and variability of return from the investment if held for the full intended duration.
- **Liquidity** of the investment. Whether there is any possibility that the cash may be required prematurely to make unexpected payments and whether there would be any costs in the event of an early termination.
- Risks associated with **early redemption**. A security which provides a fixed, risk-free return if held for the full term may prove costly if terminated early.
- **Realisation/Maturity**. In some circumstances it may be important that the investment can be realised easily. It provides a company with a reserve, or safety margin, in its cash planning.

The overall aim should be to secure the maximum interest possible, consistent with a satisfactory level of risk and the required degree of liquidity. The investing company has to balance the expected interest with the risks involved.

CASH AND FINANCIAL MANAGEMENT

Test your understanding 1

In the management of cash balances, surpluses may sometimes be forecast. These surpluses should be managed, taking liquidity, safety and rate of return into account.

(a) Describe **each** of these three factors:

   (i) liquidity

   (ii) safety

   (iii) rate of return.

(b) Briefly explain which of these three factors you consider to be the most important, giving reasons for your choice.

Test your understanding 2

The benefits of good cash management to a company are:

(a) better control of financial risk

(b) opportunity for profit

(c) strengthened statement of financial position

(d) increased confidence of customers, suppliers, banks and shareholders.

Explain how good cash management may realise any **two** of these benefits.

4 Types of investment

4.1 Bank and building society deposit accounts

One of the safest and simplest forms of investment for surplus cash is to pay it into a high street bank or building society deposit account. There is a wide variety of such accounts available. For example:

- **Instant access deposit accounts** – money can be withdrawn when required without having to give any notice. There is no loss of interest but the **interest rate** is generally **quite low**.

- **Notice deposit accounts** – money can be withdrawn after a certain period of notice, for example 7 days or 30 days. These tend to have higher interest rates than instant access accounts but, if cash is withdrawn without notice, some loss of interest will be incurred.

- **High interest deposit accounts** – these will tend to be for larger amounts, for example at least £5,000, and for a fixed term with no withdrawal of funds permitted.

For cash that is definitely not going to be required in the near future there are deposits that can be made for a fixed term of up to three months at a variable rate of interest which is linked to money market rates. This will normally yield a higher rate of return due to the lower liquidity.

An important feature of the banking system in the UK is that it is financially stable. Investment in a bank or building society deposit account offers high security with relatively low returns.

In the event of default, investors are protected by statutory compensation schemes that will refund any funds lost, but only up to specified limits. The income received depends on the type of account and in some circumstances payment of interest can be made without deduction of tax.

The risk factor on deposit accounts is very low although the real return (i.e. the return in excess of inflation) is also likely to be low. Deposit accounts are useful for short-term investment or as a readily accessible emergency fund.

4.2 Bonds

There are lots of types of bonds, examples include:

- Local authority bonds – are certificates issued by local authorities backed by the government. They are also called local authority short-term loans, which are marketable. A lump sum can be invested for a fixed term at a fixed interest rate. They are considered low risk as they are backed by the government.

- Corporate bonds – are bonds issued by a company. These are long term bonds and can be high risk as the price will fluctuate with the movements in the general level of interest rates and can also be affected by the perceived credit risk of the company issuing the bonds.

- Government bonds or gilts – see below.

A bond will normally have a nominal (par) value (e.g. £100), a coupon rate (e.g. 5%) and redemption terms (e.g. redeem at par in 20X5). The annual interest is the product of the nominal value and the coupon rate (e.g. £100 × 5% = £5 per annum).

Characteristics of a bond:

- Return – typically bonds have low returns because they are a lower risk investment.

- Risk – bonds are usually lower risk than equity. For example the bonds may be secured and the interest rate fixed.

- Timescales – the maturity is defined on the bond and varies from very short term (e.g. Treasury Bills) to long term (e.g. 25 year corporate bonds). Some bonds are redeemable but others irredeemable.

- Liquidity – if the bonds are unquoted then the investor has no choice except to wait for redemption. However, if quoted they will be easier to liquidate by selling on the bond markets. For example government bonds are usually very liquid. Note: high risk bonds will be sold at a large discount on face (nominal) value.

There are a number of different ways of calculating the yield on bonds:

- **Coupon yield.** The coupon yield is the fixed rate of interest, expressed as a percentage of nominal value. So 7% Treasury Stock 20X2 would have a coupon yield of 7%, regardless of its market price.

- **Interest yield.** The interest yield is the annual interest receivable, expressed as a percentage of the market price. For example, if 7% Treasury Stock 20X2 has a market price of 103.80, the interest yield is 6.7% (7/103.80 × 100%).

- **Redemption yield.** The interest yield measures the interest return on gilts, but ignores any capital gain or loss on investment when the gilts are eventually redeemed. Redemption yield is the interest yield plus or minus an amount to reflect the difference between the market price of the gilt and its eventual redemption value.

These calculations are covered within the next section on Government securities.

4.3 Government securities (gilts)

Government securities are also known as gilt-edged securities, gilts or Treasury stock. They are a type of bond.

Definition

Government securities or gilt-edged securities are **fixed interest securities issued by HM Treasury** which pays the holder a fixed cash payment (or coupon) every six months until maturity, at which point the holder receives the final coupon payment and the return of the principal.

The term 'gilt' or 'gilt-edged security' is a reference to the primary characteristic of gilts as an investment – the security. This is a reflection of the fact that the British Government has never failed to make interest or principal payments on gilts as they fall due.

Example

An issue of 9% Treasury stock has a par value of £100, a market value of £105.80, and it is redeemable at par in two years' time.

The **coupon rate** usually reflects the **market interest rate** at the time of the first issue of the gilt. The coupon indicates the cash payment per £100 nominal that the holder will receive per year.

This payment is made in two equal semi-annual payments on fixed dates.

For example, an investor who holds £100 nominal of 9% Treasury Gilt 20X6 will receive two coupon payments of £4.50 each year (9% × £100 = £9 split over two payments).

Gilts also have a specific maturity date.

The term can vary from less than one year up to 20 or more years. As this is a fixed rate interest, a change in base rates can affect the market price, and the attractiveness of the investment.

Interest yield

Definition

The interest yield or flat rate yield is the coupon rate of interest as a percentage of the current price of the gilt.

Example

An issue of 9% Treasury stock has a par value of £100, a market value of £105.80, and it is redeemable at par in two years' time. The interest yield on the stock is:

$$\frac{9\% \times £100}{£105.80} \times 100 = 8.5\%$$

This shows the return on the gilt if it were bought today and held for a year whereas the redemption yield is the return throughout the whole life of the security.

Redemption yield

Definition

The redemption yield is the **internal rate of return** (IRR) earned by an investor who buys the gilt today at the market price, assuming that the bond will be held until maturity, and that all coupon and principal payments will be made on schedule. Redemption yield is the discount rate at which the sum of all future cash flows from the gilt (coupons and principal) is equal to the price of the bond.

The redemption yield can be calculated for any fixed interest security. It is a way of comparing different securities and also comparing the return with the return from other forms of investment.

Example

An issue of 9% Treasury stock has a market value of £105.80, and it is redeemable at par (£100) in two years' time.

- £105.80 is the initial investment.
- Each year that the gilt is held the investor will receive 9% interest on the par value of the gilt = £9.
- At redemption the investor will receive £100.

An investor buying a quantity of the stock now at £105.80 and holding it until maturity will only receive £100 for every £105.80 of investment.

Although the investor will receive an interest yield of 8.5% per annum (see above), there will be a capital loss of £5.80 for each £105.80 invested.

Since the stock has two years remaining to maturity this represents an average loss of £2.90 each year, which is 2.7% of the investment value.

As a rough approximation, the redemption yield on the stock is 5.8% (8.5% – 2.7%).

This can also be calculated as follows:

Calculate the NPV at two different discount rates and then calculate the IRR.

Note annuity factors have been used to calculate the present value of the interest received. This could equally been done by discounting the interest received each year.

	4%	£		8%	£
T_0 £105.80	× 1.000	(105.80)	T_0 £105.80	× 1.000	(105.80)
$T_1 - T_2$ £9	× 1.886	16.974	$T_1 - T_2$ £9	× 1.783	16.047
T_2 £100	× 0.925	92.5	T_2 £100	× 0.857	85.7
Present value		3.674	Present value		–4.053

The redemption yield:

$$IRR = L + \frac{N_L}{N_L - N_H} \times (H - L)$$

$$IRR = 4 + \frac{3.674}{3.674 - -4.053} \times (8-4)$$

IRR = 5.90%

L = Low interest rate

H = High interest rate

N_L = NPV at the low interest rate

N_H = NPV at the high interest rate

This means that over the term of the investment there will be a return of 5.90%.

Government securities can either be held to maturity or sold in a secondary market if the cash is needed. If they are sold before maturity a broker may be used which will incur costs (**brokerage fees**).

In the UK Gilts are **almost risk free** and **very marketable** ensuring that they are a popular form of investment for companies. Beware that gilts in different countries may be a higher risk due to instability of governments.

 Test your understanding 3

An issue of 4% Treasury stock has a par value of £100, a current market price of £94.00. The stock has exactly three years to redemption, when it will be redeemed at par.

Required:

(a) Calculate the current interest yield on the stock.

(b) Calculate an approximate redemption yield.

 Test your understanding 4

8% Treasury Stock 20Y2 has a par value of £100 and a market price of £126.9784 at 31 March 20X6. Calculate the interest yield.

4.4 Certificates of deposit

Definition

A certificate of deposit (CD) is issued by a bank or building society which certifies that a certain sum, usually a minimum of £50,000, has been deposited with it to be repaid on a specific date.

The term can range from seven days to five years but is usually for three months (90 days). CDs are negotiable instruments; they can be bought and sold, therefore if the holder does not want to wait until the maturity date the CD can be sold in the money market.

The market in CDs is large and active therefore they are an ideal method for investing large cash surpluses. The sale value of a CD will depend on how much a buyer is willing to pay to obtain the right to the deposit plus interest at maturity.

Since CDs are negotiable, the holder can sell them at any time. This makes them far more liquid than a money-market time deposit, with the same bank.

CDs usually offer an attractive rate of interest when compared to deposit accounts and a low credit risk (as long as a reputable bank is used). They are useful for investing funds in the short term since they can be sold at any time on the secondary market.

An investor could ask the bank to make an early repayment, but there are normally penalty charges for doing this.

4.5 Shares

A share is a security that represents a portion of the owner's capital in a business. Shareholders are the owners of the business. They share in the success or failure of the business. This can be measured by the amount of dividends that they receive and by the price of the share, quoted on the stock market.

Shares in companies can be bought as an investment. Shares are bought and sold through a **broker for a fee**. Whilst being a share holder the company/person may have the right to vote in decisions and also receive **dividends** from the company they have invested in, depending on the class of shares held.

CASH AND FINANCIAL MANAGEMENT

There are two main types of shares:

- **Ordinary shares** – also called equity shares, this is the risk capital of a company. Ordinary shares give holders the rights of ownership in the company, such as the right to share in the profits, to vote in general meetings and to elect and dismiss directors. Obligations of ownership are also conferred and this may result in the loss of an investor's money if the company is unsuccessful. Ordinary shares usually form the bulk of a company's capital and have no special rights over other shares. In the event of liquidation, ordinary shares rank after all other liabilities of the company.

- **Preference (Preferred) shares** are comparable to debentures in that they yield fixed rate dividends. The main difference, however, is that dividends on preferred shares are paid provided the company makes a profit, whereas dividends on loan notes need to be paid irrespective of whether the company makes a profit or a loss.

Share prices can fluctuate depending on either, or both, the company and general market performance.

If a company is achieving good profits and has a good reputation then the return possible from shares is higher than that of the other options discussed.

Conversely if confidence in the company or in the general market drops then the loss can also be significant. Due to this, shares are considered the **most risky** of investment opportunities.

Dividend yield is a financial ratio that shows how much a company pays out in dividends each year relative to its share price. In the absence of any capital gains, the dividend yield is the return on investment for a stock.

Dividend yield is calculated as follows:

$$= \frac{\text{Annual dividend per share}}{\text{Market price per share}}$$

It is a way to measure how much cash flow you get for each pound invested in shares. Investors who require a minimum stream of cash flow from their investment portfolio can secure this cash flow by investing in stocks paying relatively high, stable dividend yields.

 Example

If a company pays annual dividends of £1 per share and the shares are trading at £20 the company has a dividend yield of 5%.

$$= \frac{1}{20} \times 100 = 5\%$$

Investing surplus funds: **Chapter 7**

 Test your understanding 5

A company pays annual dividends of £1 per share and the shares are trading at £40 each. Calculate the dividend yield.

 Test your understanding 6

Use the pick lists to complete the following sentences:

Certificates of deposit are certificates issued by [banks/local authorities/government]. They [can/cannot] be traded on a market. They are considered to be a [low risk/high risk] investment.

Government securities are also known as [gold-edged/gilt-edged/gilted] securities. They [can/cannot] be traded on a market. They are considered to be a [low risk/high risk] investment.

 Test your understanding 7

What type of investment do the following describe:

Interest rates are fixed and these types of securities are considered to be low risk because they are backed by the government.

- A   Certificates of deposit
- B   Government securities
- C   Bonds
- D   Bank deposit account

Certificates issued by banks that certify that an amount of money has been deposited and will be repaid at a specific date in the future. They can be traded on a market. They are considered to be a low risk investment.

- A   Certificates of deposit
- B   Government securities
- C   Bonds
- D   Bank deposit account

4.6 Land and property

Historically land and property were deemed to be a fairly safe investment as there is a finite supply. However in the two decades land and house values have been more volatile, sometimes resulting in a capital loss for investors. Therefore any initial investment may not be fully realised if the market value has dropped at the date of sale.

Land and property are usually seen as a long term investment and may take a long time to make a suitable return for the company. The **investment can only be realised once the land or property is sold** and the speed of this will depend upon the economic environment at the time of sale. A return could also be obtained by renting the land or property to another party.

The liquidity of the company may be adversely affected if they are unable to realise the full investment at the point of sale. It is unlikely that the return could be forecast with any certainty at the time of purchase.

4.7 Commodities

The term commodity is specifically used for an economic good or service when the demand for it has no qualitative differentiation across a market. That is there is little differentiation between a commodity coming from one producer and the same commodity from another producer; a barrel of oil is basically the same product, regardless of the producer.

Traditional examples of commodities include basic resources and agricultural products such as gold, iron ore, sugar and rice. Soft commodities are goods that are grown, while hard commodities are ones that are extracted through mining.

There are three ways to invest in commodities – either directly by buying it physically, or buying shares in commodity companies, or indirectly through a fund or an investment trust.

- Investing physically means actually buying and holding the asset; it comes with storage problems, but there are several bullion firms offering online gold dealing and safe storage of the asset. Buying physical gold coins also offers an easy way to access the metal.

- Buy shares in commodity companies for example buy shares in companies such as BP, Royal Dutch Shell or Tullow Oil. The same applies to 'soft' commodity companies, although they are less numerous on the UK indices. The investment will be subject to movements in the stock market, as well as to changes in the price of the commodity itself.

- An investment fund is an easy way to access the sector. They provide a degree of diversification, as they typically invest in a variety of commodities as well as in production companies.

There are some common risks when investing in commodities:

- **Geopolitical** risk – the world's natural resources are located in various continents and the jurisdiction over these commodities lies with sovereign governments, international companies, and many other entities. For example, to access the large deposits of oil located in the Persian Gulf region, oil companies have to deal with the sovereign countries of the Middle East that have jurisdiction over this oil.

- **Speculative** risk – commodities markets are populated by traders whose primary interest is in making short-term profits by speculating whether the price of a security will go up or go down.

- **Fraud** – the Commodity Futures Trading Commission (CFTC) and other regulatory bodies do try to protect investors there is always the possibility that you will become a victim of fraud.

Commodities come into and go out of fashion over time. Supply and demand for commodities can change **liquidity**.

For example, if there is a sudden shortage of a commodity and the price begins to move higher, it will attract speculative buying. On the other hand, if a market is suddenly hit with a huge supply, speculative selling will often appear.

While some markets like gold and crude oil attract a high number of market participants, timber and frozen concentrated orange juice futures tend to always suffer from liquidity problems.

4.8 Other ways to use surplus funds

Other than the investment opportunities mentioned above a business could choose to repay any loans early or to take advantage of a settlement discount a supplier offers. By doing this a business may be able to reduce finance charges or reduce the amount paid to payable.

Overall this could provide a greater saving in monetary terms than the monetary return the various investment opportunities provide. This may be a more suitable way of using surplus funds in certain economic conditions such as increases in interest rates.

5 Making the right decision

5.1 Organisational policies and regulation

As noted earlier in the chapter each business will have certain criteria it will consider when deciding what to invest surplus funds in:

- maturity
- return
- risk
- liquidity
- diversification.

5.2 Attitudes to risk

There are two main types of risk with investments – capital risk and return risk. When investing in short-term investments it will be necessary to consider these risks and to take into account any expected changes in the economic and financial environment.

The decision makers' attitude to risk will have a bearing on the final investments chosen:

- **Risk neutral** decision makers consider all possible options and will try to select the one that maximises the expected return for an acceptable risk level
- **Risk seekers** are likely to choose the option that will give the best return regardless of the risk involved
- **Risk averse** decision makers will consider the options and make a decision based on minimising the risk involved.

All investments should be considered by a number of people as they may each have a different view point on the 'considered' level of risk. Company policy should also be robust enough to manage the risk levels.

5.3 Costs

There are a number of costs associated with making investments. Some of which are:

- **Brokerage fees** – some investments can be bought and sold through a broker, for example shares. There will be fees charged by the broker for making the sale or purchase.

- **Early termination costs** – if money is removed from some investments before it reaches maturity or realisation there may be a fee to apply. This also applies if the decision is to use surplus cash by repaying a loan early.

- **Interest rate changes** – increases or decreases in interest rates can have an impact on the value of the investment. See the next section for more detail.

5.4 Interest rate changes

Some short-term investments will have variable rates of interest. For example, many **bank deposit accounts** have **variable** rates of interest which means that if the bank base rate goes up or down the interest earned on the deposit will also increase or decrease.

This is an **advantage** if interest rates go **up** but a **disadvantage** if they go **down**.

Other types of investment, such as **fixed rate deposit accounts and gilt edged securities**, are **fixed** rate investments.

This means that if the general rate of interest changes there is no change in the interest paid on these investments. This is an **advantage** if interest rates go **down** but a **disadvantage** if interest rates go **up**.

Example

If an investment is made in a **fixed rate deposit account** and interest rates were expected to change then this would have **no effect on the amount deposited**.

The principal amount invested will always remain the same and this is the amount that will be repaid at the end of the term of the investment no matter what happens to interest rates. What will be affected is the level of return in comparison to variable rate deposit accounts:

- If interest rates rise above the fixed rate then the investment will be returning less than a variable rate deposit account.

- If interest rates drop below the fixed rate then the investment will be returning more than a variable rate deposit account.

CASH AND FINANCIAL MANAGEMENT

 Example

An investment in **fixed rate gilts** is rather different. These are marketable securities, i.e. they can be sold on to another investor. As such, their **market value will fluctuate** with changes in underlying interest rates or the base rate.

- If a business has invested in gilts and the **interest rate increases** then the **value of the gilt will fall** in order to ensure that the return is in line with general interest rates.
- If the base rate of interest is decreased then the market value of the gilts will increase.

Therefore, the person responsible for such investments should take account of expected changes in economic and financial conditions before making an investment.

 Test your understanding 8

Four possible investment options are available:

Option 1

Investment of £60,000 required, there is a 90 day notice period, risk has been assessed as medium due to the inclusion of some shares in the portfolio and the interest rate is 5% per annum.

Option 2

Investment should be between £40,000 and £80,000, there is a 30 day notice period, interest is 3%, risk has been assessed as low as there is no inclusion of shares.

Option 3

Investment portfolio consists of stocks and shares so is high risk but with a projected interest rate of 8%. There is a minimum investment of £35,000 required and a 45 day notice period exists.

Option 4

A low risk investment opportunity with a guaranteed return of 2.5%, the minimum investment required is £40,000 and 10 working days' notice must be given for withdrawals.

Investing surplus funds: **Chapter 7**

The treasury department has the following policy for investing surplus funds:

It must be possible to access the cash invested within 45 days.

The maximum investment amount is £45,000.

The interest rate must be 2.5% above base rate, which is currently 0.5%.

The investment must be low risk.

Complete the table below and decide which policy can be invested in, if any.

	Convertible within 45 days?	Investment £45,000 or below?	Interest rate 2.5% above base rate?	Low risk?	Invest?
Option 1					
Option 2					
Option 3					
Option 4					

Test your understanding 9

A company is looking to invest £50,000 for 6 months. Four possible investment options are available:

Option 1 – Bank notice deposit account

Fixed interest is 5% per annum, there is a 60 day notice period with an early redemption cost of £1,000.

Option 2 – Bank deposit account

Fixed interest is 0.5% per month, there is a 30 day notice period, early redemption is not available.

Option 3 – Gilts

Purchase of gilts, which reach maturity in 1 year, with a fixed interest rate of 6% per annum, payable quarterly.

CASH AND FINANCIAL MANAGEMENT

Option 4 – Shares

An investment opportunity in shares with a possible return of 8% in 6 months.

The treasury department has the following policy for investing surplus funds:

It must be possible to access the cash invested within 30 days.

The investment must be low risk.

It has also been noted that the base rate is likely to rise over the next 6 months.

Which of the four options available is the most suitable for the company?

 Test your understanding 10

Task 1

Wilson Limited's long-term cash flow forecast to year ended 20X9 suggests a cash surplus of £1 million will be generated in 20X8 and £1.75 million in 20X9.

The company is considering its future cash management strategy and is considering three business strategies. For each of the following three scenarios, suggest what action you would take to manage the cash surplus and explain the reasons for your suggestion.

(a) Plans for an acquisition of a cycle parts manufacturer (value up to £5 million) when a suitable opportunity arises.

(b) Development in 20X8 and 20X9 of several new product lines requiring capital investment of £2.5 million.

(c) Phased development of two new product lines requiring capital investment of £1.25 million and the intention to acquire another cycle parts manufacturer (value up to £3 million) when a suitable opportunity arises.

Task 2

What are the main factors to consider when investing a cash surplus? Identify three factors and briefly explain their importance.

5.5 Other considerations

When considering whether to invest in a company it is also necessary to consider how the **ethics, sustainability or working practices** of the company could affect an organisation's reputation and decision making.

Issues such as the use of child labour, poor working conditions for employees, and lower than minimum wage being paid can negatively affect how a company is perceived.

If an organisation is seen to be investing in a less than reputable company this will have a negative impact on the organisation. It could be assumed that the investor condones and encourages poor business practices.

6 Summary

If a business has a short-term surplus of funds then these should be invested, rather than remaining as idle cash which is not earning any income for the business.

The main factors to consider when determining the type of investment are the risk, return and liquidity of the investment.

If a business deals with cash sales then management should ensure that basic security measures for the cash are in place.

CASH AND FINANCIAL MANAGEMENT

Test your understanding answers

Test your understanding 1

(a) (i) **Liquidity**

The ability of a company to meet its debts as they fall due. The ability to change the liquidity profile (i.e. by selling investments) to meet unforeseen circumstances.

(ii) **Safety**

Investment of surplus cash must not be vulnerable to any unacceptable risk of loss through credit, market or exchange risk.

(iii) **Rate of return**

The return on the cash investment after taking into account transaction costs, management overheads and possible gains or losses on principal.

(b) Safety is the most important factor. Most short-term cash investments can be easily liquidated, even if at a discount. The difference between rates of return on high quality cash investments will be insignificant compared with the scale of loss encountered if there is loss of principal.

Test your understanding 2

(a) **Better control of financial risk**

By determining and maintaining the proper level of cash within a company in accordance with the organisation's financial procedures and within defined authorisation limits.

(b) **Opportunity for profit**

By reducing to a minimum the opportunity cost associated with maintaining cash balances in excess of a company's operating needs. Earnings (or surpluses) are improved by freeing up surplus cash for investment purposes while reducing interest charged through minimising borrowing.

(c) **Strengthened statement of financial position**

By reducing or eliminating cash balances in excess of target balances and putting surplus cash to work by investing (e.g. in the overnight money market); by reducing or eliminating cash borrowing and keeping interest costs as low as possible.

(d) **Increased confidence of customers, suppliers, banks and shareholders**

By having access to funds to disburse to suppliers (payables), banks (interest, fees and principal payments) and shareholders (dividends) when due. By providing good instructions to customers (receivables) to enable the organisation to convert receipts into usable bank deposits.

Test your understanding 3

(a) **Interest yield**

$$\frac{4\% \times £100}{£94} \times 100 = 4.26\%$$

(b) **Approximate redemption yield**

If an investor buys the stock now at £94.00 and holds it for three years until maturity, he, she or they will make a capital gain of 100 – 94 = £6 at redemption. In other words, there will be a capital gain of £6 for every £100 of stock, or for every £94 invested. This gives an average annual gain on redemption of £6 ÷ 3 = £2 for each £94 invested, which is 2.13% of the investment value per annum.

The approximate redemption yield is therefore the interest yield of 4.26% plus 2.13%, which is 6.39%

Test your understanding 4

$$\text{Interest yield} = \frac{\text{Coupon rate}}{\text{Market price}} \times 100 = \frac{8}{126.9784} \times 100 = 6.3\%$$

Test your understanding 5

$$\frac{1}{40} \times 100 = 2.5\%$$

Test your understanding 6

Certificates of deposit are certificates issued by banks. They can be traded on a market. They are considered to be a low risk investment.

Government securities are also known as gilt-edged securities. They can be traded on a market. They are considered to be a low risk investment.

Test your understanding 7

What type of investment do the following describe:

Interest rates are fixed and these types of securities are considered to be low risk because they are backed by the government.

B   Government securities

Certificates issued by banks that certify that an amount of money has been deposited and will be repaid at a specific date in the future. They can be traded on a market. They are considered to be a low risk investment.

A   Certificates of deposit

 Test your understanding 8

	Convertible within 45 days?	Investment £45,000 or below?	Interest rate 2.5% above base rate?	Low risk?	Invest?
Option 1	N	N	Y	N	N
Option 2	Y	Y	Y	Y	Y
Option 3	Y	Y	Y	N	N
Option 4	Y	Y	N	Y	N

CASH AND FINANCIAL MANAGEMENT

Test your understanding 9

	Meets policy guidelines?	Risk	Return	Cost	Invest?
Option 1	Yes	Low	1,250	1,000	No

Comments: Can access cash in 30 days but there is a charge of £1,000, the risk is low and the return = (£50,000 × 5%) × 6/12 = £1,250. Giving a net return of £250.

	Meets policy guidelines?	Risk	Return	Cost	Invest?
Option 2	Yes	Low	1,500	0	Yes

Comments: Cash can be accessed within 30 days with no fee, the risk is low and the return = (£50,000 × 0.5%) × 6 = £1,500.

	Meets policy guidelines?	Risk	Return	Cost	Invest?
Option 3	Yes	Low	1,500	Unknown but fees may be charged for sale	No

Comments: Cash can be accessed by selling the gilts but there may be a brokerage charge for doing so. The risk is low and the return = (£50,000 × 6%) × 6/12 = £1,500. Interest rates are likely to rise so the market value of the gilt will drop.

	Meets policy guidelines?	Risk	Return	Cost	Invest?
Option 4	No	High	4,000	Brokerage fees to buy and sell shares	No

Comments: A high risk investment, with a high return = (£50,000 × 8%) = £4,000.

Option 2 is the most suitable for the company.

Option 1 has the lowest net return, Option 3 may drop in market value and has unknown fees associated with the sale, Option 4 is high risk.

Test your understanding 10

Task 1

(a) Action – Invest cash in bank deposits or marketable securities (e.g. CDs, commercial paper).

Reason: To leave Wilson Limited with sufficient liquidity to help it make the acquisition, whilst receiving a market return on its cash investments.

(b) Action – Use cash to make the necessary capital investment in the new product lines.

Reason: Unless the cash is likely to be needed for a specific reason (such as an acquisition when cash will be needed immediately) it is unlikely that Wilson Limited will receive a return on its cash investments equivalent to the cost of raising debt finance.

(c) Action – Hold the cash to make the acquisition; either borrow or raise additional equity finance.

Reason: The cash will be required for the eventual acquisition at short notice. The new product lines should be easily financed using external funds.

Task 2

Risk	To ensure the investment is of acceptable credit standing.
Liquidity	To ensure the investment has sufficient marketability to allow the maximum availability of funds.
Return	To ensure the investment offers a good yield without unduly increasing risk or credit quality.

CASH AND FINANCIAL MANAGEMENT

Impact of regulations and policies on financing and investment

Introduction

In this chapter we will consider how government policies, regulations and organisational policies and principles can impact a business's cash management processes and how they raise finance and invest surplus funds.

KNOWLEDGE

Government monetary policies (5.1)

Impact of financial regulations, guidelines and security procedures on an organisation's principles of cash management (5.2)

Raising finance and investing funds according to organisational culture and policies (5.3)

Economic conditions that could affect financial decisions (5.4)

CONTENTS

1. Government and the Bank of England
2. Financial and statutory regulations
3. Economic factors
4. Organisational culture and policies

Impact of regulations and policies on financing and investment: **Chapter 8**

1 Government and the Bank of England

1.1 Introduction

Financial regulations, government policies, economic factors (such as interest rates and foreign exchange rates) and an organisation's principles over cash management can all impact how an organisation chooses to raise new finance or invest surplus funds.

Higher interest rates may make debt a less attractive option for raising new finance or governments may make grants available to help finance energy saving machinery.

1.2 The Government and the Bank of England

The Government can affect an organisation's financing decisions by controlling the supply of money, interest rates and the availability of credit. Governments have two main ways of affecting the economy:

- **Fiscal policy** refers to the government's taxation and spending plans.

- **Monetary policy** refers to setting interest rates and the management of the money supply (the total amount of money, including currency in circulation and deposited in banks and building societies) in the economy.

The Bank of England is the UK's central or national bank charged with overall control of the banking system in the interest of the nation.

In particular, monetary policy involves the changing of interest rates or varying of the amount of money that banks need to keep in reserve. The aim of the Government's monetary policy is to **keep inflation low and to create stable economic growth**.

A change in interest rates will affect the economy through a number of routes:

- First, a change in the cost of borrowing will affect spending decisions. A rise in rates will make savings more attractive and borrowing less so, and this will tend to reduce present spending, both on consumption and on investment. Lowering interest rates makes borrowing cheaper. Consumers have more spare cash to spend, companies can raise cheaper capital, and the economy starts to accelerate again.

CASH AND FINANCIAL MANAGEMENT

- Second, a change in rates affects the cash flow of borrowers and payables. A rise or fall in interest rates affects the cash flow of those with floating interest rate assets or liabilities. For example, many households have floating interest rate deposits in banks and building societies. Floating interest rate receivables include households with mortgages, and companies. Fluctuations in cash flow may affect spending.

- Third, a change in interest rates affects the value of certain assets, notably housing and stocks and shares. Such a change in wealth may influence people's willingness to spend.

- Fourth, a particular pressure on prices comes through the exchange rate. For example, a rise in domestic interest rates relative to those overseas will tend to result in a net inflow of capital and an appreciation of the exchange rate. A rising pound will reduce prices for imports, thus increasing competitive pressures and supplementing the downward pressure on inflation arising from weakened demand.

All of these influences on demand are likely to affect prices and inflation. A rise in short-term interest rates can be expected to restrain demand for UK output in the way described. That in turn is likely to put downward pressure on UK prices and the rate of inflation.

The Government and the Bank of England will want to try to maintain a stable economy and will change tax rates and interest rates to try to balance out any boom and bust periods.

 Example

2020/21 COVID pandemic

VAT reductions and increased government spending

During and after the global COVID pandemic of 2020/21, the UK government temporarily reduced the level of VAT for hospitality and entertainment to help these industries recover. Also, loans and financial help was available to businesses from the government to help keep staff employed whilst on furlough. This had the effect of making consumers' purchases cheaper, increasing their confidence and allowing them to still buy goods

This was used as a way of stimulating the economy and boosting demand in a period when the UK economy was struggling.

Interest rates

Meanwhile, the Bank of England started significantly reducing interest rates. This was an attempt to make it cheaper for businesses to borrow funds.

The additional investment in businesses that this caused was also designed to boost demand.

1.3 The Bank of England's role

The Bank of England (the Bank) acts as banker:

(a) to the government

(b) to foreign central banks and international organisations.

All commercial banks have a bank account with the Bank which is used to settle debts between each other and to pay amounts due to the government.

The Bank of England is in the control of the UK government. The Governor, Deputy Governor and 16 directors are appointed by the Sovereign on the recommendation of the Prime Minister. Consequently, the Treasury is able to implement government policies through:

(a) the use of **monetary policy** – actions that determine the size and rate of growth of the money supply, which in turn affects interest rates. The aim of any monetary policy is to keep the economy stable

(b) the Bank's overall control of the **banking system**, and

(c) the Bank's influence over the financial institutions.

The Bank of England acts as the government's bank in the widest possible sense, i.e. examining and anticipating banking problems.

1.4 The Bank of England's operations in the markets

- The Bank ensures implementation of government policy to control the economy by controlling the money market for short-term loans by the issue of Treasury bills.

- The Bank issues long-term government debt, referred to as gilt-edged securities or gilts.

- The Bank sets interest rates (base rate) via a committee appointed by the government.

- The Bank manages the exchange rate to protect the pound. If sterling's value is too high the Bank sells sterling for foreign currencies, if its value is too low the Bank will buy sterling with its foreign currency reserves.

- The Bank meets the government's long-term borrowing requirements by open market operations on the Stock Exchange. The Bank is a lender of last resort and will provide funds for banks which are short of cash.

CASH AND FINANCIAL MANAGEMENT

 Test your understanding 1

The aim of a Government's monetary policy is to create as high economic growth as possible.

Is this statement True or False?

1.5 Impact of an organisation's cash management decisions

The Bank of England has control over interest rates, which will influence what an organisation may wish to do with any surplus funds.

When **interest rates** are **low**:

- Money is less expensive to **borrow** so people will spend more.
- This can create employment opportunities and expansion within businesses that require capital investment.
- It will also create **inflation**.

 Definition

Inflation is the rise in the prices of goods and services within an economy over time. It reduces the purchasing power of money, meaning that each £ sterling buys fewer goods and services.

Most governments want stable prices and low inflation. This is because high levels of inflation tend to have the following problems:

- As prices rise, consumers may purchase fewer goods, reducing growth in the economy.
- Employees will push for higher pay rises, in order to match price rises. This can lead to problems for businesses.
- Other costs (such as raw materials) will also rise for businesses, possibly leading to reductions in investment and production.
- Consumer confidence may be damaged due to uncertainty in the future prices of goods and services.
- People on fixed incomes (such as students or pensioners) may find themselves worse off, as their income will not rise even though the cost of goods has increased.

When **interest rates** are **high**:

- Money is more expensive to borrow which leads to higher levels of **saving or investing**.
- The government will reduce inflation rates to try to encourage people to spend money.

The interest rate position will impact on what a business decides to invest in as this will impact on the cost of capital and thus the level of return an investment makes.

If interest rates are low the organisation is likely to invest less in external opportunities as the surplus funds may be required to meet internal expansion or requirements. If interest rates are high then the treasury function is more likely to invest any surplus funds to receive a return for the future.

1.6 Quantitative easing

Quantitative easing is a relatively unconventional monetary policy that involves Bank of England buying financial assets (such as government and corporate bonds) using money that it has generated electronically.

Put more simply, the central bank has essentially printed itself new money that it can spend (although in practice it is unusual for the money to actually be printed).

This has the effect of **increasing the amount of cash within the economy**, hopefully increasing aggregate demand. However, it can cause **increased inflation and exchange rates**.

Test your understanding 2

If Government and the Bank of England wish to reduce inflation what action are they most likely to take:

A   Reduce tax rates

B   Raise interest rates

C   Lower interest rates

D   Increase government spending on infrastructure

CASH AND FINANCIAL MANAGEMENT

2 Financial and statutory regulations

2.1 Introduction

Organisations might have guidelines for their cash managers about how any surplus cash should be invested. For example, a company might have a rule that all surplus cash should be held in bank deposit accounts and available for immediate withdrawal without notice.

Alternatively, a company might have a stated policy of investing surplus cash in short-dated gilts.

Private companies are allowed to invest their own funds as they wish but there are regulations to adhere with set out in the following documents:

- The Companies Act
- Money laundering and counter terrorism financing regulations
- The Bribery act 2010

In public sector organisations, investment guidelines are likely to be very strict. This is because any surplus cash is 'public money', and a public organisation should not be exposed to the risk of large investment losses. Such organisations are therefore likely to specify how any surplus cash should be used.

Example

The following investment guidelines applied in a UK local borough council have been published on the Internet.

They provide a useful example of what the nature of investment guidelines can be.

1   Maturity and liquidity parameters.

    Minimum of 50% of the investment portfolio should have a maturity of one year or less.

    The maximum average maturity of the total portfolio should be three years.

    All investments with over three months to maturity must be in negotiable instruments (i.e. investments that can be sold if required).

    The maturity of any one investment in the portfolio must not exceed 10 years.

2. All investments must be in sterling-denominated instruments.

3. All investments must be made through banks or building societies that are on an approved list.

4. The amount invested through/with any individual bank or building society must not exceed 25% of the total value of the investment portfolio.

5. Investments must have a credit rating of no less than a certain grade. (The minimum credit rating is specified, and the authority requires all investments to have a high 'investment grade' credit rating.

6. The total value of gilts and corporate bonds in the portfolio must not exceed 50% of the value of the portfolio.

7. The maximum that can be invested with any individual borrower, with the exception of the UK government, is 10% of the value of the portfolio.

8. The investment guidelines end with a list of the types of securities that can be purchased for the portfolio. They include government securities (Treasury bills and gilts), local authority bills and bonds, bank bills, sterling CDs, commercial paper and corporate bonds.

Local authorities regularly invest short-term because they raise a large part of their taxes early in the year, and hold the money until it is needed for spending.

2.2 The Companies Act

The Companies Act 2006 forms the primary source of UK company law.

The Act provides a comprehensive code of company law for the United Kingdom. The key points are:

- the Act details certain existing common law principles, such as those relating to directors' duties

- it implements the European Union's Takeover and Transparency Obligations Directives

- it introduces various new provisions for private and public companies

- it applies a single company law regime across the United Kingdom, replacing the two separate (if identical) systems for Great Britain and Northern Ireland

- it otherwise amends or restates almost all of the Companies Act 1985 to varying degrees.

CASH AND FINANCIAL MANAGEMENT

The Companies Act 2006 can be found here:

http://www.legislation.gov.uk/ukpga/2006/46/contents

The main implication of this legislation on cash management is the responsibility of directors to act in the best interest of shareholders and therefore safeguard assets without taking excessive risks. The Act gave increased rights to shareholders, increased directors' duties in considering shareholders, employees and the environment. It also increases the rules and disclosures needed over political donations.

2.3 Money laundering and counter terrorism financing regulations

Money laundering is the process by which criminally obtained money or other assets (criminal property) are exchanged for 'clean' money or other assets with no obvious link to their criminal origins. It also covers money, however come by, which is used to fund terrorism.

The UK Anti-Money Laundering Legislation (AMLL) consists of:

- The Proceeds of Crime Act 2002 as amended (POCA)
- The Money Laundering Regulations 2007 (MLR)
- The Terrorism Act 2000 as amended (TA)

The UK legislation on money laundering and terrorist financing applies to the proceeds of conduct that are a criminal offence in the UK and most conduct occurring elsewhere that would have been an offence if it had taken place in the UK.

Anyone can commit a money laundering offence. However, the Proceeds Of Crime Act (POCA) and the Terrorism Act (TA) include additional offences which can be committed by **individuals working in the regulated sector,** that is by people providing specified professional services such as accountants or solicitors.

This means that an **accountant** (e.g. an AAT member in practice) will be personally liable for breaching POCA and/or TA if he, she or they acts as an accountancy service provider while turning a 'blind eye' to a client's suspect dealings.

The Money Laundering Regulation (MLR) imposes duties on 'relevant persons' (sole traders and firms (not employees) operating within the regulated sector) to establish and maintain practice, policies and procedures to detect and deter activities relating to money laundering and terrorist financing. It is the sole trader or firm which will be liable therefore for any breach of the MLR.

The practice, policies and procedures required by the MLR of accountancy service providers include:

- Customer Due Diligence on clients
- reporting money laundering/terrorist financing
- record keeping.

Materiality or **de minimis** exceptions are not available in relation to either money laundering or terrorist financing offences – meaning no amount is too small not to bother about. Any suspected illegal activity must be reported to the National crime Agency (NCA) and care must be taken to not 'tip off' the suspected party of the report.

You can find out more on the Gov.uk website:

https://www.gov.uk/topic/business-tax/money-laundering-regulations

2.4 The Bribery Act 2010

The Bribery Act (2010) creates the following offences:

1. Bribing a person to induce or reward them to perform a relevant function improperly (active bribery).
2. Requesting, accepting or receiving a bribe as a reward for performing a relevant function improperly (passive bribery).
3. Using a bribe to influence a foreign official to gain a business advantage.
4. Failing to prevent bribery on behalf of a commercial organisation.

Accountants need to very careful when deciding whether to accept gifts, hospitality and inducements, especially if 'excessive', as these may be perceived to be bribes.

Bribery can be viewed as a threat to objectivity and also compromises the fundamental principles of integrity and professional behaviour. It is still an offence for a UK company to participate in corrupt activity, regardless of where in the world the activity takes place.

You can find out more on the Gov.uk website:

https://www.gov.uk/government/publications/bribery-act-2010-guidance

Test your understanding 3

If an AAT qualified accountant suspects a client of money laundering they should:

A   Report it to their firm's Money Laundering Reporting Officer (or authorities if no such officer exists)

B   Speak to the client about it to request they stop the illegal activity

C   Do not report due to client confidentiality restrictions

D   Only report the matter if the amounts involved are over £500

3 Economic factors

3.1 Local vs global economies

When investing and trying to expand, a business needs to consider whether to remain in its own local economy or to expand into wider, global markets.

A business will find expanding locally much easier since it will already have an established brand name in the region, better knowledge of local competition and customer needs and a better knowledge of local regulations.

Expanding into global markets (either by buying goods from foreign suppliers or by selling products overseas) has many additional risks and costs such as extra transportation costs, import/export duties, exchange rate risk, different legal and tax regulations and less market knowledge of customers or competitors.

However, foreign suppliers may offer different products not available from local suppliers or at cheaper prices, giving a business a competitive advantage. Selling overseas gives access to global markets, often with much higher growth rates than the UK, and offers greater opportunities for a business to grow and expand much more than just selling in their local area.

Online selling, whether through a business's own website or via a platform such as Ebay or Amazon Marketplace allows easy access to a worldwide customer base, even for small businesses.

3.2 Exchange rates

One risk of buying or selling overseas is exchange rate risk. Changes in foreign exchange rates will influence both overseas sales and purchases.

If UK sterling strengthens (so £1 buys more foreign currency) then this will make it cheaper to import goods from foreign suppliers, but harder to export goods to foreign customers (since they will need to be charged a higher prices. If UK sterling weakens then the opposite is true.

Example

A UK company buys goods from a French supplier for €100 per unit. Currently the exchange rate is €1.15:£1 (so £1 = €1.15).

Therefore the cost to the UK company is £86.96 per unit (€100/1.15).

If sterling strengthens and the exchange rate moves to €1.25:£1 then the cost to the UK business will reduce to £80 (€100/1.25).

As you can see the strengthening of sterling is beneficial to UK companies buying from foreign suppliers, but a weakening of sterling (which would cause the exchange rate to decrease) would make suppliers more expensive.

Example

A UK company sell goods to an American customer for $200 per unit. Currently the exchange rate is $1.35:£1 (so £1 = $1.35).

Therefore the receipt to the UK company is £148.15 per unit ($200/1.35).

If sterling strengthens and the exchange rate moves to $1.40:£1 then the receipt to the UK business will reduce to £142.86 ($200/1.40).

As you can see the strengthening of sterling is bad for UK exporters selling to foreign customers. They either have to accept a lower sterling receipt, or increase their prices which will upset customers. Equally a weakening of sterling (which would cause the exchange rate to decrease) would make foreign sales more profitable.

CASH AND FINANCIAL MANAGEMENT

Exchange rates can also affect **inflation** since many goods sold in the UK are imported from other countries. If sterling weakens (so exchange rates fall) then foreign goods become more expensive and prices rise, increasing inflation.

Test your understanding 4

A UK business sells their product to Italian customers at a fixed price of €150.

Last year the exchange rate was €1.25:£1 but this year it has fallen to €1.12:£1.

What is the impact of this exchange rate movement on the UK business (assuming no other changes to sales or costs)?

A   No change in profit

B   Profit increases by £13.93 per unit

C   Profit decreases by £19.50 per unit

D   Profits decrease by £13.93 per unit

3.3   Interest rates

If interest rates are expected to rise then a business may prefer a fixed rate loan to a variable rate loan to protect itself from increased costs. If interest rates are low then debt becomes more attractive to businesses who wish to raise finance. If interest rates are high, then equity may be preferred.

For investors, if interest rates are high then savings in interest earning investments such as bank accounts, bonds or gilts become more attractive.

If interest rates are very low then investors may explore alternative investments such as shares, property, cryptocurrency (e.g. Bitcoin) or commodities (e.g. gold). This increased demand may boost the price of these investments.

Impact of regulations and policies on financing and investment: **Chapter 8**

4 Organisational culture and policies

4.1 Impact of economic factors on organisational policy

As noted in the two previous chapters each business will have certain criteria it will consider when deciding how to finance their business and what to invest surplus funds in:

- maturity
- return
- risk
- liquidity
- diversification.

The state of the wider economy is also likely to influence the financial decisions and policies made by an organisation.

If the economy is healthy and experiencing stable or high growth, a business will likely find it easier to obtain additional finance to grow the business. If the economy is in a recession then obtaining finance may be more difficult so a business may choose to invest surplus cash in short term investments where they can easily access their money if needed.

If interest rates are high then an organisation is more likely to use any surplus cash to repay existing debt to reduce their overall finance costs. If interest rates are low, then repaying debt may not be a priority and the business may use the surplus cash to reinvest in expanding the business, invest in other investment opportunities or take advantage of bulk or early settlement discounts from suppliers.

4.2 Ethical considerations

When considering whether to invest in another company it is also necessary to consider how the **ethics, sustainability or working practices** of the company could affect an organisation's reputation and decision making.

When raising finance a business may find it easier to attract investors if the business is based on sound ethical and environmentally friendly principles. In 2015 the London Stock Exchange became the first exchange to set up a dedicated Green Bond market, to promote bonds from green conscious and sustainable businesses. This helps investors finance environmentally sustainable businesses and at the start of 2021 over £45 billion in finance had been raised on this bond market.

Issues such as the use of child labour, poor working conditions for employees, and lower than minimum wage being paid can negatively affect how a company is perceived. This may deter customers and potential investors.

5 Summary

Economic factors such as interest rates and economic growth rates, both locally and globally should be considered when a business is choosing how to raise finance or invest surplus funds.

Government and the Bank of England will use monetary policy and interest rates to control inflation and promote stable economic growth. These policies may influence the cost of finance and the return on investments.

A company should also be conscious of growing ethical and environmental sustainability awareness from customers and investors when making business and financial decisions.

Test your understanding answers

Test your understanding 1

False

The aim of a Government's monetary policy (interest rates and the supply of money) is to create STABLE economic growth and keep inflation low.

Test your understanding 2

B

In order to reduce inflation, interest rates should be increased. This will encourage more people to save (rather than spend) and will increase the cost of borrowing, again reducing the amount people have to spend. This will reduce demand in the economy, lowering prices and inflation.

The other actions would all help stimulate economic growth but are likely to increase inflation.

Test your understanding 3

A

An AAT accountant was a duty to report any suspicious behaviour. This duty overrules any confidentiality restrictions and the amounts involved are irrelevant.

An accountant also needs to be careful not to 'tip off' the client as this is also a criminal offence.

Test your understanding 4

B

Last year €150 was worth (€150/1.25) £120 of revenue

This year €150 is worth (€150/1.12) £133.93 of revenue

Therefore, profit has increased by £13.93 per unit.

CASH AND FINANCIAL MANAGEMENT

Assumed knowledge

1 Depreciation

1.1 Introduction

Non-current assets are capitalised in the statement of financial position at the point when they are purchased. However this is not the end of the story.

1.2 The accruals concept

The accruals concept states 'costs incurred in a period should be matched with the income produced in the same period'. Non-current assets are purchased to help generate income over a long period of time. In accordance with the accruals concept the cost of the asset should be matched to the period over which income is earned.

1.3 What is depreciation?

It is the measurement of the cost of the non-current asset consumed in a period. It reflects the wear and tear of a non-current asset in a period.

1.4 Calculating depreciation

There are three key factors to consider:

- cost of the asset
- useful economic life (period over which economic benefits are expected to be derived from asset)
- residual value (amount that the asset is expected to be sold for at the end of its useful economic life).

> Assumed knowledge: **Chapter 9**

There are two main ways of calculating depreciation:

1.5 Straight line method

This method assumes that the asset is used consistently throughout its life. Accordingly the depreciation charge is the same each year and the carrying value of the asset is reduced by the same amount each accounting period.

There are two different ways that you may be asked to calculate straight-line depreciation.

 Example

$$\frac{\text{Cost} - \text{residual value}}{\text{Useful economic life}}$$

A new oven has been purchased by Ian for his cafe. Calculate the depreciation charge per year for the oven.

Cost £100,000

Residual value £25,000

Useful economic life 5 years

$$\frac{£100,000 - £25,000}{5}$$

= £15,000 per year

 Example

$$\text{Cost} - \text{residual value} \times \%$$

Roxanne's business policy for her hairdressing business is to depreciate non-current assets at 25% on cost each year.

What is the depreciation charge each year if one of the assets costs £15,000?

£15,000 × 25% = £3,750

1.6 Reducing balance method

This method assumes that an asset is used less and less the older it gets. For this reason the depreciation charge falls each year.

It is calculated by multiplying the asset's carrying amount (the cost of the asset that has not been charged to the Statement of Profit or Loss) and multiplying it by a set percentage.

Example

Fixtures and fittings in Dev's corner shop cost £40,000. His business policy is to depreciate these assets at 10% per annum on a diminishing (reducing) balance basis.

Calculate the depreciation for the first three years of ownership.

Year 1 – £40,000 × 10% = £4,000

Year 2 – (£40,000 – £4,000) × 10% = £3,600

Year 3 – (£40,000 – £4,000 – £3,600) × 10% = £3,240

2 Accruals and prepayments

2.1 Introduction

An organisation's Statement of Profit or Loss and Statement of Financial Position are prepared on the basis of the accruals concept.

Income is included on the basis of when it is earned, irrespective of whether it has been received in cash, and expenditure is included on the basis of when it is incurred, irrespective of whether it has actually been paid.

This principle applies not only to sales and purchases but also to other income and expenses.

Assumed knowledge: **Chapter 9**

2.2 Accruals

 Definition

An accrual is an expense incurred in a period but not yet paid for.

Accounting for an accrual – Journal entry

    Dr Expense account*   X
    Cr Accruals   X   (current liability in SoFP)

*Will depend on the expense to which the accrual relates.

 Example

A business has a year end of 31 December 20X6. The last phone bill received and paid during the year covered the period to 31 October 20X6.

Post year-end an invoice that covered November, December 20X6 and January 20X7 was received. The phone charge for that period was £600.

Required

Calculate the year-end accrual for the phone expense.

Solution

£600 ÷ 3 × 2 = £400

 Example

A business has a year-end of 31 December 20X5. The last gas bill received and paid covered the period from 1 January 20X5 to 31 July 20X5. The bill was for £1,400.

Gas is expected to accrue evenly over the year.

Required

Based on the information provided, estimate the gas accrual for the year to 31 December 20X5.

Solution

£1,400 ÷ 7 × 5 = £1,000

2.3 Prepayments

Definition

A prepayment is a payment made in advance – the expense relates to a period following the current accounting period.

Accounting for a prepayment – Journal entry

Dr Prepayments   X (current asset in SoFP)

Cr Expense account*   X

*Will depend on the expense to which the prepayment relates.

Example

Andrew's year-end is 31 December 20X6.

The bank statement shows that Andrew paid £1,500 for premises insurance during 20X6, to cover the period 1 January 20X6 to 31 March 20X7.

Required

Calculate the prepayment as at 31 December 20X6.

Solution

£1,500 ÷ 15 × 3 = £300

Example

Jason's year end is 31 December 20X8.

Jason paid road tax of £120 during 20X8. This was for the period 1 July 20X8 to 30 June 20X9.

Required

Calculate the prepayment as at 31 December 20X8.

Solution

£120 ÷ 12 × 6 = £60

> Assumed knowledge: **Chapter 9**

2.4 Opening accruals and prepayments

If there is a closing accrual or prepayment it will need to be brought down to be an opening accrual or prepayment for the next period.

Example

The electricity account for the year ended 30 June 20X3 included an accrual for £650. The bank payments for the next 3 months were £12,100. There was an accrual at the end of September of £550.

Write up the electricity expense account clearly showing the accrual balance brought forward and the balance carried forward for the three months ended 30 September 20X3.

Electricity account

Date	Detail	£	Date	Detail	£
30/06/X3	Closing accrual	650			
30/09/X3	Bank	12,100	1/07/X3	Opening accrual	650
30/09/X3	Closing accrual	550	30/09/X3	Expense for the period	12,000
		12,650			12,650

Example

The insurance account for the year ended 30 June 20X3 included a prepayment for £300. The bank payments for the next 3 months were £4,300. There was a prepayment at the end of September of £600.

Write up the insurance expense account clearly showing the prepayment balance brought forward and the balance carried forward for the three months ended 30 September 20X3.

Insurance account

Date	Detail	£	Date	Detail	£
			30/06/X3	Closing prepayment	300
1/07/X3	Opening prepayment	300	30/09/X3	Expense for the period	4,000
30/09/X3	Bank	4,300	30/09/X3	Closing prepayment	600
		4,600			4,600

3 Revaluation of property, plant and equipment

3.1 IAS 16 requirements

IAS 16 permits (it is not compulsory) companies to revalue property, plant and equipment if a policy of revaluation is adopted, although in practice, this is only applied to land and buildings.

If a company decides to revalue its land and buildings, it must then keep the valuation up to date by having periodic revaluations, perhaps at intervals between three and five years to ensure that amounts stated in the financial statements continue to be relevant and reliable for users of the financial statements.

All assets of the same class must be revalued. For example, if land and buildings were to be revalued, this would not require the revaluation of plant and machinery, but would require the revaluation of all (rather than some) land and buildings held.

If a revalued asset has a finite useful life, such as a building, it should continue to be depreciated over its remaining estimated useful life, based upon the new revalued amount and the remaining expected useful life. Following revaluation, the carrying amount at each reporting date will be the fair value from the latest valuation less any subsequent accumulated depreciation and any subsequent accumulated impairment losses.

3.2 Accounting for a revaluation

When accounting for revaluation of property, plant and equipment, the following procedure should be adopted:

- restate the asset to the revalued amount (rather than at cost)
- eliminate the accumulated depreciation to date on that asset
- establish or update the revaluation reserve.

> Assumed knowledge: **Chapter 9**

 Example

A building was purchased at a cost of £200,000 on 1 January 20X8. It is depreciated over its useful life of 20 years on a straight line basis down to a nil residual value. At 31 December 20X8 the building was revalued at £247,000. The company does not make the annual transfer from revaluation reserve to retained earnings.

Show how this revaluation should be dealt with in the financial statements as at 31 December 20X8 and 20X9.

Solution

In the year ended 31 December 20X8, depreciation of $\frac{200,000}{20} =$ £10,000 would be charged so the carrying value at the date of revaluation is £190,000.

The revaluation gain is £57,000 (from a carrying value of £190,000 up to £247,000). This gain would be reported in other comprehensive income for the year and shown in the statement of financial position as a revaluation reserve within equity.

The revaluation is accounted for as follows:

	£	£
Dr Building (247 – 200)	47,000	
Dr Accumulated depreciation	10,000	
Cr Revaluation reserve		57,000

The revised depreciation charge for 20X9 would be £247,000/19 years = £13,000.

At 31 December 20X9, the amounts to be included in the statement of financial position would be:

Carrying value of property (£247,000 – £13,000) = £234,000

Revaluation reserve £57,000

A company which has revalued property, plant and equipment can choose whether or not to make an annual transfer from revaluation reserve to retained earnings for the amount of the 'excess depreciation' i.e. the increase in the depreciation charge as a result of the revaluation.

In effect, this treats part of the revaluation reserve as being realised and can then be regarded as part of retained earnings from which dividends may be paid to shareholders.

CASH AND FINANCIAL MANAGEMENT

If a company chooses to make this annual transfer, it must do so every year so that the financial statements are prepared using consistent accounting policies. The transfer is made within the statement of changes in equity as follows:

Dr: Revaluation reserve   Cr: Retained earnings

 Example

Continuing with information from the previous example when the building has been revalued to £247,000, calculate the amount of the 'excess depreciation' charged as a result of revaluing the building and state the accounting entries required to account for the transfer within the statement of changes in equity for the year ended 31 December 20X9.

Solution

The 'excess depreciation' is £3,000 (£13,000 – £10,000).

The accounting entries required are as follows:

	£	£
Dr Revaluation reserve	3,000	
Cr Retained earnings		3,000

Balance on revaluation reserve = £54,000 (£57,000 – £3,000)

3.3 Reporting valuation gains and losses

Valuation gains are recorded in other comprehensive income for the year and held in a revaluation reserve within the equity section of the statement of financial position.

Losses are recognised in the statement of profit or loss unless there is already a balance in the revaluation reserve for that asset.

In this case, the loss is taken first to other comprehensive income which will reduce the revaluation reserve in the statement of financial position. Any loss in excess of the balance on revaluation reserve for that asset is taken to profit or loss.

Assumed knowledge: **Chapter 9**

4 Disposals

4.1 Introduction

When a non-current asset is disposed of (i.e. sold or scrapped), it is unlikely that the proceeds from sale will be equal to the carrying value of the asset in the statement of financial position.

The difference between the carrying value and the sale proceeds will be either a profit or a loss on the disposal of a non-current asset.

- Profit – this will occur where the sales proceeds exceed the carrying value.

- Loss – this will occur where the sales proceeds are lower than the carrying value.

4.2 Steps to disposing of a non-current asset

Firstly open a disposal T Account, then:

- Step 1 – Remove the original cost of the disposed asset from the asset account

    Dr Disposals

    Cr Non-current asset cost

- Step 2 – Remove the accumulated depreciation of the disposed asset from the accumulated depreciation account

    Dr Non-current asset accumulated depreciation

    Cr Disposals

- Step 3 – Enter the sale proceeds received/receivable for the disposed asset

    Dr Bank/Receivable

    Cr Disposals

- Step 4 – Balance off the ledger accounts and calculate whether a profit or loss has been made on disposal

CASH AND FINANCIAL MANAGEMENT

 Example

Veronica has a motor vehicle with a carrying value of £2,800. The motor vehicle had originally cost £7,000. Veronica sells the asset for £3,000 cash.

Required

Show the journal entries to dispose of the non-current asset above and calculate the profit or loss on the disposal of the non-current asset.

Solution

	£	£
Dr Disposal account	7,000	
Cr Motor vehicles cost account		7,000
Dr Accumulated depreciation – MV	4,200	
Cr Disposal account		4,200
Dr Cash	3,000	
Cr Disposal account		3,000

Disposal

Motor vehicles	7,000	Accumulated depreciation	4,200
Profit on disposal	200	Cash	3,000
	7,200		7,200

4.3 Part exchange of assets

You may come across a situation where instead of selling a non-current asset for cash, an old asset is taken by the supplier in part exchange for a new asset. A cheque/cash is paid for the net cost of the new asset, after offsetting the part exchange value of the old asset.

It is important that the new asset is recorded at its full cost, not the net amount for which a cheque/cash is paid. So in this situation you have got to deal with both the sale of one asset and the purchase of another.

Assumed knowledge: Chapter 9

Journals for part exchange

		£	£
1	Dr Disposal account	X	
	Cr Non-current asset cost account		X
2	Dr Accumulated depreciation	X	
	Cr Disposal account		X
3	Dr Non-current asset cost account (part exchange value)	X	
	Cr Disposal account		X
4	Dr Non-current asset cost account	X (net cost)	
	Cr Bank/trade payables		X

Example

During the year Sarah part exchanged a machine that had originally cost £20,000 and had accumulated depreciation of £17,000.

The new machine cost £15,000 and a cheque for £14,000 was written for the remaining balance.

Required

Prepare the journal entries to account for the disposal and purchase of the assets and write up the disposal account to calculate the profit or loss on disposal.

Solution

	£	£
Dr Disposal account	20,000	
Cr Machine cost account		20,000
Dr Accum dep'n – machines	17,000	
Cr Disposal account		17,000
Dr Machine cost account (part exchange)	1,000	
Cr Disposal account		1,000
Dr Machine cost account (net cost)	14,000	
Cr Cash		14,000

Disposal account

Machine	20,000	Accumulated depreciation		17,000
		Part exchange		1,000
		Loss on disposal		2,000
	20,000			20,000

5 Irrecoverable debts

5.1 Introduction

Trade receivables should only be included as assets in a statement of financial position if they are expected to settle the amounts due from them. The prudence concept requires an organisation to recognise future losses as soon as it becomes aware of their existence.

This means that as soon as an organisation is aware that a debt may not be settled, then the asset value should be reduced by an adjustment being put through the accounts.

5.2 Irrecoverable debts

This is a debt that the business believes will NOT be recovered. It should be completely removed from the ledger accounts and therefore from the statement of financial position.

Double entry to account for an irrecoverable debt:

Dr Irrecoverable debt   X (SoPL)

Cr SLCA   X (SoFP)

5.3 Doubtful debts

This is a debt about which there is some question as to whether or not the amount will be settled.

We must recognise this doubt in the accounts but we should not write off the debt completely, because the cash may be received. In any event we need to keeping pressing for it to be settled. Therefore we still need to show the debt as outstanding.

> **Assumed knowledge: Chapter 9**

> **Example**
>
> Shauna has trade receivables at her year-end of £25,000.
>
> There is concern about whether £5,000 of this will be settled.
>
>   Dr Irrecoverable debt expense   5,000 (SoPL)
>
>   Cr Allowance for doubtful debts   5,000 (SoFP)
>
> The allowance for doubtful debts is offset against the trade receivables balance in the statement of financial position.
>
> **Statement of financial position extract**
>
> Trade receivables   25,000
>
> Less allowance for doubtful debts   (5,000)
>
>   20,000
>
> This treatment clearly shows that there is doubt as to whether the debt will be received but does not write it off and we can continue chasing it.

5.4 Types of allowance for doubtful debts

There are two main types:

- **Specific allowance** – calculated by reference to a particular invoice or trade receivables balance.

- **General allowance** – this is an allowance against trade receivables as a whole, normally expressed as a percentage of the trade receivables balance.

CASH AND FINANCIAL MANAGEMENT

6 The Statement of Financial Position

	£	£
Non-current assets		
Property, plant and equipment		X
Goodwill		X
Investments in associates		X
		X
Current assets		
Inventories	X	
Trade and other receivables	X	
Cash and cash equivalents	X	
		X
Total assets		**X**
Equity		
Share capital		X
Share premium account		X
Retained earnings		X
Revaluation reserve		X
Total equity		X
Non-current liabilities		
Loans or debentures		X
Current liabilities		
Trade and other payables	X	
Bank overdrafts	X	
Tax payable	X	
		X
Total liabilities		X
Total equity and liabilities		X

Assumed knowledge: **Chapter 9**

7 The Statement of Profit or Loss

	£
Revenue	X
Cost of sales	(X)
Gross profit	X
Distribution costs	(X)
Administrative expenses	(X)
Operating profit	X
Finance costs	(X)
Profit before tax	X
Tax	(X)
Profit for the period	**X**
Other comprehensive income	
Gain on revaluation of land	X
Total comprehensive income for year	X

8 Net assets

8.1 The accounting equation

The basic accounting equation is that:

Net assets = Capital

Remember that net assets = business assets – business liabilities

This can be expanded to:

Increase in net assets = Capital introduced + profit – drawings

This is important: any increase in the net assets of the business must be due to the introduction of new capital and/or the making of profit less drawings.

CASH AND FINANCIAL MANAGEMENT

8.2 Using the accounting equation

If the opening net assets of the business can be determined and also the closing net assets then the increase in net assets is the difference.

Therefore if any capital introduced is known together with any drawings made by the owner, then the profit for the period can be deduced.

Alternatively if the profit and capital introduced are known then the drawings can be found as the balancing figure.

 Example

Archibald started a business on 1 January 20X1 with £2,000. On 31 December 20X1 the position of the business was as follows:

	£
It owned	
Freehold lock–up shop, at cost	4,000
Shop fixtures and equipment, at cost	500
Inventory of goods bought for resale, at cost	10,300
Debts owing by customers	500
Cash in till	10
Cash at bank	150
It owed	
Mortgage on shop premises	3,000
Payables for goods	7,000
Accrued mortgage interest	100

Archibald had drawn £500 for personal living expenses.

The shop fixtures are to be depreciated by £50 and certain goods in inventory which had cost £300 can be sold for only £50.

No records had been maintained throughout the year.

You are required to calculate the profit earned by Archibald's business in the year ended 31 December 20X1.

KAPLAN PUBLISHING

Solution

This sort of question is answered by calculating the net assets at the year-end as follows:

Net assets at 31 December 20X1

	Cost £	Depreciation £	CV £
Non-current assets			
Freehold shop	4,000	–	4,000
Fixtures and fittings	500	50	450
	4,500	50	4,450
Current assets			
Inventory at lower of cost and net realisable value (10,300 – 300 + 50)		10,050	
Trade receivables		500	
Cash and bank balances (150 + 10)		160	
		10,710	
Current liabilities			
Trade payables	7,000		
Mortgage interest	100		
		(7,100)	
			3,610
			8,060
Mortgage			(3,000)
Net assets			5,060

The profit is now calculated from the accounting equation.

Note that the opening net assets will be the cash paid into the bank when the business was started on 1 January 20X1.

Change in net assets	= Profit + capital introduced – drawings
£5,060 – 2,000	= Profit + Nil – 500
£3,060	= Profit – 500
Profit	= £3,560

CASH AND FINANCIAL MANAGEMENT

 Example

Jones and Sons is a firm of builders who have been trading for just over a year. The tax authorities have just raised a tax assessment on the firm based on profits of £42,000. The owner David Jones does not believe that the firm has done that well because they have an overdraft at the year end. He needs a profit figure with which to counter the claim by the tax authorities. Unfortunately proper accounting records have not been kept. However the following facts have been established in respect of the year end.

- Depreciation needs to be charged at 25% on a straight line basis against the van. The van cost £12,000.
- Sundry building tools purchased in the year cost £4,000 of which £1,000 is to be written off.
- Inventory of cement and sand at cost £1,000.
- Owed by clients – £26,000. A debt of £1,000 is to be written off for work in dispute and a receivables allowance of 2% is required.
- There is an overdraft of £2,000.
- Trade payables amount to £7,000.
- There are accrued expenses of £150.
- The Jones family introduced £10,000 at the start of the year and have drawn out an average of £2,000 per month.

Calculate the profit of Jones and Sons for the year, based upon the above information.

Solution

Year end Statement of Financial Position

	£
Van (12,000 – (12,000 × 25%))	9,000
Tools (4,000 – 1,000)	3,000
Cement and sand	1,000
Receivables (26,000 – 1,000)	25,000
Less allowance ((26,000 – 1,000) × 2%)	(500)
Overdraft (remember this is negative)	(2,000)
Trade payables	(7,000)
Accrued expenses	(150)
Net assets at year end	28,350

Assumed knowledge: **Chapter 9**

Profit calculation

	£
Net assets at end of year	28,350
Less net assets at beginning of year	(nil)
Increase in net assets	28,350
Less capital introduced in the year	(10,000)
Add drawings for the year (12 months × £2,000)	24,000
Profit for the year	42,350

9 Internal rate of return

9.1 Definition

> **Definition**
>
> The **IRR** calculates the **rate of return** (or discount rate) that one project is expected to achieve if it **breaks even** i.e. no profit or loss is made. The IRR is therefore the point where the **NPV of an investment is zero**.

For one investment, a graph of NPV against discount rate looks like the following:

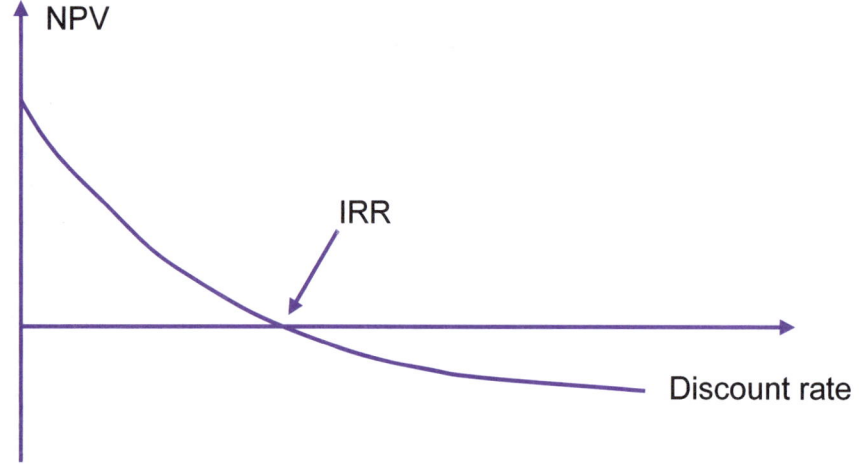

As the discount rate gets higher, the NPV gets smaller and then becomes negative. The cash flows are being discounted by a higher percentage therefore the present value of the cash flows becomes less.

CASH AND FINANCIAL MANAGEMENT

The internal rate of return (IRR) is the discount rate that will cause the cash flow of a project to have a net present value equal to zero.

To decide on whether to invest using the IRR you need to compare the IRR with the discount rate that the company would like to use. If the chosen discount rate was somewhere between 10% and 15%, and the IRR of a project was 22% then we can still accept the project as our rate is less than the IRR, giving a positive NPV.

9.2 Calculation of the IRR

The approximate IRR of a project can be estimated by considering how close the NPVs are to zero.

The method used to estimate the IRR is as follows:

- Calculate two NPVs for the investment at different discount rates.
- Estimate the IRR with reference to the NPV values.

Example

A machine costs £150,000 now. We expect the following cash flows:

	Year 1 (t = 1) £000	Year 2 (t = 2) £000	Year 3 (t = 3) £000	Year 4 (t = 4) £000	Year 5 (t = 5) £000
Scrap value					30
Sales revenues	40	50	60	50	40
Variable costs	(10)	(12)	(15)	(13)	(11)

Estimate the IRR of the investment.

Solution

1. NPV with a discount rate of 10% = £4,400
2. NPV at a discount rate of 20% = –£31,000
3. Estimate the IRR

    The IRR will be closer to 10% then 20% as £4,400 is closer to zero than –£31,000. As indicated by the diagram below:

    From this we could estimate the IRR as approximately 11% or 12%

Assumed knowledge: Chapter 9

The IRR of an investment can also be calculated using linear interpolation i.e. it uses two known points on a graph and joins them with a straight line. The point where the line crosses the x-axis will be calculated to provide the IRR.

The method used to calculate the IRR is as follows:

- Calculate two NPVs for the investment at different discount rates
- Use the following formula to find the IRR:

$$\text{IRR} (\%) = L + \frac{N_L}{N_L - N_H} \times (H - L)$$

Where:

L = Lower rate of interest

H = Higher rate of interest

N_L = NPV at lower rate of interest

N_H = NPV at higher rate of interest

CASH AND FINANCIAL MANAGEMENT

 Example

A machine costs £150,000 now. We expect the following cash flows:

	Year 1 (t = 1) £000	Year 2 (t = 2) £000	Year 3 (t = 3) £000	Year 4 (t = 4) £000	Year 5 (t = 5) £000
Scrap value					30
Sales revenues	40	50	60	50	40
Variable costs	(10)	(12)	(15)	(13)	(11)

Calculate the IRR of the investment.

Solution

1. NPV with a discount rate of 10% = £4,400 positive

2. NPV at a discount rate of 20% = £31,000 negative

3. Using the formula – you need to remember the rules of maths. Remove the brackets first, then deal with and division or multiplication and finally addition and subtraction (BODMAS)

$$IRR = L + \frac{N_L}{N_L - N_H} \times (H - L)$$

$$IRR = 10 + \frac{4{,}400}{4{,}400 - -31{,}000} \times (20 - 10)$$

$$IRR = 10 + \frac{4{,}400}{35{,}400} \times 10$$

$$IRR = 10 + 0.1243 \times 10$$

$$IRR = 10 + 1.243 = 11.24\%$$

Assumed knowledge: **Chapter 9**

MOCK ASSESSMENT

CASH AND FINANCIAL MANAGEMENT

1 Mock Assessment Questions

Task 1 (10 marks)

(a) **Buying a new delivery van is an example of:** (1 mark)

   A   A regular revenue payment

   B   Drawings

   C   An exceptional payment

   D   A capital payment

(b) **Identify whether the following items affect cash, profit, or both cash and profit.** (3 marks)

Item	Cash	Profit	Cash and profit
Prepaying business insurance for next year			
Paying dividends to shareholders			
Writing off an irrecoverable debt			

The following information has been extracted for company R:

Item	Period 8 £	Period 9 £
Receivables	2,350	2,945
Credit sales	20,487	21,892

(c) **Calculate the cash received from customers in period 9.** (2 marks)

The cash received from customers is £ _____

Mock Assessment Questions

Company X disposes of a non-current asset that originally cost £10,500 and which had accumulated depreciation of £7,800 on the date of disposal. Company X recorded a loss on disposal of £950 on this asset.

(d) **Calculate the disposal value of the non-current asset.** (2 marks)

The disposal value is £ _____

As of 30 June 20X1, current liabilities showed a balance of £12,750 owed to the tax authorities. The financial statements for the year ended 30 June 20X2 show a tax expense of £15,000 and a tax liability of £13,500.

(e) **Calculate the money paid in respect of tax during the year to 30 June 20X2.** (2 marks)

£ _____

Task 2 (15 marks)

A company is preparing its forecast sales and purchase information for April.

The sales volume trend is to be identified using a 3-point moving average based on the actual monthly sales volumes for the current year.

(a) **Complete the table below to calculate the monthly sales volume trend and identify any monthly variations using the additive model.** (4 marks)

	Sales volume (units)	Trend	Monthly variation
November	425		
December	570	540	30
January	625		
February	545		
March	690		

Additional information

The production cost per unit has been set at £13.

Assume that the increase in the trend is constant and the seasonal variations are cyclical.

CASH AND FINANCIAL MANAGEMENT

(b) **Using the trend and the monthly variations identified in part a, calculate the forecast production cost for April.** (1 mark)

The forecast production cost for April is £ _____

Additional information

The company uses an index to forecast future monthly wage costs. The January monthly wage cost of £11,700 was calculated when the wage index was 100.

(c) **Create an index (to one decimal place) for the wage cost for February and March with January as the base period.** (2 marks)

Month	January	February	March
Price	£11,700	£12,004	£11,928
Index			

The cash budget for Walldoor for the three months ended June has been partially completed. The following information is to be incorporated and the cash budget completed:

- A bank loan of £60,000 has been negotiated and this will be paid into the business's bank account in April. The loan principal will be repaid in 48 monthly instalments beginning in May.

- The loan attracts 5% interest per annum calculated on the amount of the loan principal advanced in April. The annual interest charge is to be paid in equal monthly instalments beginning in May.

- A share issue raising £143,750 is planned in May.

- The company has contracted to purchase plant and machinery for £80,000. The supplier has agreed hire purchase terms. The hire purchase interest is 3% of the purchase price. The interest and instalments will be paid in 10 equal monthly amounts starting in April.

- At 1 April the balance of the bank account was £5,214.

Mock Assessment Questions

(d) Using the additional information above, complete the cash budget for Walldoor for the three months ending June.

(8 marks)

Note:

- Cash inflows should be entered as positive figures.
- Cash outflows as negative figures (use brackets or minus sign).
- Round to the nearest whole £ throughout.
- If a cell does not require an entry, leave it blank.

	April £	May £	June £
RECEIPTS			
Cash sales	2,700	3,450	3,900
Credit sales	15,300	19,550	22,100
Proceeds from share issue			
Bank loan			
Total receipts			
PAYMENTS			
Purchases	−13,200	−14,400	−16,800
Wages	−10,541	−10,685	−10,852
Expenses	−5,541	−5,745	−6,785
Hire purchase of plant and machinery			
Bank loan capital repayment			
Bank loan interest			
Total payments			
Net cash flow			
Opening bank balance			
Closing bank balance			

CASH AND FINANCIAL MANAGEMENT

Task 3 (10 marks)

A cash budget has been prepared for Boxlid Ltd for a new product the next four periods.

The budget was prepared based on the following sales volumes and a selling price of £180 per item.

	Period 1	Period 2	Period 3
Sales volume (items)	800	850	875

The pattern of cash receipts used in the budget assumed 50% of sales were received in the month of sale and the remaining 50% in the month following sale.

	Period 1 (£)	Period 2 (£)	Period 3 (£)
Original value of forecast sales	144,000	153,000	157,500

Boxlid needs to make adjustments to its cash budget to take account of the following:

- The selling price will be reduced by 15% per item.
- The pattern of sales receipts changes to 30% of sales received in the month of sale, 50% in the month following sale and the remaining 20% two months after sale.

(a) **Complete the table below to calculate the sales receipts expected in periods 1 to 4 if the selling price and receipts pattern changes (round down to the nearest £).** (6 marks)

	Adjusted forecast sales value £	Sales receipts Period 1 (£)	Period 2 (£)	Period 3 (£)	Total
Period 1 sales					
Period 2 sales					
Period 3 sales					
Revised forecast sales receipts					

KAPLAN PUBLISHING

Mock Assessment Questions

(b) **Complete the sentence below.** (1 mark)

If the selling price and receipt patterns change, total receipts from sales in periods 1 to 3 will increase/fall by _____% (2 decimal places)

(c) **Complete the sentence below.** (2 marks)

Company Z has budgeted to make and sell 3,000 units for £25 each. Company Z often gives discounts to customers. In the cash budget, Company Z expects to receive £70,500 in respect of these sales.

The average level of discount Company Z gives its customers (to 1 decimal place) is _____%.

(d) **Which ONE of the following is an example of a controllable factor** (1 mark)

A   Changing to a more expensive supplier

B   Increases in prices due to a global pandemic

C   A change in interest rates

D   A change in demand of a product

Task 4 (15 marks)

(a) The quarterly budgeted and actual figures for an organisation are provided below:

	Budgeted £	Actual £
Receipts from receivables	95,142	97,158
Cash sales	25,541	23,475
Payments to payables	–54,214	–52,965
Cash purchases	–6,951	–7,841
Capital expenditure	–18,000	–24,850
Wages and salaries	–20,100	–19,540
General expenses	–18,654	–19,876
Net cash flow	2,764	–4,439

The following information has also been provided:

- Due to high levels of competition, the organisation began to offer slightly longer credit terms to its customers.

- The organisation changed supplier for some of its materials in the year.

CASH AND FINANCIAL MANAGEMENT

- Some older machinery was replaced in the year with newer, more efficient machinery.
- Only variances in excess of 7% are deemed significant and require investigation.

(i) **Identify the significant variances and calculate the percentage change in these variances.** (3 marks)

(ii) **Explain one potential reason for each of these variances.** (3 marks)

(iii) **Identify an action that could be taken to rectify these variances, and to reduce the likelihood of recurrence.** (3 marks)

Significant variance and % change from budget	Possible reasons for variance	Potential corrective action

Mock Assessment Questions

(b) **Explain TWO potential consequences of a business failing to meet its loan repayments on time.** (2 marks)

(c) **Explain what is meant by overtrading and identify signs that a company may be overtrading.** (4 marks)

CASH AND FINANCIAL MANAGEMENT

Task 5 (15 marks)

The following figures are from the financial statements of a company for the year ended December 20X3.

Statement of profit or loss	20X3	Statement of financial position	20X3
	£000		£000
Revenue	10,000	**Non-current assets**	
Cost of sales	6,000	Property, plant and equipment	5,800
Gross profit	4,000	**Current assets**	
Distribution costs	1,000	Inventory	1,300
Administration costs	1,200	Trade receivables	1,300
Operating profit	1,800	Cash	700
Finance costs	200	**Total assets**	9,100
Profit before taxation	1,600	**Equity**	
Tax	500	Share capital	600
Profit for the year	1,100	Retained earnings	3,300
		Total equity	**3,900**
		Non-current liabilities	
		Loans	4,400
		Current liabilities	
		Trade payables	800
		Total equity and liabilities	**9,100**

(a) **Calculate the following (to 2 decimal places)** (2 marks)

   The current ratio is _____ :1

   The quick ratio is _____ :1

(b) **Calculate the following (to the nearest day):** (3 marks)

   The inventory holding period is _____ days

   The trade receivables collection period is _____ days

   The trade payables payment period is _____ days

(c) **Using your answers to part (b) calculate the working capital cycle for the company.** (1 mark)

   The working capital cycle is _____ days

Mock Assessment Questions

(d) **Identify whether the following statements are true or false about quantitative easing.** (2 marks)

Statement	True	False
It generates high inflationary pressure		
It increases the supply of cash in the economy		

(e) **Identify whether the following statements are true or false.** (5 marks)

Statement	True	False
The Companies Act says that companies must disclose political donations		
Money laundering regulations only cover solicitors		
The Bribery Act only covers the actions of UK companies within the UK		
Under Money Laundering regulations, only suspicious transactions over £1,000 need to be reported		
The treasury function of a business is responsible for preparing the year end financial statements		

(f) **Identify which two comments are true about the Bank of England** (2 marks)

Activity	Tick
It controls interest rates	
It controls exchange rates	
It regulates the supply of money in the economy	
It will carry out the Government's fiscal policy	
It aims to keep growth and inflation at high levels	

CASH AND FINANCIAL MANAGEMENT

Task 6 (10 marks)

(a) **A bank has offered to lend a company £96,000 to be repaid in 12 monthly instalments of £8,400 per month.** (1 mark)

The flat rate of interest being charged is _____ %

(b) **Which two of the following methods of raising finance does not affect the gearing of a company?** (2 marks)

Activity	Tick
Bank loan	
Invoice discounting	
Hire purchase	
Increasing trade payables	

(c) A company has a bank overdraft of £328,000 and the average monthly interest is £2,596.67.

The annual interest rate (to 1 decimal place) is _____ %
(2 marks)

(d) CD uses factoring to manage its trade receivables. The factor advances 80% of invoiced sales and charges interest at a rate of 12% per annum. CD has estimated sales revenue for next year of £2,190,000. The average time for the factor to receive payment from customers is 50 days.

The estimated interest charge for next year payable to the factor will be £ _____ (2 marks)

(e) In times of increasing inflation, which would be the best option? (1 mark)

    A   Variable rate borrowing

    B   Fixed rate borrowing

Mock Assessment Questions

(f) **Select if the following statements are true or false:** (2 marks)

Statement	True	False
With invoice discounting, the company is no longer responsible for collecting the money due from customers.		
A with-recourse debt factoring agreement means the debt factoring company is responsible for any irrecoverable debts.		

Task 7 (10 marks)

(a) **Calculate the approximate yield to redemption of a 5% Treasury Stock with a current market price of £110, redeemable in 4 years at par.** (2 marks)

The approximate redemption yield is (to 2 decimal places):

 %

(b) **Which of the following investments is likely to provide the lowest level of return?** (1 mark)

A   Gilts

B   Certificates of deposit

C   Local authority bonds

D   Shares

A company is to pay a dividend of £3.50 per share and the current market price of each share is £48.40.

(c) **What is the dividend yield per share? Show your answer to two decimal places.** (1 mark)

 %

CASH AND FINANCIAL MANAGEMENT

(d) **Identify whether each of the following statements is true or false.** (3 marks)

Statement	True	False
Investing in property is considered to be high risk		
Local Authority bonds are considered to be high risk		
Risk averse decision makers will consider the options and make a decision based on minimising the risk involved		

Saanvi has invested in a portfolio of investments. The current value and expected return is shown below.

(e) (i) **Complete the table (to the nearest whole pound)** (2 marks)

Statement	Value (£)	Expected return (%)	Expected return (£)
Investment A	200,000	6.25	12,500
Investment B	350,000	4.30	
Investment C	100,000	2.75	
Total	650,000		

(ii) **Calculate the expected overall return on the portfolio to two decimal places.** (1 mark)

_____ %

Task 8 (15 marks)

A company has £750,000 surplus cash and the finance director estimates that the cash is free to be invested for up to two years.

Option 1

A four year fixed rate bond with a High Street bank paying interest of 6% per annum.

Option 2

A local business is looking to expand and is asking for help financing this expansion. The company is selling shares at £8.50 per share. The expansion will create new jobs in an area of unemployment.

Mock Assessment Questions

Option 3

Invest in a foreign gold mine. Shares are £12.00 each. Research shows that gold is in abundance but there are rumours of child labour and health and safety issues surrounding the mine's owners.

(a) **Identify ONE economic factor the finance director should consider for each of the options.** (3 marks)

Investment option	Economic factor to consider
Fixed rate bond	
Local business	
Gold mine	

(b) **Discuss the risks and returns of the three investment options.**

You should also consider any ethical or moral issue(s) that may be needed to be taken into account, or any benefits there might be for the local economy, if relevant. (12 marks)

1   **Fixed rate bond**

2 Shares in a local business

Mock Assessment Questions

3 Gold mine investment

CASH AND FINANCIAL MANAGEMENT

2 Mock Assessment Answers

Task 1

(a) **D** – Buying a new van is a **capital payment**

(b)

Item	Cash	Profit	Cash and profit
Prepaying business insurance for next year	✓		
Paying dividends to shareholders	✓		
Writing off an irrecoverable debt		✓	

(c) The cash received from customers is **£21,297**.

Cash received = opening receivables + sales – closing receivables

Cash received = 2,350 + 21,892 – 2,945 = 21,297

(d) The disposal value is **£1,750**.

Disposal value = carrying value – loss on disposal

Disposal value = (10,500 – 7,800) – 950 = 1,750

(e) The cash paid in respect of tax is **£14,250**.

Cash paid = opening payable + expense – closing payable

Cash paid = 12,500 + 15,000 – 13,500 = 14,250

Mock Assessment Answers

Task 2

(a)

	Sales volume (units)	Trend	Monthly variation
November	425		
December	570	540	30
January	625	580	45
February	545	620	−75
March	690		

(b) The forecast production cost for April is **£9,685**

Trend = 620 + 40 + 40 = 700 units

Variation = 700 + 45 = 745

Cost = 745 × £13 = £9,685

(c)

Month	January	February	March
Price	£11,700	£12,004	£11,928
Index		102.6	101.9

(d)

	April £	May £	June £
Receipts			
Cash sales	2,700	3,450	3,900
Credit sales	15,300	19,550	22,100
Proceeds from share issue		143,750	
Bank loan	60,000		
Total receipts	78,000	166,750	26,000

CASH AND FINANCIAL MANAGEMENT

Payments			
Purchases	−13,200	−14,400	−16,800
Wages	−10,541	−10,685	−10,852
Expenses	−5,541	−5,745	−6,785
Hire purchase of plant and machinery	−8,240	−8,240	−8,240
Bank loan capital repayment		−1,250	−1,250
Bank loan interest		−250	−250
Total payments	−37,522	−40,570	−44,177
Net cash flow	40,478	126,180	−18,177
Opening bank balance	5,214	45,692	171,872
Closing bank balance	45,692	171,872	153,695

Task 3

(a)

	Adjusted forecast sales value £	Sales receipts			
		Period 1 (£)	Period 2 (£)	Period 3 (£)	Total
Period 1 sales	122,400	36,720	61,200	24,480	
Period 2 sales	130,050		39,015	65,025	
Period 3 sales	133,875			40,162	
Revised forecast sales receipts		36,720	100,215	129,667	266,602

Mock Assessment Answers

(b) Total receipts from sales in periods 1 to 3 will fall by **29.05%**

Working

	Period 1 (£)	Period 2 (£)	Period 3 (£)	Total
Original value of forecast sales	144,000	153,000	157,500	
Original sales receipts	72,000	148,500	155,250	375,750

(375,750 – 266,602) ÷ 375,750 × 100 = 29.05%

(c) The average level of discount Company Z gives its customers (to 1 decimal place) is **6.0%**.

The sales are 3,000 × £25 = £75,000. Company Z only expects to receive (70,500/75,000) 94% of this amount, hence a 6% discount.

(d) **A** – It is the company's choice to change supplier.

Task 4

(a)

Significant variance and % change from budget	Possible reasons for variance **NOTE: only 1 reason is needed for each variance**	Potential corrective action **NOTE: only 1 action is needed for each variance**
Cash sales 8.1% under budget (adverse)	This could be due to a decrease in selling price or a decrease in volume sold that has not been budgeted for. Another reason could be that more customers are taking advantage of paying on credit, given the extended credit terms being offered.	Credit sales need to be investigated to see if more customers are taking up credit terms and future budgets need to be adjusted. A variance of 0.04% for total income (from cash sales and receivables) is not a concern.

CASH AND FINANCIAL MANAGEMENT

Cash purchases 12.8% over budget (adverse)	This could be due to an increase in purchase price or volume. It could also be due to a change in payment terms offered by our new suppliers. Payments to payables have decreased so it is quite likely that we are paying sooner than we had planned in the budget. It may be that we are taking advantage of a settlement discount as overall purchase payments have decreased from £61,165 in the budget to £60,806 actual. Alternatively the new suppliers may have lower prices.	Confirmation of the credit terms we are paying to are required and should be incorporated in the next budget. Investigate the potential to move to a cheaper supplier, or try to negotiate credit terms with the new suppliers.
Capital expenditure 38.1% over budget (adverse)	The most likely cause is the purchase of a new assets which was not budgeted for. This may have been caused by an error in the budgeting process or an unexpected need for a new/replacement piece of equipment. The new machinery may also be more efficient, which would help explain the slight underspend on wages and salaries.	Investigation is needed to see if this was an oversight at the time the budget was put together or whether the purchase of new machinery was unexpected. This in the biggest variance in both actual money spent and in percentage terms so this needs to be looked in to carefully to try to prevent it happening again.

Mock Assessment Answers

(b) **Explain TWO potential consequences of a business failing to meet its loan repayments on time.**

- Bank may cancel the loan and demand immediate repayment
- Bank may seize and sell secured assets
- Potential penalty charges and increased interest costs
- Fall in credit rating making it harder to raise finance in the future

(c) **Explain what is meant by overtrading and identify signs that a company may be overtrading.**

Overtrading occurs when a business expands rapidly with insufficient working capital to support it.

Signs of overtrading include:

- Rapidly growing sales
- Increase in receivable collection periods
- Decline in liquidity ratios
- Fall in cash levels
- Longer payables payment periods.

CASH AND FINANCIAL MANAGEMENT

Task 5

(a) Current ratio = (1,300 + 1,300 + 700) ÷ 800 = 4.13:1

Quick ratio = (1,300 + 700) ÷ 800 = 2.50:1

(b) Inventory holding period = 1,300 ÷ 6,000 × 365 = **79** days

Trade receivables collection period = 1,300 ÷ 10,000 × 365 = **47** days

Trade payables payment period = 800 ÷ 6,000 × 365 = **49** days

(c) Working capital cycle is 79 + 47 – 49 = **77** days

(d)

Statement	True	False
It generates high inflationary pressure	✓	
It increases the supply of cash in the economy	✓	

(e)

Statement	True	False
The Companies Act says that companies must disclose political donations	✓	
Money laundering regulations only cover solicitors		✓
The Bribery Act applies to the actions of UK companies regardless of where in the world the corruption takes place	✓	
Under Money Laundering regulations, only suspicious transactions over £1,000 need to be reported		✓
The treasury function of a business is responsible for preparing the year end financial statements		✓

(f)

Activity	Tick
It controls interest rates	✓
It controls exchange rates	
It regulates the supply of money in the economy	✓
It will carry out the Government's fiscal policy	
It aims to keep growth and inflation at high levels	

Mock Assessment Answers

Task 6

(a) The flat rate of interest being charged is (8,400 × 12 – 96,000) ÷ 96,000 × 100 = 5%

(b)

Activity	Tick
Bank loan	
Invoice discounting	✓
Hire purchase	
Increasing trade payables	✓

(c) The annual interest rate (to 1 decimal place) is 9.5%

Annual interest = 12 months × £2,596.67 = £31,160

Interest rate = 31,160/328,000 = 9.5%

(d) **£28,800**

80% of invoiced sales	= £2,190,000 × 80% = £1,752,000
Outstanding trade receivables	= £1,752,000 × 50/365
	= £240,000
Interest at 12% per annum	= £240,000 × 12%
	= £28,800

(e) **B**

(f) **Select if the following statements are true or false:**

Statement	True	False
With invoice discounting, the company is no longer responsible for collecting the money due from customers.		✓
A with-recourse debt factoring agreement means the debt factoring company is responsible for any irrecoverable debts.		✓

CASH AND FINANCIAL MANAGEMENT

Task 7

(a) **2.28%**

Interest yield = 5 ÷ 110 × 100 = 4.55%

Capital loss = £10 ÷ 4 = £2.50 per year

Represents 2.5 ÷ 110 × 100 = 2.27% of investment value

Approximate redemption yield = 4.55% − 2.27% = 2.28%

(b) **A** – Gilts have the lowest risk so will generally give the lowest return

(c) £3.50 ÷ £48.40 × 100 = **7.23%**

(d)

Statement	True	False
Investing in property is considered to be high risk	✓	
Local Authority bonds are considered to be high risk		✓
Risk averse decision makers will consider the options and make a decision based on minimising the risk involved	✓	

(e) (i)

Statement	Value (£)	Expected return (%)	Expected return (£)
Investment A	200,000	6.25	12,500
Investment B	350,000	4.30	15,050
Investment C	100,000	2.75	2,750
Total	650,000		30,300

(ii) Calculate the expected overall return on the portfolio to two decimal places

4.66 %

Overall return = £30,300/£650,000 = 4.66%

Mock Assessment Answers

Task 8

(a)

Investment option	Economic factor to consider
Fixed rate bond	Interest rates
Local business	Economic growth, current economic cycle
Gold mine	Commodity prices, exchange rate fluctuations, any political uncertainties in the country where the mine is located

(b) The notes below cover a range of possible points that you may include in your written response.

These examples are not intended to be exhaustive and other valid comments may be relevant.

Option 1

- Fixed rate so a return is guaranteed.
- The return is 6%.
- Liquidity depends on the terms of the investment. This option is a fixed term of 4 years. It may be possible to redeem the investment early if the money is required but there is a risk of incurring early redemption charges/penalties, usually a couple of months' interest but the capital amount is safe.
- Traditionally bank deposit accounts were seen as risk free from the perspective of the loss of capital value. However in light of the global financial crisis there is a risk of loss of capital value if the deposit is not covered by a government backed guarantee scheme.
- It may be possible to sell the bond before maturity.

Option 2

- High risk investment.
- The company may not be a FTSE100 company so selling the shares may be difficult affect the liquidity of this investment.
- Share prices may increase but equally they could fall so the return is very uncertain.
- A thorough investigation will need to be carried out on the company in question to analyse profits and profile. Will dividends be distributed?
- Helping this company to expand may well help the local area to improve by providing much needed employment which in turn may improve the image of the investing companies. If it fails then this may have a negative impact on the investing companies.

Option 3

- Very high risk investment.
- Need to investigate the report regarding the abundance of oil as if the report is false the entire investment could be lost.
- As with option 2 – it may be difficult to sell the shares if this company is not a FTSE100 company affecting liquidity.
- A thorough investigation, including a site visit, will need to be carried out on the company in question to analyse profits and profile.
- Ethical issues/damage to reputation for any investor if the claims of child labour and poor health and safety are true.

Mock Assessment Answers

CASH AND FINANCIAL MANAGEMENT

Glossary

Term	Description
Accrual	An expense that has been incurred during the period but has not been paid for by the end of the period.
Annual percentage rates (APR)	The APR is annual rate that is charged for borrowing (or made by investing), expressed as a single percentage number. It represents the actual yearly cost of funds over the term of a loan. This includes any fees or additional costs associated with the transaction.
Broker	A broker is an individual or party that arranges transactions between a buyer and a seller, and gets a commission when a deal is executed.
Capital receipts/payments	Receipts/payments that relate to the disposal/acquisition of non-current assets.
Capped interest rates	A capped interest rate means that there is an upper limit on the level the interest charge can go to.
Depreciation	An annual internal charge to the income statement that spreads the net cost of a non-current asset over the number of years of its useful life.
Exceptional receipts/payments	Receipts/payments that are not expected to occur on a regular basis.
Fiduciary duty of banks	The bank is expected to act with the utmost good faith in relationship with the customer.
Fixed charge	A fixed charge is where the security is a specific and identifiable asset or group of assets.
Fixed interest rate	A fixed interest rate provides an unchanging percentage charge over the length of the borrowing period.
Flat rate interest	Interest rate is calculated based on the loan principle. It is applied to the whole of the loan every year and does not take into account any repayments.

Glossary

Term	Description
Floating charge	A floating charge is where the security is supplied by a group of assets of the relevant value which can change in make-up i.e. inventory or receivables.
Loan principal	The amount that is borrowed.
Maturity date	The final payment date of a loan.
Money markets	A market for the buying and selling of short term, highly liquid investments.
Personal guarantee	A form of security offered by an individual.
Prepayment	A payment made during the period that relates to an expense in a future period.
Regular receipts/payments	Receipts/payments that are expected to occur frequently.
Simple interest rate	This can be calculated by taking the total interest as a percentage of the original principal.
Term loans	A term loan is a loan from a bank for a specific amount that has a specified repayment schedule and a variable interest rate. Term loans almost always mature between one and 10 years.
Variable interest	A variable interest rate changes over the period of the borrowing, usually in line with base rate.
Yield	The return from an investment.

INDEX

A

Accounting equation, 304

Accruals, 8, 12, 292
    concept, 289

Acid test ratio, 193

Additive, 50, 55, 56

Adverse variance, 156

Annual percentage rate, 209

Anti-Money Laundering Legislation, 279

APR, 209

Attitudes to risk, 259

B

Bank and building society deposit accounts, 248, 284

Bank
    loan, 214
    of England, 274
    overdraft, 213

Base
    interest rate, 208
    year, 70

Basic trend, 42

Bonds, 223, 249

Bribery Act (2010), 277, 280

C

Capital
    employed, 191
    payments, 3
    receipts, 2

Capped interest rate, 209

Cash
    budget, 86
    deficits, 132
    flow and profit, 5
    flow control reports, 156
    flow(s), 2, 9
    inflows, 2
    operating cycle, 186
    outflows, 3
    payments, 157
    receipts, 157
    surpluses, 133

Centred moving averages, 46

Certificate of deposit, 254

Characteristic movements, 42

Closing
    payables, 99
    receivables, 90

Commodities, 257

Companies Act 2006, 277, 278

Compound interest, 208

Corporate bonds, 223, 249

Costs, 8

Coupon, 223
    yield, 249

Current ratio, 192

Cyclical variations, 43

D

De minimis, 280

Debt factoring, 216

Depreciation, 8, 20, 106, 289

Diminishing (reducing) balance, 291

Discounts
    allowed, 97
    received, 101

Index

Disposals, 298

Diversification, 246

Dividend yield, 255

Doubtful debts, 8, 301

E

Effective interest rate, 209

Equity shares, 225, 226

Exceptional cash flows, 3

Exchange rates, 109

External influences, 241

F

Favourable variance, 156

Fiduciary relationship, 232

Finance
 choosing the right form, 227
 leases, 17
 reasons for, 206

Financing transactions, 9

Fiscal policy, 272

Fixed
 charge, 212
 interest rate, 208

Flat rate interest, 208

Floating charge, 212

Forecast, 39

G

Gearing, 196, 207

Gilts, 249, 250

Government, 272
 bonds, 249
 securities, 250

H

High interest deposit accounts, 248

Hire purchase, 219

I

Index numbers, 69

Inflation, 67, 275

Input VAT, 108

Instant access deposit accounts, 248

Interest, 210
 rate(s), 207, 242, 260, 277
 received, 110
 yield, 249, 251

Internal rate of return, 308

Inventory, 26, 103
 holding period, 188

Investing – requirements, 240, 272

Investment
 types, 248, 284
 objectives, 242, 281
 strategy, 241

Invoice discounting, 218

IRR, 308

Irrecoverable debts, 96, 149, 301

Irregular cash inflows, 2

L

Labour, 104

Lagging, 89, 98

Land and property, 257

Leasing, 220

Liquid assets, 184

Liquidity, 184, 185, 244, 246

Loans, 116

Local Authority bonds, 249

CASH AND FINANCIAL MANAGEMENT

M

Margins, 75

Mark-ups, 74

Maturity, 244, 246, 283

Monetary policy, 272, 274

Money Laundering Regulations 2007 (2007 Regulations), 279

Money laundering, 277, 279

Monitoring, 132

Moving averages, 44, 65

Multiplicative, 50, 52, 58, 59

N

Net assets, 304

Nominal
  interest rate, 209
  value, 223

Non-cash items, 20

Non-current assets, 8, 14

Notice deposit accounts, 248

O

Opening
  payables, 99
  receivables, 90

Operating profit percentage, 193

Output VAT, 108

Over-capitalisation, 200

Overdraft interest, 111

Overtrading, 199

P

Part exchange, 299

Payables, 11, 26

Payments, 98, 151

Percentage(s), 67, 134

Period expenses, 22

Prepayments, 8, 13, 293

Private organisations, 206

Proceeds of Crime Act 2002 (POCA), 279

Proforma for a cash budget, 87

Proportional, 50

Public organisations, 206

Q

Quantitative easing, 276

Quick ratio, 193

R

Random variations, 43

Realisation, 246

Receipts, 89, 141

Receivables, 10, 25

Reconciliation, 160

Reconciling profit to cash flow, 24

Redemption, 223
  yield, 250, 251

Regression
  analysis, 65
  equation, 65

Return on, 245, 246
  capital employed, 191
  shareholders' funds, 194

Revaluation, 295
  reserve, 18

Index

Revenue, 8
    payments, 3
    receipts, 2

Risk, 243, 246, 282
    averse, 259
    neutral, 259
    seekers, 259

ROCE, 191

S

Sale and leaseback, 222

Seasonal variations, 42, 50

Security, 212

Sensitivity, 133

Settlement discount(s), 146, 155

Shares, 225, 226, 254

Simple interest, 208

Standard rated, 108

Statement of
    financial position, 6
    profit or loss, 6

Straight line depreciation, 290

T

Tax, 20

Terrorism Act 2000 (TA 2000), 279

Terrorism Act 2006 (TA 2006), 279

The Statement of Financial Position, 303

The Statement of Profit or Loss, 304

Time series, 41
    series graph, 41

Trade
    payable collection period, 188
    receivable collection period, 188

Treasury, 241
    stock, 250

V

Variable interest rate, 208

Variance, 164
    analysis, 132

W

Working capital, 186
    cycle, 186